Stella Andromeda

ASTRO
BIRTHDAYS

What Your Birthdate Reveals
About Your Life & Destiny

Hardie Grant

BOOKS

Published in 2021 by Hardie Grant Books,
an imprint of Hardie Grant Publishing

Hardie Grant Books (London)
5th & 6th Floors
52–54 Southwark Street
London SE1 1UN

Hardie Grant Books (Melbourne)
Building 1, 658 Church Street
Richmond, Victoria 3121

hardiegrantbooks.com

British Library Cataloguing-in-Publication Data. A catalogue record for this book
is available from the British Library.

AstroBirthdays
ISBN: 9781784884598

10 9 8 7 6 5 4 3 2 1

Publisher and Commissioner: Kajal Mistry
Project Editor: Kate Burkett
Design, Art Direction and Illustrations: Evi-Studio
Copy-editor: Caroline West
Proofreader: Lucy Rose York
Production Controller: Sabeena Atchia

Colour reproduction by p2d
Printed and bound in China by Leo Paper Products Ltd.

'To every thing
there is a season,
and a time to
every purpose
under the heaven'

(Ecclesiastes, Book 3, Verse I)

Introduction

To every thing there is a season, and this includes a time to be born. Our birthday is where we begin our life on Earth and this resonates with information, not just from the position of the planets at that moment in time, on that specific date and in that particular place, but also from being part of a family heritage and a cosmic whole. Every year, from now on, we will measure our lives. No wonder we all have a fascination with our birthdays and see these as something to celebrate.

As an astrologer, I start with the sun signs of the zodiac, which gives me an insight into where to begin, but there's also numerology associated with your birthday and then the wisdom of the Tarot. It's all here, with a reading for 366 days of the year.

Further information about your astrological profile can be gleaned from a birth chart if you know your time and place of birth, but here your reading will give you a personal insight into how you respond to life and its challenges, what predisposition you may already be aware of or what will be revealed as you mature, and the way you approach your closest relationships. This snapshot could be the beginning or the confirmation of a journey towards self-discovery. And, of course, you can also check the birth dates of those you love or work with, family, friends and colleagues.

Short Guide to Each Zodiac Sign

The primary source of birth date information is from the zodiac sign in which it falls, headed by an intuitive sense of what key characteristics encapsulate that date. I have worked to divine key traits for each, focusing on how a significant birth date can provide insight via astrology by using knowledge of the celestial body that also rules the sign and how this might play out for an individual.

♈ Aries
21 March–20 April

Key words for those born under Aries are independent, pioneering and outgoing. Generally straightforward, sometimes to the point of bluntness, there is something childlike about Aries in their immediate enthusiasm and openness to new ideas and action. This is because Aries is the first sign of the zodiac, representing the birth of the New Year. It is also a fire sign, and Aries can often spark activity and motivation in others but, like fire, they need to be constantly refuelled both by new ideas and the support of others to get things done.

Ruled by Mars, the warrior planet associated with the Roman god of war (his Greek equivalent was the god Ares). The month of March was named after him.

♉ Taurus
21 April–20 May

Those born under Taurus are dependable, tenacious and hardworking. Sometimes depicted as the strong, silent type, Taurus may sound rather boring, but their solid reliability is like a prize, fertile bull balanced by a practical and compassionate nature: Taurus in Earth-Mother mode will be the one turning up with a thoughtful home-cooked meal for that friend sick in bed. For Taurus, security lies mainly in material possessions and they are not suited to a nomadic existence, preferring to put down roots and create a stable home life wherever they are. This need for security means that they are often good with money, making it and keeping it and spending it on their home, creating a secure place for themselves and their beautiful purchases. Taurus likes to feel contained and is very self-contained in many ways, to the point of appearing reserved and keeping their feelings private.

Ruled by Venus, the planet associated with the Roman goddess of beauty and love (her Greek equivalent is Aphrodite).

♊ Gemini

21 May–20 June

Gemini are airy, communicative, versatile, energetic in mind and adaptable by nature. There's something quixotic – mercurial – about them, too, which fascinates others. Occasionally rather lax or discreet about the truth of a situation, this is less about deliberately lying than skirting around the issue when it suits them. Considered rather capricious as a consequence, there is a duality to Gemini's make-up, which is depicted in the sign's representation by the mythological twins Castor and Pollux, who were born of the same mother but two different fathers. This duality can be seen in an ability to assume two (or even more) roles, which is made possible by an easy adaptability as Gemini is a mutable sign. This can also make Geminis restless, seeing them flit from one idea, one role, or job, or occupation to another – a sort of hyperactivity that can result in a dissipation of energy.

Ruled by the planet Mercury, the messenger of the gods. Mercury moves swiftly on winged feet and is linked to communication and travel (his Greek equivalent is Hermes).

♋ Cancer

21 June–21 July

Loyal, kind, sympathetic – all this is true of Cancer, but they can also appear a little 'crabby', contradicting what people think they know about them because, like the crab, there is a very gentle and soft interior that occasionally needs quite a hard exterior to hide and safeguard their feelings. The crab is at home on land as well as in water, so is comfortable in the real world and also in the shifting seas of their imagination. Make no mistake, Cancer is all about feelings and, ruled by the Moon, those shifting tides of feeling can fluctuate very strongly below the surface. Still waters run deep, but Cancer is also a cardinal sign, with a strong, ambitious engagement with the real world, and very much a people person, too. They are all about relationships, with their lover especially, but also with their family and friends. Once they make a commitment they hang on tight, which gives them that other well-known characteristic of the sign of the crab – tenacity.

Ruled by the Moon and its rhythms, which also influences the tides of the sea. The Greek goddess of the Moon was Selene (in Roman mythology aligned to Luna), who drove a silver chariot across the night sky.

♌ Leo

22 July–21 August

Leos like to shine on their world, radiating energy and exuding cheerfulness like a sunny day. That energy often makes them strongly creative, whether in artistic or business endeavours, and even with an eye to their own legacy, sometimes to the extent of wanting to be immortalised in some way through their creation of something of lasting value. If you hear a man or woman being dubbed a 'golden boy or girl', or living a 'gilded life', then chances are they're Leos, but they are very likely to be achieving this through their own efforts in their chosen field. Leos are also idealists with a strong, almost childlike inner vision and self-belief that's difficult to thwart. Even if circumstances challenge this, they believe things will go well and will make them so; they believe in their own positive destiny. Their view of life is generally optimistic, and this often makes them extremely generous and straightforward, magnanimous in attitude and willing to share their own good fortune. It's partly this that makes them successful.

Ruled by the Sun, the primary lifegiving force in the zodiac and representative of the father, or where we all come from, hence the phrase 'sun sign', which is applicable to all astrological signs.

♍ Virgo

22 August–21 September

Traditionally represented by the virgin (or chaste corn maiden), there is something of a paradox about Virgo because this sign is also linked to the creative and fertile Earth Mother, so we could say Virgo is all about abundance, but an abundance that is often kept in check. Practical but discriminating, conscientious but warm, adaptable but reserved, they are a unique combination of opposites that can sometimes clash and cause them stress. That reserve is all part of their *modus operandi*, as keeping something back (in reserve) means they are always prepared. Need a piece of string or a clean pair of socks? Virgo won't let you down. There's something very fastidious, analytical and detail-oriented about Virgo, too, as they go about making their lists, finessing their spreadsheets and ensuring things happen to schedule and on time. They are a wonderful employee but can sometimes get stuck as a 'handmaiden' rather than a boss, which would be a mistake, as they are very good at running their own show, too.

Ruled by the planet Mercury, the messenger of the gods. Mercury moves swiftly on winged feet and is linked to communication and travel (his Greek equivalent is Hermes).

♎ Libra
22 September–21 October

Key words for Libra are balance, harmony and diplomacy. Generally inclined to creating peace, using silver-tongued words to soothe and placate, they are also good listeners and the least argumentative sign of the zodiac. That doesn't mean Libra doesn't enjoy debating issues; in fact, they relish it, weighing up the pros and cons of a situation and trying to balance both sides according to their astrological sign, the scales. There's a huge sense of fairness which drives them and also an objectivity that allows Librans to see both sides. They have an ability to prioritise rational thought over feelings, which can often work in their favour, but may sometimes make them appear a rather reserved, cool customer. In fact, in extreme instances, this ability to see all sides can work against them, as others might distrust the Libran inclination to try to please all the people, all the time. That balancing act can sometimes look a little too much like sitting on the fence and so Libra needs to remember that it's also important to say what is actually thought and felt in order to communicate well, even at the risk of ruffling a few feathers.

Ruled by Venus, the planet associated with the Roman goddess of beauty and love (her Greek equivalent is Aphrodite). The Libran love of luxury can also incline towards indulgence.

♏ Scorpio
22 October–21 November

Scorpio is considered one of the most powerful (and occasionally difficult) signs: a real poker player; there's just so much going on inside that's not always obvious to those around them. They also need solitude to process all that internal activity and this occasional need to withdraw, to disappear emotionally, can give them a reputation for being moody. Another facet of Scorpio that's not always easily understood is their idealism. They actually believe in the best and can be very positive about life. This also stems from a sense of regeneration, that anything can be improved upon or made anew, even if this seems impossible to everyone else. Scorpio is one of the kindest, most loyal and even gentlest of signs, which can be unexpected, for as much as they thrive in sexual relationships, their friendships are equally important and often as intense.

Ruled by Pluto, the ancient god of the underworld and death. This represents the powerful connection between Scorpio and the regeneration and the cycle of life.

♐ Sagittarius
22 November–21 December

Sagittarius is all about independence of mind, body and spirit, and this lies at the heart of their approach to life. Positivity radiates from them because in Sagittarius' world, anything and everything is possible: they are seriously optimistic about life and somehow this seems to open doors for them, not least because their positivity is hard to resist. All this makes them very attractive to be around, but the downside is that they may not be around for long. This independence of spirit can make Sagittarius very restless, always in pursuit of new ideas, places and people. Essentially, they are the sign of the explorer and philosopher, and an interesting mix of animal instinct and enlightened thinking.

Ruled by Jupiter, one of the most important of the Roman gods, the ruler of the heavens and representing optimism, good fortune and abundance.

♑ Capricorn
22 December–20 January

Sometimes considered a rather boring sign, but it would be a mistake to dismiss Capricorn in this way. Cool, creative, ambitious, diligent and with a wry sense of humour – dig a little deeper and they are anything but boring. Capricorn is an interesting combination of practical, due to being an earth sign, and possessing strong initiative, courtesy of being a cardinal sign.

Ruled by Saturn, the most distant of our planets and the zodiac's taskmaster, who was named after the Roman god responsible for the sowing and reaping of seeds, representing hard work and the patient wait for a return.

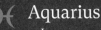 Aquarius
21 January–19 February

Independent, thoughtful, innovative and tolerant are all key words associated with Aquarius, whose capacity for ideas and adventure (both actual and in the mind) means they are never boring. Those born under this sign are also humanitarian and equalitarian, concerned with humanity as a whole and with big ideas for improving life for everyone, in practical rather than spiritual ways. Freedom of thought, expression and movement are all dear to their heart and Aquarius will avidly support free speech, freedom of information and human rights.

Ruled by the planet Uranus, a planet named after the ancient Greek god. This association represents disruption, change and the unexpected. It's all about innovation and invention.

Pisces
20 February–20 March

Imaginative, empathic, intuitive and sometimes spiritual to the point of being mystical, Pisces has a quicksilver mind, like fish catching the light as they dart through the watery depths in which they thrive. This, the twelfth astrological sign of the zodiac, is all about the deep spiritual regeneration that heralds the new (as embodied in the sign that follows, Aries). And as a water sign, Pisces links the two worlds of internal and external life, existing at a point on the cusp of reality and in the realms of imagination, making them one of the most naturally creative of the signs.

Ruled by Neptune, named after the Roman god of the sea (whose Greek equivalent is Poseidon). This planet is the farthest from the Sun and appears to be deep, fluctuating blue in colour. Neptune is all about fantasy, mystery and possible deception.

Short Guide to Cardinal, Fixed and Mutable Signs

The 12 zodiac signs can be grouped into three different ways in which their energies may act or react, giving further depth to each sign's particular characteristics.

Cardinal
Aries • Cancer • Libra • Capricorn

These are action planets with an energy that takes the initiative and gets things started. Aries has the vision, Cancer the feelings, Libra the contacts and Capricorn the strategy.

Fixed
Taurus • Leo • Scorpio • Aquarius

Slower but more determined, the signs work to progress and maintain those initiatives that the cardinal signs have fired up. Taurus offers physical comfort, Leo loyalty, Scorpio emotional support and Aquarius sound advice. You can count on fixed signs, but they tend to resist change.

Mutable
Gemini • Virgo • Sagittarius • Pisces

Adaptable and responsive to new ideas, places and people, mutable signs have a unique ability to adjust to their surroundings. Gemini is mentally agile, Virgo is practical and versatile, Sagittarius visualises possibilities and Pisces is responsive to change.

Short Guide to Sun Signs

It takes 365 (and a quarter, to be precise) days for the Earth to orbit the Sun and in so doing, the Sun appears to us to spend a month travelling through each sign of the zodiac. Your Sun sign is therefore an indication of the sign that the Sun was travelling through at the time of your birth. Knowing what Sun signs you and your family, friends and lovers are provides you with just the beginning of the insights into character and personality that astrology can help you discover.

If your birthday falls close to the end of one Sun sign and the beginning of another, it's worth knowing what time you were born. There's no such thing, astrologically, as being 'on the cusp' – because the signs begin at a specific time on a specific date, although this can vary a little year on year. If you are not sure, you'll need to know your birth date, birth time and birth place to work out accurately to which Sun sign you belong. Once you have these, you can consult an astrologer or run your details through an online astrology site program to give you the most accurate birth chart possible.

Short Guide to Numerology

Your birth date also yields a representation of personality through its number. An observation of the numerical patterns of our lives gives us additional insight into the workings of our inner world, too. Whether you are born on a single digit number, or double, this can be reduced to a single digit manifestation. This, in turn, reveals the deepest values to which you instinctively aspire and some of the challenges to these that you may have to face. The revelations provided by this increase the tools you have to work with as you forge your way through life.

At its simplest, the numerical value of the date of the month on which you were born is shown below. (You can take this further and combine it with the numerical value of the month and the year you were born.) An outline for the numbers is given for each birth date in the book.

No. 1: Born on the 1st, 10th, 19th or 28th
No. 2: Born on the 2nd, 11th, 20th or 29th
No. 3: Born on the 3rd, 12th, 21st or 30th
No. 4: Born on the 4th, 13th, 22nd or 31st
No. 5: Born on the 5th, 14th or 23rd
No. 6: Born on the 6th, 15th or 24th
No. 7: Born on the 7th, 16th or 25th
No. 8: Born on the 8th, 17th or 26th
No. 9: Born on the 9th, 18th or 27th

In addition, using the letters of your given name, you can also work out your Destiny Number by running through the alphabet and allocating a numerical value to each letter.

1 = A, J, S	4 = D, M, V	7 = G, P, Y
2 = B, K, T	5 = E, N, W	8 = H, Q, Z
3 = C, L, U	6 = F, O, X	9 = I, R

Short Guide to Tarot Cards

Reading tarot cards is a form of cartomancy, which means using cards for divination. When we say that 'It's all in the cards', we are alluding to the possibility of seeing what the cards can psychically reveal to and about us. The cards used in this book to divine a reading for each birthday are taken from the Rider Waite Tarot Deck, which was conceived by esoteric and psychic researcher Arthur Edward Waite (1857–1942), designed by Pamela Colman Smith (1878–1951) and first published by William Rider & Son in 1909. Each card represents an archetype, channelled originally by a process of divination, with a meaning that the reader interprets according to the signs and symbols depicted. The cards are readily available to buy and own or, alternatively, illustrative reference can easily be found online for each card in the Rider Waite deck.

A Tarot deck consists of 78 cards in total: 22 Major Arcana and 56 Minor Arcana cards. The 22 major cards include the Sun, Moon, Empress, Emperor, Fool, Magician, Devil, Wheel of Fortune, Lovers, Death and Hanged Man. Each card has a specific meaning which is used to interpret life's psychic force in a spread. Likewise, the 56 minor cards are divided into four suits, Cups, Pentacles, Wands and Swords, each containing 10 cards, plus a King, Queen, Knight and Page, which are used to interpret our daily trials and tribulations.

I focused on each birth date as I selected a card, blind, from a shuffled pack, using psychic divination to see what this might reveal.

January 1st

Insightful pioneer

As befits the first day of the year, the Roman god Janus could look backwards and forwards, and individuals born on the first day of the calendar year combine great insight with a Capricorn dedication to the upward climb of the year. You're also likely to show tenacity and a willingness to take the world in your stride, which means that, like the proverbial mountain goat, you're resilient when it comes to tolerating stress. This will stand you in good stead across many different career choices, where dealing with other people is a key feature – from retail, to teaching, to working in medical settings, you are well disposed to delivering under pressure. You're probably the first to volunteer to support others, whether through mentoring a colleague or babysitting a friend's child. This sort of equanimity means you're valued both at work and at home. In love, you can be quite a cool character, but kind, and, if you're really interested in someone, you're more than capable of playing a long game. Because a harmonious domestic life is important to you, once you've made a commitment, you're unlikely to change your mind.

Numerology

No. 1: A powerful entity and results-oriented force, all about initiating action and getting things done.

Tarot

Page of Cups: The suit of Cups is representative of our emotions and the youthful page isn't quite sure what to do with the contents of his chalice. You may sometimes wonder about the nature of your own feelings and should be reassured that over time these will mature and become easier to understand.

Famous birthdays

J.D. Salinger American writer
E.M. Forster British writer
Verne Troyer American actor

January 2nd

Careful individualist

Your approach to life is unlikely to be like the rest of the herd as you tend towards a more individualistic approach. This is reflected in the choices you make, from the clothes you wear to the holidays you take. There's a carefulness about these choices, too, which suggests a thoughtfulness about how you want to live your life. Because of this, you may find that it takes time to find out what it is you really want to do as a career. Almost by a process of finding out what doesn't appeal, you will eventually find the right role for your talents. This may also mean working not in a large organisation, but for a small start-up where it's easier for your individuality to fit in. However, because of your diligent approach, you are likely to be a valued colleague whatever you choose. You probably take a similar approach to your more intimate relationships and even though people often say opposites attract, you will likely only really consider a life partner who has a similar take on life to your own.

Numerology

No. 2: Shows resilience and power in gentleness, often provides the role of mediator, and linked to psychic abilities.

Tarot

Ten of Swords: The Swords are about action and although this card depicts quite a violent image, it suggests that your actions shouldn't pin you down. Although decisiveness is generally valued, don't always feel obliged to act, because it's sometimes better to wait and see whether this is absolutely in your best interest.

Famous birthdays

Cuba Gooding Jr American actor
Christy Turlington American model
St Therese of Lisieux French saint

January 3rd

Astute charmer

There's something rather canny about those born on the third day of the first month and, like a lot of Capricorns, something very sure-footed about your approach to life. You have probably already learned that you can charm more flies with honey than vinegar, and this is often how you approach a problem, making you something of a smooth talker. Luckily, there is usually some substance behind your words, as you are astute enough to realise that you cannot fool people, especially when it comes to delivering at work, and your career is important to you. You're likely to find work in a role where you can manage people, possibly at quite a senior level, and your ability to graft really pays off here. Family means more than just blood relatives to you and your friends can often be of equal or even greater importance. That said, your most intimate relationships often arise from initial friendships because you value having a solid basis on which to build something as important as a family.

Numerology

No. 3: Creative with the gift of imagination and an ability to communicate through writing, art or speech.

Tarot

Queen of Wands: Wands are always depicted in leaf, and as such represent life and being rooted in something enduring. There's a strong and mature quality to this card, suggesting something quite solid that can be relied upon, much as those around you know they can rely on you.

Famous birthdays

Mel Gibson Australian actor
J.R.R. Tolkien British author
Greta Thunberg Swedish environmental activist

January 4th

Charismatic explorer

Those born on this date have a tendency to go straight to the heart of things. Whether this is a problem or a journey, it's all the same. You probably tend to look outwards, taking a pragmatic and long-term view of situations, as if focused on a horizon that others can't yet see, which is a characteristic of Capricorn's view from the metaphorical mountain. Strongly grounded, you are someone who often enjoys a slower, more methodical approach to life, and are unfazed by more airy temperaments that appear, initially, to make faster progress. Your approach makes you well suited to those professions requiring attention to detail, such as research, editing or project management, within different arenas. If this sounds a little dull, remember that you can be highly effective across the most creative of industries and you are also blessed with a sense of fun that breathes life into the most mundane of tasks. All of which gives you an attractive charisma that will have many wanting to be your friend or lover. When it comes to your love life, your instinct is for monogamy and a secure base from which to explore.

Numerology

No. 4: Invested in the physical world, centred earth energy that is practical in application.

Tarot

Nine of Pentacles: The Pentacles represent our resources, and this particular card suggests an abundance of such a useful trait, which will aid you in self-sufficiency, financial independence and successful accomplishment. What's more, the value of joining forces to combine resources, and achieve more in partnership than alone, is also noted.

Famous birthdays

Sir Isaac Newton British physicist
Julia Ormond American actress
Michael Stipe American singer-songwriter

January 5th

Spontaneous idealist

For those born on this date, idealism is combined with spontaneity. But because you also know that putting in the hours is part of what it takes to realise your dreams, long after others have given up, you are the one likely to achieve your aims. Spontaneity is part of the picture because your quick mind probably reacts fast, but you also believe that smart decisions come from doing your homework. Yours is a creativity that likes to see tangible results, where there is some sort of finished product at the end; whether this is a successful campaign to save a park or the perfectly made birthday cake, you'll find your niche. The same applies to work. Not for you something ethereal and inconclusive in terms of a career; you are much happier when you can map out the beginning, middle and end of a piece of work, making you an extremely effective team player when needs be. In love, you don't like game-playing and can be straightforward to a fault. Don't forget that romance sometimes needs an edge of mystery and anticipation, too.

Numerology

No. 5: Impulsive and restless by nature, spontaneous and likes to discover the world through the senses.

Tarot

Seven of Cups: The Cups contain our emotions, and this number suggests you have plenty, but there's also a tendency towards wishful thinking. This may be because your imagination dreams up great ideas and you need to work out how to achieve them. It can help to remember that the attainment of desire requires determination.

Famous birthdays

Bradley Cooper American actor
Umberto Eco Italian writer
Diane Keaton American actress

January 6th

Grounded empath

As an earth sign, like others born on this date you have empathy which is rooted in something solid that can actually carry you and those you love forward in life. This is good because it means you're less likely to be overwhelmed by your empathic response to others. You're also likely to have empathy for the Earth, with an acute understanding of how we affect our environment. This instinctive knowledge may find you attracted to working in environmental or climate protection in some way, even if only as an activist in your local community. You know that we can all do our bit, but you may want to find a career that also supports this, perhaps in sustainable garden design or something similar. Your love and concern for the Earth is likely to extend to those who inhabit it alongside you, and indeed family and friends are very important to you. It may take you some time to find that one special person with whom to share your life, not least because they need to have the same aspirations as you and this may take some maturity.

Numerology

No. 6: Empathic and nurturing, can problem-solve in an emotional and physical way, responsible and cares deeply about family and friends.

Tarot

Judgement: This card is a powerful one from the Major Arcana and suggests the ability to make good and well-informed judgements, rather than knee-jerk reactions. The power also comes from flexibility and an ability to review ideas as circumstances change, and not take things at face value. This sort of wisdom often takes time to emerge.

Famous birthdays

Eddie Redmayne British actor
Joan of Arc French saint
Nigella Lawson British foodie writer

January 7th

Aspiring strategist

There's an entrepreneurial side to those born on this date, and you're likely to be a keen thinker who aspires to achieve their life goals and knows that it may take hard work to achieve them. As strategies go, hard work is just one of them because you also have the ability to visualise what you aspire to and, once in your sights, you will work out what it takes to get there. Vision and graft are the touchstones of many an entrepreneur and if at some point in your working life you find you are planning your own start-up to realise your dreams, then your chances of success will be better than most, whether this is online or on your local high street. Added to this, you are probably open to a wider range of influences than many from which to formulate your ideas – whether in the arts, health, finance or science, there's a diversity of interests matched with a sense of purpose. You may find you are applying this approach to your love life, but maybe not with as much success. It's worth remembering that intimate relationships take a lot more give and take and a little more compromise to work day to day.

Numerology

No. 7: Very analytical and detail-oriented, likes to observe and investigate things, and has a keen, inventive eye.

Tarot

Four of Cups: This card presents something of a quandary because the Cups are containers for emotions, and here someone is being offered one cup while eyeing up another three. Is it an either/or situation, or can you accumulate all four? It may take time and maturity to resolve this issue.

Famous birthdays

Lewis Hamilton British F1 racer
Christian Louboutin French shoe designer
Nicolas Cage American actor

January 8th

Enthusiastic reformer

Looking at a situation and seeing how it could be done better comes easily to those born on this day. It may be a mystery to everyone else, but you're likely to have the organisational flair and creative vision that makes reform, improvement and change easy to accomplish. It's a rare skill to be able to balance what needs to be changed and how, or even at all. It may take time to mature, but it shouldn't be ignored and needs to be nurtured to flourish. How might this work in your life? It may be that the practical nature of Capricorn brings this to bear in a career in education or social services, or even politics with either a large or a small 'P'. Trying to improve things for people, whether in a local community or on the world stage, will probably emerge during your working life. It's the same at home. You'll work happily in a partnership with someone you love to make your home life function as well and efficiently as possible, wanting to make improvements where you can. All this industry is probably tempered with good humour because you're an optimist at heart, too.

Numerology

No. 8: Sees the big picture and aims for it, linked to abundance and material wealth, and uses financial success to give back to others.

Tarot

King of Wands: The Wands are always depicted as alive, sprouting leaves, representative of our power. The King of Wands is undoubtedly powerful, but he's also honest and conscientious, and maybe rather austere yet tolerant. As ruler, we can expect good things from him, and this suggests that your role in life is a similar one.

Famous birthdays

David Bowie British singer-songwriter
Stephen Hawking British theoretical physicist
Shirley Bassey Welsh singer

January 9th

Wise counsellor

Some people have to reach maturity to achieve wisdom, but some are what we call 'old souls' from birth and this is probably something that was said about you as a child. When it comes to supporting those around you, whether workmates, friends or family, your counsel is often sought because of the thoughtfulness behind your response to someone's dilemma. That you are likely to be a practical soul also gives you the edge here, because whatever counsel you offer is rooted in a solution that makes good sense to its recipient. This natural inclination may take you into a career that involves helping to solve problems of an emotional nature, attracting you to roles in occupational health, human resources or psychotherapy. You just seem to know how to get at the nub of a problem and are also able to communicate your ideas effectively and easily. In your closest relationships, however, you may be inclined to take on too much responsibility for another's happiness. Remember that, in love, receiving support is as important as giving it.

Numerology

No. 9: An old soul that looks to spiritual awareness to solve life's problems and likes to help others to do so in the same way.

Tarot

Two of Swords: The Swords are about action and they also provide protection for those who seek help. The two swords are in balance and being held in each hand by someone in a blindfold, which suggests purpose and no judgement about those who need support. It's not always an easy life for someone to position themselves in this way in the service of others.

Famous birthdays

Catherine Middleton Duchess of Cambridge
Simone de Beauvoir French writer
Richard Nixon 37th President of the United States

January 10th

Ambitious performer

The view from the top is very much what you probably want to see, no matter how high the mountain you have to climb to get there. You're likely to be ambitious, but it's your ability to 'try on' personas for size that helps you to see how you need to adapt and find the courage and imagination in order to achieve the outcome you desire. Performance is part of this and may sometimes be an end in itself. Whether you pursue a career where you literally perform to an audience or not, performance in some way may be part of it – there's an element of performance in many people's working lives, and for the military, police or medical services there's even a 'costume'. What is important, however, is to know when not to perform. It can sometimes be something of a defence, hiding our real selves, and in our more personal relationships it's important to trust those we love with more vulnerable aspects of ourselves. In addition, the route to the top shouldn't be at the expense of our family and friends because when the audience departs, we will need their support.

Numerology

No. I: A powerful entity and results-oriented force, all about initiating action and getting things done.

Tarot

Ace of Pentacles: This is very much a card for someone who sees themself as numero uno in life, if not now, then in the future. The Pentacles suggest our resources, both material and emotional, and this card depicts the offer of one as a gift. The gift of a positive state of mind is a resource that will enable you to achieve your dreams.

Famous birthdays

Rod Stewart British singer
George Foreman American boxer
Abbey Clancy British model and TV presenter

January 11th

Articulate strategist

There are no flies on you, and when what's needed is someone who can cut through the emotional turmoil and make a reasoned and rational decision, you are the person for the job. You may sometimes be seen as a little aloof, but this is only because that razor-sharp intellect will be working overtime when you meet someone new. In fact, you are a loyal lover and friend once you have ascertained someone deserves your time and attention. Astute and cool-headed, you're well suited to an academic career, medicine or legal work. Watch that obstinate streak, which can alienate people who only want to help, and don't hide that huge loving heart away.

Numerology

No. 2: Shows resilience and power in gentleness, often provides the role of mediator, and linked to psychic abilities.

Tarot

The Six of Swords: You are adept at slicing your way through and navigating choppy waters, and will always make your way, slowly and surely, to greater happiness, thanks to your determination and uncanny ability to quickly assess the best course of action.

Famous birthdays

Kyle Richards star of *The Real Housewives of Beverley Hills*
Mary J. Blige American singer-songwriter
Rachel Riley *Countdown* presenter

January 12th

Quick-witted charmer

Ok, let's get the worst trait out of the way first – that short temper of yours. You're a natural leader, charming and seductive, but impatient. You may have a tendency to cut your losses and move on too quickly, which can mean missing out on a gem of a work project or love partner. But once you accept not everyone moves through life at the same lightning speed and that honey attracts more flies than vinegar, you will discover you have everything you need to live the good life. Money loves you just as much as you love it and, for you, spending is as much of a pleasure as good sex. You are excellent company, artistic and fun, and so won't ever be short of friends or people to party with and enjoy the finer things in life.

Numerology
No. 3: Creative with the gift of imagination and an ability to communicate in writing, art or speech.

Tarot
Temperance: One of the Major Arcana cards, Temperance signifies a link with higher consciousness. You know, deep down, that things are unfolding exactly as they should, and you are on the right life path. You may just need to learn to be patient.

Famous birthdays
Jeff Bezos Amazon founder
Pixie Lott British singer
Melanie Chisholm British singer

January 13th

Shy pragmatist

Not for you a laissez-faire attitude to other people, your social life and your work responsibilities – you take all these very, very seriously, often putting the needs of others before your own. You can get caught on the hamster wheel of work, work, work, but when you make time for play, you show your witty side and are great fun to be around. Shy but intensely sensual, you may take your time to commit to love, but when you do find your soulmate, you'll be signing on for a life-long passion and loving commitment to your mate. Ensure you make time for play and don't let yourself become overwhelmed by all the things you'd like to change to create a fairer society.

Numerology

No. 4: Invested in the physical world, centred earth energy that is practical in application.

Tarot

The Magician: Possibly the single most powerful card in the 78-card Tarot deck, the Magician uses his or her powers to bring about change for good, calling on all the resources at their disposal, including intuition and spiritual connection.

Famous birthdays

Orlando Bloom British actor
Bill Bailey British comedian
Liam Hemsworth Australian actor

January 14th

Ethical warrior

Social justice is your field and while fiercely individualistic in terms of how you set about bringing greater fairness to the world stage, improving things for the downtrodden is your primary mission in life. The ultimate humanitarian, where you sense injustice you will fight passionately for redress, sometimes expending so much energy on the collective that you neglect to take the same care of yourself and your own relationships. It may be that you are holding work colleagues and prospective love interests to your impossibly high ethical standards or that you simply fear being tied down, but whatever the block to forming stronger personal relationships, it is important you recognise what this could cost you in the long term – loneliness – if you don't try to cultivate standards that are less exacting for others.

Numerology

No. 5: Impulsive and restless by nature, spontaneous and likes to discover the world through the senses.

Tarot

The Star: The healing card of the Major Arcana, the message of the Star to you is to heal yourself before diving in to heal others. It will make you more effective in your campaigning and activism because when you speak, it will be and also sound authentic.

Famous birthdays

Carl Weathers American actor
Emily Watson British actress
Jack Jones American jazz singer

January 15th

Wise humourist

You already know money, which you are not overly concerned about, cannot buy you love and that laughing someone into bed is always a great start to being happy, with that happiness becoming the foundation of a loving home. You're not afraid to send yourself up or show your vulnerability, and the wisdom which underpins such a healthy attitude to what's most important in life is such an attractive quality that you won't ever be short of company or companionship. You love teamwork, so may be drawn to teaching, the armed forces or other careers where your humour and innate wisdom will soon have you recognised for a well-deserved promotion ... if you want one.

Numerology

No. 6: Empathic and nurturing, can problem-solve in an emotional and physical way, responsible and cares deeply about family and friends.

Tarot

Two of Cups: A card that is all about the happiness you create when you build the life you want with the one you love. For you, life is all about emotions, the most important one being happiness.

Famous birthdays

Martin Luther King Jr American civil rights activist
Claudia Winkleman British TV show host
Chad Lowe American actor and director

January 16th

Gifted problem-solver

With an enviable gift for communicating and sharing important ideas, coupled with fine diplomatic skills, it is easy to see how and why you have so much respect from both your immediate family and wider social networks, including work colleagues. It is as if you are able to integrate the rational and the slightly more mystical to troubleshoot and solve problems that would leave others flailing by the wayside. As you mature through life and your career, expect people to seek you out for your guidance and opinions. You will make a gifted teacher, whatever your chosen field, but don't neglect your own personal life when you are so busy helping others to find the right path and such elegant solutions to the challenges that come their way.

Numerology

No. 7: Very analytical and detail-oriented, likes to observe and investigate things, and has a keen, inventive eye.

Tarot

Knight of Wands: The Wands in the Tarot deck are all about communication, and this card signifies a powerful, often highly innovative and fearless communicator who will garner respect by saying out loud what others may not notice or may fear to admit.

Famous birthdays

Kate Moss British model
John Carpenter American director and composer
James May British TV presenter

January 17th

Confident leader

If being direct is the mark of a leader, then you have leadership qualities in spades. You have a strong sense of purpose and drive and also the tenacity to keep going to reach your goals. Having such strong convictions will inspire others to happily put you in charge, but a good leader is also a good listener and actively open to the ideas of others, which is a quality you will need to cultivate. It cannot be 'my way or the highway' all the time! You are gregarious, so enjoy teamwork and a lively social life. Watch the urge, though, to throw a temper tantrum if things don't go your way; nobody likes a dictator or a brat.

Numerology

No. 8: Sees the big picture and aims for it, linked to abundance and material wealth, and uses financial success to give back to others.

Tarot

The Wheel of Fortune: One of the very positive Major Arcana cards and a sign that the world really is lining up to give you everything your heart desires, as long as you learn to regulate your emotions and keep that temper in check.

Famous birthdays

Michelle Obama Attorney and former First Lady of the United States
Jim Carrey Canadian actor
Eartha Kitt American singer

January 18th

Psychic empath

You may not think of yourself as psychic, but you know that hunch you had about which horse would win the Derby and which Christmas cracker had the tiny scissors inside? You are so intuitive (and almost always right) that you may as well accept you have psychic gifts and carry on using them for the greater good, as well as your own protection. You instinctively know what others are feeling, which makes you popular at work and among friends; people really do like and respect you. And trust those hunches we mentioned because they will help you land the right job, find the right soulmate and, if you are planning a family, know when the time is exactly right to start one. You can sometimes struggle to show your deeper feelings, but this will get easier once you fully commit to someone.

Numerology

No. 9: An old soul that looks to spiritual awareness to solve life's problems and likes to help others to do so in the same way.

Tarot

Six of Pentacles: Pentacles signify money and wealth, and this card depicts a wise man sharing alms, which reflects your deep-seated empathy for the plight of others. If you can help, in whatever way, you will.

Famous birthdays

Leo Varadkar Irish politician
Estelle British singer and rapper
Kevin Costner American actor and director

January 19th

Unconventional visionary

Naturally curious and with the determination to look everywhere for the answers to the questions you may have, you would make a brilliant academic researcher, artist or musician because you simply don't see the world in the same way as everyone else. For those less courageous and farsighted, this can make you a challenge to be around, but you are never going to swap your originality for conventionality just to fit in. Make sure you surround yourself with people who appreciate what a rare gift you have, instead of fearing it, and, although it's true you do your best work in solitude, don't let that preference for your own company allow you to become so isolated you cannot find your way back to close connections with the people you love.

Numerology

No. 1: A powerful entity and results-oriented force, all about initiating action and getting things done.

Tarot

Eight of Swords: This is a difficult card because it depicts a woman bound and blindfolded and imprisoned by swords, but as always with the Tarot, things are not as bleak as they may at first seem. For you, this card is simply a warning not to get so caught up in your extraordinary vision that you leave everyone behind and find yourself alone, isolated and trapped in a prison of your own making.

Famous birthdays

Dolly Parton American singer-songwriter and businesswoman
Edgar Allan Poe American writer
Janis Joplin American singer-songwriter

January 20th

Rebellious change-maker

You're ambitious but more for the changes you want to see in the world than for yourself and, luckily, you have the charm to gently persuade others to see your point of view and help you realise your goals for the greater good. You are an unconventional thinker but have a sociable nature which means you work best in a team and can happily find a path that combines business and pleasure. Having such lofty ideals can sometimes make you impatient with others who may be slower to catch on, including romantic partners, so it's important you build a life with someone who shares some of those ideals or you will end up resenting each other.

Numerology

No. 2: Shows resilience and power in gentleness, often provides the role of mediator, and linked to psychic abilities.

Tarot

Ten of Wands: This card depicts a young man struggling to carry ten large sticks towards a town in the far distance; the Wands represent communication, so this card signifies the burden you may be feeling trying to get your ideas where you need them to be heard to effect change. Slow down and trust they will reach the right ears at the right time.

Famous birthdays

Gary Barlow British singer-songwriter
Buzz Aldrin American astronaut
Skeet Ulrich American actor

January 21st

Kind mentor

Drawn to the arts – music, painting, writing and design – you bring new ideas to your chosen speciality and, although sometimes a bit unpredictable, will be seen by others as multi-talented and someone whose advice and guidance is worth seeking out. You know the value to others of praising and encouraging their efforts, and you are often selfless in supporting and comforting other people, including and especially children. You are kind and idealistic and so may already be working on setting up a charitable foundation to help others or some other kind of initiative that will allow you to champion those who need it most. If you're not already doing this, don't be surprised if something similar finds its way to you out of the blue and is the perfect fit for the next chapter of your life.

Numerology

No. 3: Creative with the gift of imagination and an ability to communicate in writing, art or speech.

Tarot

Ace of Cups: This fantastically positive card tells you everything is aligning to give you the life you imagine for yourself; a life full of wonderment, love and, just as importantly for you, magical opportunities to use your creative gifts to truly help and support others, making a difference in the lives of everyone you meet.

Famous birthdays

Grigori Rasputin Russian mystic and visionary
Geena Davis American actress
Christian Dior French fashion designer

January 22nd

Enthusiastic environmentalist

You love the natural world and the great outdoors, but not simply as a spectator. You understand the damage we have done to the planet and even if you have taken a different career path, you will likely be doing something on a voluntary basis that will help raise awareness of the need to change our ways and better protect our planet and all who share it. Your enthusiasm is infectious, so you are good at getting the 'yes' you need from others to get the job done, but you get bored easily and are sometimes a bit guilty of thinking the grass is greener and of abandoning a worthwhile project halfway through for the sparkle of something shiny and new. All you need to remember is that the grass is actually greener where we choose to water it and that every project or ambition will present challenges that you are more than capable of working through. Look for a stable and grounded soulmate who won't let you spin enthusiastically out of control.

Numerology

No. 4: Invested in the physical world, centred earth energy that is practical in application.

Tarot

The Page of Cups: The young man in this card is holding a gold chalice with a fish swimming inside, which signifies that with you, emotions really do run very deep. Your enthusiasm can often disguise just how concerned you are, but this is also a card depicting resilience, so know that whatever you decide to take on in life, you have the resources and power you need to cope.

Famous birthdays

John Hurt British actor
Sam Cooke American soul singer
Diane Lane American actress and producer

January 23rd

Intelligent rebel

Quick-witted and equally quick-thinking, you're an engaging storyteller and entertainer, playing up, rather than playing down, your own quirky nature and eccentricities. You've a huge thirst for knowledge and a passion for learning, and you're just as likely to be an historian as a futurologist. You know the rules but don't much care for them: personal freedom is your goal and heaven help anyone who tries to change you or tie you down because you'll be gone in a puff of smoke, slipping quietly away out of a side door. You are impulsive but intuitive with it and know that, for you, friendship and common interests, rather than a romantic intensity, will give your loving relationship the foundation it needs to survive all of this quirkiness. Once you do commit, you will be a loyal and honourable partner through life.

Numerology

No. 5: Impulsive and restless by nature, spontaneous and likes to discover the world through the senses.

Tarot

Ten of Cups: Joy, Joy, Joy! One of the most uplifting cards in the entire 78-card Tarot deck, the Ten of Cups depicts a happy couple watching their children skipping under a rainbow with their happy home nestled in the background between protective trees. This is a card of immense love, joy and complete fulfilment in all you undertake and dream of.

Famous birthdays

Addison Russell American baseball player
Chesley Sullenberger American airline pilot
Tiffani Thiessen American actress

January 24th

Independent animal lover

It's not that people don't find you attractive or want to be with you, it's more that if you were really honest, you'd admit you can sometimes rate lust more highly than love and, put quite simply, just like being on your own or, better still, in the peaceful company of animals that you can care for. Others find you intriguing, mysterious even, especially if you've left your heart-breaker teens and twenties behind and are settled into a peaceful life in some far-flung corner of the world where the fact you keep yourself to yourself only serves to add more intrigue to the mystery of who you are and where you come from. You may meet your soulmate, marry, settle down and live happily ever after, but if that doesn't happen you won't be shedding any tears for a life you never really gave a second thought to. You are a caring and thoughtful friend, and you will enjoy deep connections with those you choose to stay close to, all of whom will accept that you may just be the least 'needy' and most independent person they have ever known.

Numerology

No. 6: Empathic and nurturing, can problem-solve in an emotional and physical way, responsible and cares deeply about family and friends.

Tarot

King of Pentacles: Pentacles signify financial stability. The King of Pentacles is a self-made figure who has carved his own way through life gathering all the material resources he needs to now live stress-free and enjoy his own company. He likes the finer things in life and has earned them, but his feet are firmly on the ground and he is not likely to be swayed by shiny objects. This is a kind person who, just like you, relishes his own company but equally, if he appreciates you, he is very, very nice to be around.

Famous birthdays

Neil Diamond American singer-songwriter
Adrian Edmondson British comedian
Edith Wharton American writer

January 25th

Sensitive carer

You are so attuned to the feelings and needs of others that you have a sensitivity bordering on a psychic gift. Most days, this will feel like a blessing in your life, especially if you work in the caring professions, but you may feel occasionally overwhelmed by all the pain and hurt in the world and beat a hasty retreat into solitude. This can be confusing for those who, until now, have only met the caring and sociable version of you. They will wonder what happened? If you start feeling swamped by a sense of fatalism, remind yourself that a glass half full looks the same as one half empty but feels a whole lot better, and surround yourself with positive people to help you stay on track.

Numerology

No. 7: Very analytical and detail-oriented, likes to observe and investigate things, and has a keen, inventive eye.

Tarot

Strength: One of the Major Arcana, this card depicts a woman gently closing the mouth of a male lion. Her strength, like yours, lies in the gentle and caring way she is handling a wild animal that could easily overwhelm her. It is a reminder that you too are stronger than you think and when you feel overwhelmed, know that this feeling, as with all feelings, will pass.

Famous birthdays

Robert Burns Scottish poet
Etta James American blues singer
Virginia Woolf British writer

January

January 26th

Charismatic powerhouse

You exude such a powerful aura of self-confidence that it can feel hypnotic to those who cross your path, all of whom will quickly recognise your commanding personality. You have such a strong sense of right from wrong that you will naturally land in some kind of leadership role where you are not afraid to invent new rules to replace the ones you don't like, or to forge ahead in a completely new direction. You have the dogged determination to navigate choppy waters and when you succeed, you expect the right level of appreciation for your efforts. You may, initially, find intimacy a bit uncomfortable, but once your trust has been won, you are a loyal and loving partner who is devoted to their mate.

Numerology

No. 8: Sees the big picture and aims for it, linked to abundance and material wealth, and uses financial success to give back to others.

Tarot

The Emperor: One of the Major Arcana, this card depicts a mature man who embodies gravitas and wisdom, signifying your potential to become a truly great person as you navigate the path you have chosen through life. You will likely be a great protector of others already and will be someone who people love, admire and describe as inspirational once you reach your dotage.

Famous birthdays

Ellen DeGeneres American TV show host
Eddie Van Halen American guitarist
José Mourinho Portuguese football coach

January 27th

Maverick mystic

If anyone is going to leave their mark on the world, it will be those born on this day. You're a born mentor with a deft touch for helping others to realise their dreams and when not working, you will be delving into the mysteries – known and unknown – of life. You are driven and self-motivated and work best alone without the irksome need for supervision. Spiritually curious, you are unlikely to conform to any conventional stereotypes and, as a result, may find the emotional demands of others a bit smothering and restrictive. Make sure you choose a life partner as independent as you are, especially if your real goal is to contribute something important to the world.

Numerology

No. 9: An old soul that looks to spiritual awareness to solve life's problems and likes to help others to do so in the same way.

Tarot

The High Priestess: With her deep sense of spiritual connection and love of learning, the High Priestess is flanked by two temples of wisdom and is the female match to the Magician. She will not pass through this world without leaving her mark, and neither will you.

Famous birthdays

Wolfgang Amadeus Mozart Austrian composer
Daisy Lowe British model
Edward Smith British naval officer and Captain of RMS *Titanic*

January 28th

Dreamy romantic

Astute in business and among the best wheeler-dealers of the zodiac, there's nothing that can distract this good-looking Aquarian from their search for true love. For those born on this day, love is everything; love is all they really care about. More dreamy-romantic than go-getting Romeo or Juliet, the only problem is that this intense yearning to find and give love lies deep inside a shy outer shell. This means that, although love really is the thing they care about most, they will sit back passively waiting for fate to intervene and send the perfect partner their way. And so, unless family and friends take it upon themselves to act as matchmaker, it may take quite a while to find that longed-for soulmate.

Numerology

No. I: A powerful entity and results-oriented force, all about initiating action and getting things done.

Tarot

The Lovers: What other card could signify the deep yearning of those born on this day to find their soulmate and true love? The naked man and woman depicted on the card represent the blending of the male and female energies in a perfectly balanced and magical union the alchemists would refer to as 'the sacred marriage'. It is sacred and this is why finding that love is so important to you.

Famous birthdays

Henry VII Tudor King of England
Nicolas Sarkozy French politician
Gianluigi Buffon Italian goalkeeper

January 29th

Determined campaigner

Always the first in line to volunteer for a charitable cause or goal, you have the gifts of a quick wit and reasoned thinking with which to convert people to the causes that you champion. You have a natural sense of justice which may propel you from the start into a career as a politician or campaigner and, with some real-world experience under your belt, you can become a formidable operator in both fields. Preferring reasoned persuasion to outright confrontation, it is hard to say no when you come knocking and it can be a struggle for you to restore your equilibrium if someone does turn you down, because you take rejection very personally. Look for a mate who will bring a breezy happiness to the relationship and stop you tipping over into martyrdom.

Numerology

No. 2: Shows resilience and power in gentleness, often provides the role of mediator, and linked to psychic abilities.

Tarot

Seven of Cups: All the Cups in the Tarot deck reflect an emotional state and with this destiny card, you, more than most, will realise how material possessions fade to insignificance once you understand the importance and value of the things that money cannot buy and which we cannot and would not want to live without: things like justice and equality, fairness and love.

Famous birthdays

Oprah Winfrey American TV show host
Anton Chekhov Russian playwright
Tom Selleck American actor and producer

January 30th

Persuasive leader

Whether it's a career in the arts or the military services, where you lead, people will happily follow. This is as much about the fact that you hate being told what to do as it is about your natural ability to motivate others. Indeed, even in your romantic relationships, there's a tendency to sulk and use passive-aggressive manipulation when you don't get your own way: it's not exactly 'my way or the highway' but it comes close, and while your talent for persuasion is impressive, you need to learn to allow others to express themselves instead of being instantly dismissive if their views differ from yours – there are many riches to be gained from diversity and, you never know, you may even learn something useful, too! You'll demand unwavering love and support from your family and friends, and you will be more than happy to give that back to them.

Numerology

No. 3: Creative with the gift of imagination and an ability to communicate in writing, art or speech.

Tarot

Four of Pentacles: You may have a hard time trusting you can hang on to the good stuff that comes your way. Pentacles are all about resources, both financial and emotional, and the man in this card is hanging on tightly to his. Relax your grip, let go and see what new opportunities come your way.

Famous birthdays

Christian Bale British actor
Franklin D. Roosevelt 32nd President of the United States
Phil Collins British drummer and singer-songwriter

January 31st

Psychically gifted

All Aquarians have strong intuition, but if you're born on the last day of this month, it's likely your gift is too strong to ignore or dismiss as a good imagination. Don't be surprised if you know what someone is going to say before they open their mouth or that you will know far more about them than they are saying. These gifts will work well for you if you choose a career in the healing arts. If you plan on developing them, then find a trusted mentor who will help you put boundaries in place, so you don't end up doing all the giving and surrounded by people who just can't get enough of you and your unconventional wisdom.

Numerology

No. 4: Invested in the physical world, centred earth energy that is practical in application.

Tarot

The Magician: Surprise, surprise! Well, not really. The Magician, with his/her strong psychic abilities, navigates easily between worlds to work their magic for the greater good and keep the portals to the Ancient Mysteries open. If you choose, this can be your path, too.

Famous birthdays

Jackie Robinson American baseball player
Minnie Driver British actress
Derek Jarman British director

February 1st

Pioneering humanitarian

Non-conformist and highly intuitive, you'll happily step in where angels fear to tread if you think some good will come of it. This means, in both work and play, you'll often spot opportunities to make a difference that others may have missed. February 1st is Imbolc – the pagan feast of the waxing light and one of the four annual fire festivals. You'll know all about that fire in the belly which makes you the one to get things done, whatever the obstacles ahead. You prefer to work unsupervised and alone, and in romantic unions, you will rate friendship and companionship just as highly as love and be looking for a life partner who is happy to let you 'do' you.

Numerology

No. 1: A powerful entity and results-oriented force, all about initiating action and getting things done.

Tarot

The Sun: One of the Major Arcana and a glorious card depicting the warmth of the Sun shining down on all your endeavours throughout life. This is a card that shows vitality and promises both abundance and success.

Famous birthdays

Harry Styles British singer-songwriter and actor
Langston Hughes African-American poet and activist
Lisa Marie Presley American singer-songwriter

February 2nd

Practical thinker

Those born on this day may not be the first to offer a hug or a sympathetic ear, but this rational Aquarian will be the first to slip a little something into your bank account if you fall on hard times and also the first to turn up with a drill to help you put up shelves when you move house. Those who don't really know you may find you a bit buttoned-up, but those that do and love you for your steadiness would never swap you and your love for someone more flighty. You are bossy but get things done, and most of your bossiness is well-intentioned. You're a hard worker and an unconditional lover who gives without expecting anything in return, and once people understand that with you, actions will always speak louder than soft words or even empathising emotions, they will fight to keep you interested in them and in their corner.

Numerology

No. 2: Shows resilience and power in gentleness, often provides the role of mediator, and linked to psychic abilities.

Tarot

Three of Wands: In the Tarot deck, Wands are the suit of communicators and with this card, a successful merchant, standing on higher ground, is looking out across the desert to a far-flung land where his ships, full of hard-earned riches, are sailing. He has been successful through hard work and perseverance and knows actions matter more than pleasing words.

Famous birthdays

Shakira Colombian singer-songwriter
Farrah Fawcett American actress
Christie Brinkley American model and actress

February 3rd

Free spirit

It can be hard for you to suppress a chuckle when others tell you that they are free spirits who dislike being tied down. You'll look at their safe lifestyle choices, think about your own more adventurous ones, and know that to be truly free-spirited and an independent thinker is a very rare thing indeed. It's not that you don't want a close connection and loving relationship with another person, you just have to find someone you can have that with minus any sense of being suffocated by them and their demands on you. Sensitive and original, you probably work in the arts or if you have chosen science, you will be off developing and testing your own original hypothesis. You really are a one-off!

Numerology

No. 3: Creative with the gift of imagination and an ability to communicate in writing, art or speech.

Tarot

Ten of Pentacles: People love you and you love people (just as long as they don't smother you), and this card shows just how joyous your life is going to be when you find your soulmate and set up a base together from which you can fly off to explore other worlds and dreams, always returning home to ground yourself. The card shows a happy couple dancing at their homestead, their union watched approvingly by a snowy-haired, wise old man.

Famous birthdays

Amal Clooney Lebanese lawyer
Ferdinand Magellan Portuguese explorer
Warwick Davis British actor

February

February 4th

Idealistic adventurer

Don't be fooled by the quirky, fun-loving character of those born on this day because although they are adventurous, they have a strong sense of self-determination and practical purpose, which makes them one of the hardest working people you will ever meet. As long as you don't mistake fun-loving for frivolous, you'll get on just fine with this industrious Aquarian who will likely be involved in some humanitarian endeavour, either professionally or as a volunteer, and give their all to making things better wherever there is social injustice or unfairness. If you do tangle with them, make sure they remember all work and no play is not a recipe for well-being. Also remind them to stop and smell the roses, or they might wake up one morning and find they've faded and it's too late to drink in their heady scent.

Numerology

No. 4: Invested in the physical world, with a centred earth energy that is practical in application.

Tarot

The Fool: One of the Major Arcana, there's nothing foolish about the Fool who, armed with provisions and a little white dog for company, is stepping out to discover the world and find his place in it. The dog represents his (your) instinct, so rest assured you are travelling through life and all those adventures with the best protection you could ask for – your own sense of right and wrong and what will be best for you and yours.

Famous birthdays

Rosa Parks American civil rights activist
Charles Lindbergh American aviator
Natalie Imbruglia Australian singer-songwriter

February 5th

Talented multi-tasker

You are one of those souls that seems to have been here before. Whatever you turn your hand to, you'll seem effortlessly good at it and, just to make everyone a teeny bit more jealous, you not only have more than your share of charisma, you're also a very kind person, too. If this all sounds too good to be true, it can sometimes feel that way because one of the downsides of being able to turn your hand to anything is that it can make you restless and unable to decide what it is you actually want to give your energy to and spend your life working on. You may be drawn to journalism and broadcasting where you can legitimately hop between disciplines. Don't be surprised if you hit middle age and suddenly change tack entirely. You'll be ready to reinvent yourself – yet again – but this time with more of an emphasis on a mature understanding of how important spirituality is to you.

Numerology

No. 5: Impulsive and restless by nature, spontaneous and likes to discover the world through the senses.

Tarot

The Tower: Not the prettiest card in the pack, but don't panic; it may look like the apocalypse but what the Tower, one of the important Major Arcana, signifies for you is that when everything collapses, then everything can start again. We've already seen that you're likely to up sticks and change course completely mid-life; you may even do this multiple times throughout your life, with each time you make a big change being reflected by the Tower card.

Famous birthdays

Cristiano Ronaldo Portuguese football player
Bobby Brown American R&B singer-songwriter
Michael Sheen Welsh actor

February 6th

Fiercely independent

Employ that original intelligence of yours in the field of scientific research or, if you are more artistically inclined, musical composition, and you will succeed where others, who may have a more limited way of looking at the world, may not. Ever curious, you have a forensic ability to ask the right questions to lead you to the answers you are seeking, and this is a skill you can and will use in your personal life as well as at work. This deep thirst for knowledge can translate into 'gets bored easily and moves on', so take care not to get a name for being someone who doesn't stick around long enough to make a real difference. Others will find you intriguing, if not inspiring, and you may find yourself voted into some kind of leadership role, even if this wasn't something you were thinking about or seeking for yourself. When you're ready to settle down with a life partner, find someone who has so many layers to their personality that you'll never get bored trying to get to the very last one.

Numerology

No. 6: Empathic and nurturing, can problem-solve in an emotional and physical way, responsible and cares deeply about family and friends.

Tarot

Five of Cups: Cups depict our deep-seated, often hidden, true emotional nature and in this moving card an older brother is offering the gift of his undying love and protection to a younger sister. These two have been through some sorrows and share an unspoken pact to help each other heal. You too may carry hurts from childhood, but you will use your fierce intelligence and independent spirit – perhaps through having therapy – to ask the right questions about, as well as better understand and heal from, these hurts. Or you may use these skills and your amazing insight into the motivations of others to become a therapist yourself.

Famous birthdays

Bob Marley Jamaican reggae singer-songwriter
Ronald Reagan 40th President of the United States
Zsa Zsa Gabor Hungarian actress and socialite

February 7th

Thoughtful communicator

You intrigue others with the strange mix of a magnetic and gregarious personality, which people find hard to resist, and your need to disappear, on a regular basis, into solitude and silence to work out your original thoughts in private. Gentle and sensitive to the needs and plight of others, you may choose to work in the media or campaigning, where your ability to analyse and powerfully communicate the problem, but then also to visualise the solution to an injustice or hardship, will catch people's attention on a global scale and galvanise them to help. You are a wonderful and loyal friend, but you may idealise romantic relationships and end up disappointed when you discover that your lover has feet of clay. You want a close connection, but you are so scared of losing your independence that you may push someone who is right for you away. Talk about this fear with them before it happens.

Numerology

No. 7: Very analytical and detail-oriented, likes to observe and investigate things, and has a keen, inventive eye.

Tarot

The World: One of the Major Arcana, the world is both your stage and your oyster if you manage to get the right balance between being a magnetic force for the greater good and someone who needs to retreat and recharge through solitude. When the time is right, you will get the opportunity to make a contribution that really will expand our collective consciousness and help us right long-established wrongs in society. Whether you take this opportunity will be up to you.

Famous birthdays

Charles Dickens British writer and social critic
Laura Ingalls Wilder American writer
Eddie Izzard British comedian

February 8th

Creative country-dweller

You may currently be stuck in the city for work, but given half the chance, you'd be living in the countryside in a heartbeat. You thrive in your own company and in both the peace and pace of a rural lifestyle where there's no shortage of creative activities to make you happy, from gardening and growing, to writing and classical music. Marriage has never been high on your wish list; you may make a long-term and faithful commitment if the right person comes along, but the solo life suits you and you'll cope better than most if you find yourself parenting children without a partner. You have a way with words, so may write for a living or just for fun, and those will be real books, especially books on poetry and nature writing, on the bookshelves in your quaint cottage home. You are nice, but no pushover, and don't tolerate fools too gladly, either.

Numerology

No. 8: Sees the big picture and aims for it, linked to abundance and material wealth, and uses financial success to give back to others.

Tarot

Seven of Cups: We all need enough money to pay our bills, but you already know that no amount of material riches can make you happy or emotionally fulfilled in the same way as living happily in your own skin. This card shows a shadowy figure stepping away from all the material charms of life and turning their back on those shiny objects that just leave us craving more.

Famous birthdays

James Dean American actor
John Williams American composer
Dmitri Mendeleev Russian chemist

February 9th

Gifted counsellor

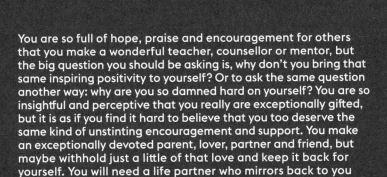

You are so full of hope, praise and encouragement for others that you make a wonderful teacher, counsellor or mentor, but the big question you should be asking is, why don't you bring that same inspiring positivity to yourself? Or to ask the same question another way: why are you so damned hard on yourself? You are so insightful and perceptive that you really are exceptionally gifted, but it is as if you find it hard to believe that you too deserve the same kind of unstinting encouragement and support. You make an exceptionally devoted parent, lover, partner and friend, but maybe withhold just a little of that love and keep it back for yourself. You will need a life partner who mirrors back to you all the faith, love and encouragement you give them. The only person still thinking that you don't deserve just as much as you give out is you. Try a little less giving and a little more taking – you may just be surprised by how good that feels.

Numerology

No. 9: An old soul that looks to spiritual awareness to solve life's problems and likes to help others to do so in the same way.

Tarot

Two of Pentacles: Pentacles depict our resources, which can be money, but they can also be our emotional resilience, compassion and empathy, and our self-worth. The young man depicted on this card is juggling the equal and opposite weights of the two pentacles captured in the infinity sign he is holding. He is scared to stop in case he drops one or the other. You carry this same fear, which comes from measuring yourself against an impossibly high standard. Drop one of those pentacles and surprise yourself by learning that you will survive to tell the tale!

Famous birthdays

Joe Pesci American actor
Carole King American singer-songwriter
Natsume Sōseki Japanese writer

February 10th

Fervent crusader

A bundle of high energy, with you what you see is what you get. There's no sly side or secret agenda; it's all out in the open for anyone to see, and while you are so good-natured that you rarely take umbrage or hold a grudge, if someone does betray your trust, you'll drop them from your life forever. Romantic relationships are important to you, as is the welfare of your family, so although you may appear to bounce from one passion to the next, your concern about those you love and have loved is deep and genuine. You are an idealist and a fervent crusader for the rights of others, and you have such an innovative mind – nobody will ever accuse you of being logical – that you often come up with ingenious ideas which are light years ahead of their time.

Numerology

No. 1: A powerful entity and results-oriented force, all about initiating action and getting things done.

Tarot

Four of Cups: The young man depicted on this card is sitting under a tree with his arms folded defensively, looking suspiciously at the cup that is being offered to him by the hand of Spirit. If he (you) can reach forward and accept that cup, life will open all its magical pathways to you. There is an opportunity with your name on it; take it and see the difference this makes to so many lives around the world.

Famous birthdays

Holly Willoughby British TV presenter
Bertolt Brecht German playwright and poet
Laura Dern American actress

February

February 11th

Original thinker

It's not that you think the rules don't apply to you, it's more that you don't think about the rules at all. Luckily for you, talent is not tied to conformity, so where others may get into trouble for turning up late, missing deadlines and generally marching to the original beat of their own drum, you are somehow excused and forgiven (which will often infuriate those around you who will complain, quite rightly, that it really isn't fair). Fairness is not really a concern of yours, either. You're too busy squeezing the life out of every minute of every day and every experience that comes your way to stop and think about falling into line and conforming. The reason you're forgiven for your rule breaking is because you're an original thinker with some very big and brilliant ideas, which, if you want them to, will take you right up the ladder to the very top of your chosen career. Tune in to your mostly hidden psychic gifts and it won't be hard to make this happen.

Numerology

No. 2: Shows resilience and power in gentleness, often provides the role of mediator, and linked to psychic abilities.

Tarot

Page of Swords: Just like the red-booted young man depicted on this card swinging his sword, you like to cut a swathe through the tedium of everyday life and its conventions to find and walk your own path. But don't expect everyone to get smartly out of your way just because you have that sword in your hand. Not everyone will appreciate what an original you are and so there may be times when you need to tone it down in order to take your next step.

Famous birthdays

Thomas Edison American inventor
Jennifer Aniston American actress
Sheryl Crow American singer-songwriter

February 12th

Confident leader

Driven and ambitious, you are well suited to a career in the military, politics or any other field where you can feel you are fighting on the side of 'right'. There are no greys in your world – there's black and white, and you're not wasting time with any discussion suggesting otherwise. You believe actions speak louder than words and however you start, you will end your chosen career in a position of seniority with people looking up to you. Your passion for social justice is admirable, but you are no killjoy because you are equally passionate about enjoying the finer things in life – including good company. Your life partner will need to be your equal and match you in your appreciation of these things, so you can enjoy sharing them together when you're not out there changing the world.

Numerology

No. 3: Creative with the gift of imagination and an ability to communicate in writing, art or speech.

Tarot

Three of Pentacles: In this card, a young apprentice is being congratulated by senior guild members and is, literally, elevated to a higher status by standing on a bench. You can expect not just success in everything you commit to, but also public recognition at some point for your contribution to the changes that help improve the lives of others. You may not seek or want it, but there is a good chance fame will find you later in life.

Famous birthdays

Charles Darwin British naturalist, biologist and geologist
Jennifer Stone American actress
Lee Byung-chul South Korean founder of the Samsung Group

February 13th

Rising star

With your talent for writing, music, dancing, theatre and directing, you're almost certainly likely to be working in the world of entertainment where you'll be known as a classy act, and one people will seek out to work with again and again. The whole world really is your stage and sipping champagne in the first-class cocktail lounge at the airport is all in a normal day's work for you. You're so impossibly glamorous, people will assume you've no time for the 'little people' you've left trailing in your wake, but nothing could be further from the truth. You're happy to play your part in public, but you're even happier to catch up with family or friends over a pizza at the local eatery. Love is important to you, but you're looking for something long-lasting, and while others may make lust and sex their top priority, you'll be just as happy hanging out with a lover who is also a best friend walking the dogs round the park or just sitting in the local coffee shop people-watching and chatting about the latest Oscar-nominated movies.

Numerology

No. 3: Creative with the gift of imagination and an ability to communicate in writing, art or speech.

Tarot

Ace of Cups: This stunning card shows the hand of Spirit offering you absolutely everything you could ever dream of or desire in life; all you have to do is show up, offer your talents to the project or your heart to the loved one, and everything else will just fall into place. Abundance on all levels, material and spiritual, leading to happiness and complete emotional fulfilment lies in wait for you.

Famous birthdays

Robbie Williams British singer-songwriter
Leslie Feist Canadian singer-songwriter
Peter Gabriel British singer-songwriter

February 14th

Articulate aesthete

Witty and driven, you have seemingly boundless energy and drive to get things done, which can often intimidate those who just can't think as quickly on their feet as you can. Be careful not to push these people away, especially with your biting humour, and remember one person's banter may be another's hurtful wounding. You are so articulate that you'll do well in whatever career you choose, whether in the arts or science, but the thing that makes your heart really happy is beauty – whether a painting, a piece of music, a chef's innovative signature dish or a finely crafted piece of pottery. You like to explore the world through all the senses and this fierce love of an aesthetic nicely balances that fierce intellect of yours, so make sure you nurture and encourage it. You may be a maker (manufacturer) yourself and if you are, then your business will be making something that is not only useful but also beautifully designed and aesthetically pleasing. Your life partner is likely to be good to look at, as well as your intellectual equal.

Numerology

No. 5: Impulsive and restless by nature, spontaneous and likes to discover the world through the senses.

Tarot

King of Swords: An intimidating character, the King of Swords sits on his throne ready to slice through time-wasting ideas and nonsense. Or he may just use his weapon to poke fun at those who take themselves too seriously. Handsome, well-dressed and comfortable in his own skin, he knows the value of beauty in uplifting the soul and is unlikely to be swayed from the comfortable path he has chosen and earned the right to follow.

Famous birthdays

Jimmy Hoffa American labour leader
Mike Bloomberg American businessman and politician
Simon Pegg British actor

February 15th

Charismatic visionary

You can just see it – what needs to happen and why – and so you work best with those who are already on the same page, although with your charisma, it's not hard for you to persuade others to join you. The original 'popular kid' in school, your warm and outgoing nature means you will likely have lots of friends and acquaintances, but you know when it comes to love that less is often more, and so you value the importance of close family and friends who provide a safe and quiet haven for you to recharge between each whirlwind of activity. You're not fazed by the obstacles or challenges standing in the way of turning your vision into a reality and you'll never give up on anyone you think you can help out of a bad patch. Fundamentally an optimist, you should look for the same attitude in a life partner to make a long-lasting and mutual love match.

Numerology

No. 6: Empathic and nurturing, can problem-solve in an emotional and physical way, responsible and cares deeply about family and friends.

Tarot

Death: One of the Major Arcana cards, Death actually signifies transformation – usually the end of one thing and the start of something new – so there is no need to be fearful of this auspicious card. In your case, it relates to your ability to have a vision and then take action to transform that vision into reality. It is your greatest strength!

Famous birthdays

Galileo Galilei Italian astronomer
Lillian Disney American illustrator and wife of Walt Disney
Jane Seymour English actress

February 16th

Cautious realist

Nobody is ever going to accuse you of jumping in either feet first or where angels fear to tread, because you won't make a move, in any direction, until you've weighed up all the pros and cons and considered what the worst possible outcome could be. This does not mean you are a pessimist, just someone who wants to make sure they've thought through all the angles and explored all the options before making a decision based on solid information rather than hopes and dreams. You're a talented all-rounder, which makes you a love match for wildly different types, and it's not unheard of for you to wake up one morning and decide the person you are currently with is no longer your type at all. Maybe don't keep a tally of the broken hearts you've left in your wake. Happily, when you do find a life partner who can keep your interest, you can expect a joyous union, even though you'll never be persuaded to believe in miracles!

Numerology

No. 7: Very analytical and detail-oriented, likes to observe and investigate things, and has a keen, inventive eye.

Tarot

Six of Wands: Crowned with a laurel wreath, which denotes a triumphant procession through life, this card depicts a well-deserved winner riding into town to claim his reward for a job well done. Wands signify the importance of good communication in achieving a successful outcome and because you leave nothing to chance, your communication, like the staff in the young man's hand, is reliable, trustworthy and solid.

Famous birthdays

Ice T American rapper
Christopher Eccleston British actor
John McEnroe American tennis player

February 17th

Empathic activist

Building a better world is the reason you get up in the morning, so it's likely you will work full-time as an activist channelling all that determination of yours into persuading others to implement the ideals that really will make the world a better, safer and fairer place and to unshackle those living under a cloud of injustice and fear. You've had to learn to build a thicker skin to protect your soft heart, and although you may now come across as tough, there's no hiding your sensitivity from those who really know and love you. You'll need a collaborative and enlightened workplace to thrive since you don't like being shackled, either, and it will be your kindness that draws the right life partner to you at the right time – probably in the short time you take a break between your campaigns to save the world and everyone in it.

Numerology

No. 8: Sees the big picture and aims for it, linked to abundance and material wealth, and uses financial success to give back to others.

Tarot

Eight of Cups: The Cups represent emotions and in this card the figure walking away from us across a mystical landscape and by the light of a saddened Sun and crescent Moon appears bent in sorrow, too. This simply means you have the resilience and fortitude to face the sorrows you see and learn of in the material world but the determination to head for a better place which offers fairness to all. You may have to climb that mountain depicted in the background to get there, but you have a sturdy staff for support.

Famous birthdays

Ed Sheeran British singer-songwriter
Michael Jordan American baseball player
Rene Russo American actress and producer

February 18th

Persuasive reformer

OK, when we say oddball here, we mean it as a compliment. What's unusual about you is you have a world view – and a drive to make things better – that is a mix of strong scientific thinking with heady metaphysical ideas, but what really spurs you on is your belief in yourself and your own instinctive hunches. Immensely charitable, you've made no secret of the fact you want to serve the world, but you're not a selfless martyr, either, so if you can do this in a way that benefits you too, all the better! A caring, compassionate and romantic nature makes you attractive to others, and when you embark on an intimate relationship with someone, you'll pour your heart and soul into it. You can be too idealistic, which leads to disappointment when you discover all human beings are flawed, so don't ditch someone just because they fail to live up to your impossible expectations. See through the flaws and love them for who they are, not who you want them to be.

Numerology

No. 9: An old soul that looks to spiritual awareness to solve life's problems and likes to help others to do so in the same way.

Tarot

The Star: One of the 22 Major Arcana cards in the Tarot deck, the Star depicts a naked woman pouring water from the primordial pool of collective consciousness onto the earth and topping up that pool with a second jug of aqua. She is balanced just so between the material and the spiritual lives, and is telling you that if you wish, you have all the protection you need to do something truly extraordinary with your life. Take action and watch a miracle unfold.

Famous birthdays

John Travolta American actor
Mary I Tudor Queen of England
Enzo Ferrari Italian racing driver and car maker

February 19th

Original hippie

If you're not already living in the countryside, you will be one day. You have a strong understanding of, and appreciation for, 'the other', and probably talked to fairies and elves at the bottom of the garden in your childhood. Wherever you settle there will be a glint of crystal catching the light in the window, the rustle of the feathers of a dreamcatcher in the bedroom and a faint scent of patchouli trailing in your wake. You are an original hippie child and could not be happier living out your alternative lifestyle irrespective of what others may think of you. You care about people and the environment and will put yourself out to join a protest march or seek alternative therapies for ailments. In fact, you'll do just about anything to avoid conventional medicine and the doctor's surgery. You're happiest living with and among a community of like-minded people and since, for you, sex is as much about the soul as the body, you'll have no problem keeping your partner drawn to you both in and out of the bedroom.

Numerology

No. I: A powerful entity and results-oriented force, all about initiating action and getting things done.

Tarot

Nine of Pentacles: Just like the woman who is in a beautiful garden and lavishing attention on her pet bird in this card, you know how to gather your resources (Pentacles) and make them work for you. That doesn't necessarily mean money; you may prioritise emotional resources and the stability they will bring. The good news is that however you decide to go about it, contentment is your goal, and this card shows it is, literally, on/in the cards for you.

Famous birthdays

Smokey Robinson American singer-songwriter
David Gandy British fashion model
Lee Marvin American actor

February 20th

Artistically gifted

You know that person who wins every prize for any artistic endeavour – from cake-making to garden design – well, that's you! You may have no idea just how creative and artistically gifted you are, but everyone else can see it. If you are not an art teacher, you will be working in some way that allows you to use and even teach these gifts to others, although a full-time job can be something of a challenge when what you really want to do is pack a small case and travel the world to see and experience life – especially art – abroad. A little shy and reserved, you may not push yourself forward for praise and accolades, but you appreciate being appreciated and having your talents recognised and acknowledged, so don't think twice about submitting work for that prize! You are kind and caring, and family will be important to you, and while you may be a little shy at first in any kind of romantic relationship, once you commit, you will be devoted to your loved one for life.

Numerology

No. 2: Shows resilience and power in gentleness, often provides the role of mediator, and linked to psychic abilities.

Tarot

The Fool: No, this card does not mean you're daft or easy to take advantage of; instead, it signifies setting out on the adventure of life and lapping up every new experience you can, which, for you, then feeds into your artistic world view and, of course, your art itself. Family ties may prevent you from taking off – the young man in this card is literally about to step off the edge of a cliff – but that won't stop you travelling in your mind and planning trips and adventures for that time in your life when you can just take off and explore the wider world.

Famous birthdays

Kurt Cobain American singer-songwriter
Rihanna Barbadian singer and actress
Cindy Crawford American model and businesswoman

February 21st

Flighty butterfly

You take people-pleasing to a whole new level which, although it makes you nice to be around, can land you in hot water because you're so busy helping everyone else, it can be difficult for others to work out what's important to you and who you really are. You are fun to live and work with – until you get bored, that is, and boy, do you get bored easily. If you're not chopping and changing career paths, you're probably chopping and changing life partners and lovers. It's unlikely you'll be married just once because even when you fancy yourself to be in love, there's always part of you wondering if you might be missing out on someone else who's just around the corner. Fortunately, you're better at committing to your children than your mate and will stick around in a partnership to honour those family values and raise good and happy kids. You'll work hard to create a harmonious, beautiful and happy home, and maybe even stay with a partner who has learned not to reveal all of themselves to you if they want to keep you interested.

Numerology

No. 3: Creative with the gift of imagination and an ability to communicate in writing, art or speech.

Tarot

Eight of Wands: Wands are all about communication and with eight of them all aligned to help you make your point and communicate what's important to you, there won't be anyone left in any doubt about what's going to happen next and why. In fact, your verbal skills are second to none, which not only helps you get what you want but also means you are often the best person to communicate a more difficult message, both at home and at work.

Famous birthdays

Nina Simone American jazz singer and civil right activist
Michael McIntyre British comedian
Ashley Greene American actress

February 22nd

Reliable protector

Compassionate and kind, you are the one family, friends and colleagues all turn to for support and guidance, and you never let them down. You have both strong energy and such good mental clarity that you can see all sides of an argument and then think your way to a resolution that will appease all parties involved. Sensitive to the needs of others, you use your rational thinking skills to help those who may currently be in a less fortunate position and your ability to suggest a well-considered action plan more than explains why everyone turns to you. The only problem is, if you are the one suggesting all the solutions, who do you turn to in your time of need? You may have become so invested in having all the answers for everyone else that you find it hard to show your own vulnerability and confusion. Try and show the same compassion and protective support to yourself that you're so happy to give to others, and when you decide to share your life with a partner, don't shut them out every time you find yourself struggling to be that better version of you that you can be. You, like the rest of us, are only human!

Numerology

No. 4: Invested in the physical world, centred earth energy that is practical in application.

Tarot

The Devil: Not someone you want to invite into your life or home, but in the Tarot deck this card represents the chains that you may feel are shackling you are chains that have been put in place by someone you know well – you! It may be that you have chained yourself so tightly to those lofty ideals of yours that you cannot break out and breathe, or perhaps you're stuck in a partnership in which both parties have grown apart and need to move on. Work out where you feel chained and use your fantastic strategising ability to make a plan of action and free yourself.

Famous birthdays

George Washington First President of the United States
Julie Walters British actress
Steve Irwin Australian naturalist and TV presenter

February 23rd

Caring listener

We have two eyes and two ears, but only one mouth, and you already know the value of staying quiet: of listening and observing without having to share every thought passing through your mind. This trait is so important that it makes you almost psychically sensitive to those around you. It's almost as if you know what they mean – which may not be what they are saying – long before they do. Your caring nature makes you an authentic humanitarian. You're a gifted networker with the ability to get on with people from all walks of life and all cultures, and with your easy, breezy ability to mix business and pleasure it should be no surprise to find yourself in a leadership role, whatever your chosen career. You have a restless nature and would hate to be desk-bound, so it's likely you are freelance or work on a contract basis, which allows you the freedom to pick and choose projects. You are a generous and passionate lover, but know that for a long-term partner, you need someone who shares your interests and can be a good friend as well as lover.

Numerology

No. 5: Impulsive and restless by nature, spontaneous and likes to discover the world through the senses.

Tarot

Ace of Wands: All that active listening coupled with your genuinely caring attitude is about to pay dividends (although that's not why you do it, of course). The Ace of Wands is telling you that whenever you do the right thing, you will always be supported, and that Spirit is always on your side. You have an abundance of creativity to share with the world, so don't hold back: step forward and let yourself be counted.

Famous birthdays

Emily Blunt British actress
Peter Fonda American actor and director
Kelly Macdonald Scottish actress

February 24th

Lucky optimist

You're one of those people who is always somehow in the right place at the right time. They say fortune favours the brave and you're certainly not afraid to celebrate or share all the good luck that comes your way. If you get engaged, you'll want the biggest and blingiest ring; if you throw a party, it will be champagne and caviar all the way. It would be tempting for others to resent your immense good luck, but they don't because you understand just how blessed you are and that those 'perfect' moments when it feels everything is aligned to deliver the life you want and deserve are fleeting and precious and can be whipped away in a heartbeat. You're also a fantastic life partner: loyal, faithful, caring and loving, and with your eye very firmly set on celebrating your Diamond Wedding anniversary with a bottle of vintage Cristal champagne!

Numerology

No. 6: Empathic and nurturing, can problem-solve in an emotional and physical way, responsible and cares deeply about family and friends.

Tarot

The Lovers: No surprises here. Love, as we've seen, is so important to you that it runs through all that you think and do, and when you find your soulmate you will be committing to a lifetime of loving them with your whole soul and, happily, being loved just as much in return.

Famous birthdays

Steve Jobs American entrepreneur and co-founder of Apple
Billy Zane American actor
Kristin Davis American actress

February 25th

Passionate champion

Although you'll champion any underdog and fight tooth and nail to get justice where you see injustice, there's a good chance that it will be animals you fight for the hardest. Fiercely protective, you'll feel enraged by animal cruelty of any kind, and won't care who you need to offend to get an animal out of danger and somewhere loving and safe. You can sometimes trip yourself up by bulldozing into situations that require a more nuanced approach and there may be times your passion comes across as radicalism, which can alienate those you need on your side. Try to adopt a more patient and measured approach, and instead of being contemptuous of those who don't 'get it' straightaway, use your excellent brain to explain, rationally, why they should care the way you do.

Numerology
No. 7: Very analytical and detail-oriented, likes to observe and investigate things, and has a keen, inventive eye.

Tarot
Three of Swords: Not one of the softest or easiest of the cards in the Tarot deck, but then you've not chosen an easy or soft path. Even among other campaigners it will be agreed there are less heart-breaking causes to champion than those you are drawn to. This is a card of heartbreak, but it's this very deep-seated sorrow that spurs you on to try and stop the cruelty you want gone from the world for good.

Famous birthdays
George Harrison British member of The Beatles
Pierre-Auguste Renoir French Impressionist artist
Sylvie Guillem French ballet dancer

February 26th

Artistic philanthropist

You want to leave the world a better place and so while you may not be in a position to create a philanthropic foundation or fund until your later years, you will be working slowly and surely towards that goal, using your artistic talents to get noticed and encourage people to think about change for the good. Your family, friends and long-suffering life partner may wish you spent a little less time at work and a little more time at play, but they understand your noble intentions and that you need to get all your ducks lined up before you can sign others up to your vision of change for the greater good. You are a big softie at heart and crave romantic love and attention. A devoted and generous partner, you can feel hurt when those feelings are not reciprocated to the same extent and can take your time to forgive those slights, intended or otherwise.

Numerology

No. 8: Sees the big picture and aims for it, linked to abundance and material wealth, and uses financial success to give back to others.

Tarot

The Moon: A deeply emotional card. You can sometimes find yourself feeling confused about what is really going on, what you're not seeing and what's not being said. You are not the most confident person when it comes to trusting both your own emotions and those of others, so maybe take a little time away from work to explore how you can stand your ground more firmly and feel less swayed (hurt) by the thoughtless actions of others.

Famous birthdays

Johnny Cash American singer-songwriter
Michael Bolton American singer-songwriter
Victor Hugo French poet and novelist

February 27th

Generous team player

Some people wince at the word 'nice' but, actually, it's a compliment and describes you pretty accurately. Kind and clever, you'll be the first to volunteer to be a good neighbour, look after someone's pet and just help out where you can because you live by the maxim: 'There's no "I" in team'. You're the best boss, although intolerant of anyone you think isn't pulling their weight, and then your bark will be just as bad as your bite! You don't like gossip and when you do help out, you do it unconditionally with no expectation of thanks or favours in return. See? You really are that nice! Steadfast, reliable, fun to be around and loving, you have all the qualities that will support a healthy, happy and productive relationship built on the foundation of a kind and caring happy home.

Numerology

No. 9: An old soul that looks to spiritual awareness to solve life's problems and likes to help others to do so in the same way.

Tarot

Three of Cups: This card depicts a joyful gathering of three friends, colleagues or family members who are celebrating their connection and all they can and do achieve together. It's a card that tells us what you already know – namely, there is great joy to be found in being part of something bigger than yourself, whether that's a neighbourhood or a global movement for change.

Famous birthdays

Elizabeth Taylor British actress
John Steinbeck America writer
Henry Wadsworth Longfellow American poet

February

February 28th

Endearing hedonist

You're here for the adventure and excitement of a life well-lived and bounce from one enthusiasm to the next with barely a pause for breath. This makes you exciting, but sometimes exhausting, to be around. Although you have the kind of get-up-and-go energy that will attract steadier types, they won't be able to keep up with you and your action-packed agenda or tolerate your somewhat 'fluid' approach to relationships. Travel and tourism are the fields that best match your astro-personality, giving you a legitimate reason to be off with your bags packed every chance you get. Others find your extravagant emotional and financial generosity endearing, but those who love you best may need to sit you down and explain why you should put the brakes on from time to time, especially if they fear you're getting so carried away that you may be on a one-way ticket to self-destruction.

Numerology

No. 1: A powerful entity and results-oriented force, all about initiating action and getting things done.

Tarot

Temperance: One of the Major Arcana, this card shows an angelic figure pouring a divine liquid between two golden chalices. The message here, especially for you, is all about balance and the need to recognise when you are becoming emotionally unbalanced and need to take steps to regulate yourself. There may come a time when, as much as you don't want to hear it, someone will talk to you about the benefits of 'everything in moderation'. It's a mantra that will keep you happy and healthy for longer.

Famous birthdays

Ainsley Harriott British chef and TV presenter
Bugsy Siegal American gangster
Stephen Spender British poet

February 29th

Successful rarity

You were born on a leap day, which means a 'proper' birthday comes along just once in every four years, and yet you are simply not bothered. In fact, you quite like being this special and if that means you only get a party every four years, well then let's make it the best party of the year. Money loves you and you've a knack for making more of it than you'll ever need. What you like best of all is getting money out of other people, but not in any underhand or unacceptable way – you like the game of the exchange to be fair and so it may be that you work in the antiques trade or an auction house or on a market stall. However you do it, there's no question that you'll do it well; you'll go on doing it and get to enjoy the reward of the finer things in life because thanks to this particular gift, you can afford them. You're a loyal life partner, will stay with one person for life and will pine to the end of your days if for some reason you become parted.

Numerology

No. 2: Shows resilience and power in gentleness, often provides the role of mediator, and linked to psychic abilities.

Tarot

King of Pentacles: This is the card that shows the self-made man (or woman) who has been so materially successful in life they can now sit back on their throne and take an early retirement. Put simply, they've made it, made it big, and made it in a such a rare way that nobody got ripped off or was offended or left the transaction feeling used. Now that's some skill.

Famous birthdays

Gioachino Rossini Italian composer
Tony Robbins American life coach and motivational speaker
Pedro Sanchez Spanish politician and prime minister of Spain

March 1st

Stylish homemaker

There's a fortune to be made if you take this talent for creating a beautiful and stylish home wherever you go in the direction of a career; name your price and those without your flair for interior design will happily pay it. Working solo, especially as your own boss, suits you, and since you can be guilty of just a teeny bit of snobbery, it could even give you access to a level of social status you envy and would like for yourself. You may give your time and talents for free to some charitable cause because you do care about the plight of others or you may be using your gift for coming up with creative solutions via a job in the media. Whatever direction you take for work, when it comes to marriage and choosing your life partner, the only direction is up! You'll look for a mate who will improve your social standing because it's important to you to be part of that upwardly mobile set and you'll do what it takes not to get left behind. Deep down, you'd like a successful partner who'll leave the beautiful homemaking to you and promise to take care of you for the rest of your life.

Numerology

No. I: A powerful entity and results-oriented force, all about initiating action and getting things done.

Tarot

Three of Wands: This card is all about success and social standing; a wealthy merchant stands on higher ground watching the ships carrying his merchandise sailing off to far-flung lands to sell their goods and bolster his fortunes. He is a gifted businessman, admired and respected for his success which has been built on being able to communicate original ideas and translate those into merchandise.

Famous birthdays

Justin Bieber Canadian singer-songwriter
Ralph Ellison American novelist
Frédéric Chopin Polish composer and pianist

March 2nd

Quiet introvert

A dreamy introvert, it's likely you'll be more engaged with your own rich interior world than the brash and noisy exterior one which, when it does intrude, has a habit of bursting your peaceful and protective bubble. It's not that you don't care about social issues and the like, you do, but not an angry protest march or chaining yourself to fences to stop the diggers. You'll want to register your protest, but you'll do it your own way through writing or music or some other artistic endeavour. You may work behind the scenes in the caring professions or in a supporting role for the political party you support. So, you are present, but not in the spotlight. You are a fiercely loyal lover who wants and needs unconditional love back from your chosen one. Be careful that your utter devotion doesn't slide into smothering the people you care about because smothered people can't breathe and won't stay smothered. Try and cultivate a little more independence in your most intimate relationships.

Numerology
No. 2: Shows resilience and power in gentleness, often provides the role of mediator, and linked to psychic abilities.

Tarot
The World: It may seem, on the surface, to be a contradiction that someone so wary of the real world should have this important card but, as you already know, there are many worlds, many dimensions and, in your case, your creativity stems entirely from the richness of your internal world, not whatever is going on outside your front door. This is one world you can control, so take joy in knowing you carry this glorious world with you throughout your life, wherever you go.

Famous birthdays
Dr Seuss American children's author
Daniel Craig British actor
Mikhail Gorbachev Russian politician and Soviet leader

March 3rd

Prodigious achiever

Good-natured and highly sociable, there's a fierce intelligence hidden behind the happy-go-lucky first impression you make, and you are anything but superficial. Clever and ambitious, with a fantastic sense of humour, you really are a force to be reckoned with and whether you bring your considerable talent to the sciences or the arts, when you put your mind to it, you can accomplish three times what others can in half the time. You have learned to juggle time and commitments, so you can cram as much into a day as humanly possible, but be careful not to spread yourself too thin or you risk leaving people feeling short-changed. You know you're prone to flying off on a tangent, so when looking for a life partner, choose someone who can ground you, without clipping your enthusiasms, and prove to you that making a commitment to each other does not have to mean giving up all your freedoms.

Numerology
No. 3: Creative with the gift of imagination and an ability to communicate in writing, art or speech.

Tarot
Ten of Cups: You're so full of life and *joie de vivre* you sometimes feel you're bursting at the seams with the excitement of it all, but when it comes to making a proper commitment you can take up the kind of defensive, protective position depicted by the man sitting with his arms folded in front of all his treasures in this card. Drop your guard and remind yourself that the sharing of your treasures is not the same as them being stolen from you.

Famous birthdays
Alexander Graham Bell Scottish scientist and inventor of the telephone
Bonnie Dunbar American astronaut
Jean Harlow American actress

March 4th

Empathic teacher

You walk a fine line between being so empathic that you are able to inspire others to see the wrongs in a situation and help you change it for the better and being so empathic, it's hard to see what's in front of you because you can't stop crying about it all. There will always be hurt, cruelty and injustice in the world, and it's not your job to either try and fix it all, all at once, or, if you can't do that, cry yourself to sleep about it every night. You are so sensitive you may need to channel all those feelings through the creative arts, or you may harness all that empathy and caring and throw yourself into teaching where it will be obvious from your first day in the classroom that you are someone who understands and cares about your students. In love, it's not so much the partnership that has you firing on all cylinders, it's the babies that can be or are already the result of that union. When it comes to babies, you can't get enough, so don't be surprised to find yourself, when the time is right, at the helm of a large and unconventional family.

Numerology

No. 4: Invested in the physical world, centred earth energy that is practical in application.

Tarot

The Empress: There's a hint of the Earth Mother about this woman who is sitting on her luxuriant throne in the height of summer, surrounded by an abundant landscape, including a rich and prosperous crop of wheat. This card shouts fecundity and reproduction, but as ever with the Tarot, that can apply to many endeavours close to your heart, other than starting a family. Your life really is pregnant with all the possibilities you can imagine for yourself.

Famous birthdays

Khaled Hosseini Afghan-American novelist and humanitarian
Brooklyn Beckham British model
Draymond Green American basketball player

March 5th

Spiritually gifted

That voice in your head urging you to follow your heart and explore what is already a deep spiritual connection further is your soul telling you that you're not imagining it, you really do have a calling. For some of you, that will mean joining an established religious or faith group and taking this as a career path; for others it will simply mean joining fellow worshippers and doing good works throughout the community and your parish. You will be an effective fundraiser for any charitable cause you believe in and, since you are skilled with your hands, won't mind pitching in to build a float for the local carnival or make a cake for some other charity event. Thanks to your highly sociable nature, you'll enjoy all types of community events and if you're currently living a city life because of work commitments, don't be surprised if you change direction completely in your middle years, move out to the countryside and find a faith group to become part of there. You are highly attractive to others and a natural flirt, but when you settle down, you'll wave goodbye to an underlying restlessness and honour your spiritual beliefs by remaining faithful to your partner.

Numerology

No. 5: Impulsive and restless by nature, spontaneous and likes to discover the world through the senses.

Tarot

Ace of Pentacles: What this card tells you is that if you can dream it, you can make it happen because guess who is and always has been on your side? Spirit. Pentacles symbolise resources, which doesn't just mean money but can also mean spiritual contentment, and all the aces tell us you are on the right path and will be supported in all the choices you make. Expect a grounded but deeply fulfilled life.

Famous birthdays

Madison Beer American singer-songwriter
Elaine Paige British singer and actress
Rex Harrison British actor

March 6th

Committed idealist

The pursuit of excellence and high ideals in all things is truly commendable but comes at a cost because when people fail to live up to those same ideals – and turn out to have very heavy feet of clay – the disappointment, for you, can be shattering. You dream of creating an ideal world and while others can appreciate this noble ideal, they won't appreciate you turning into a diva in your bid to try and turn your vision into reality. Try and be a little less demanding to keep people onside and also remember that you catch more flies with honey than vinegar. Beauty, in all its forms, is important to you and you may work in the arts or simply champion those artists whose work you find the most uplifting. You may struggle to commit to a life partner because they won't be able to live up to your unrealistic expectations but if you can moderate your demands and learn to accept people as they are and not as you want them to be, there's no reason why you shouldn't build a meaningful and long-term relationship with someone like-minded.

Numerology
No. 6: Empathic and nurturing, can problem-solve in an emotional and physical way, responsible and cares deeply about family and friends.

Tarot
The Sun: One of the Major Arcana, the Sun card signifies vibrancy, warmth and success and shows that your efforts to change the world for the better are acknowledged and appreciated, even when you are sometimes too demanding for your own good. This is a happy card. You will never attain perfection – none of us can – but you can grow, evolve and learn so much about both yourself and others as you strive to be a better person living in a better world.

Famous birthdays
Michelangelo Italian Renaissance painter and sculptor
David Gilmour British guitarist
Gabriel García Márquez Colombian writer

March 7th

Determined achiever

Your dogged determination to imagine a goal or solution to a problem, and then throw all you have at it – and more – to achieve the outcome you have envisioned, is to be admired, but maybe from afar because this tunnel vision of yours can make you pretty tricky to live with full-time. Your single-minded focus makes you well suited to the legal profession or a career in sports, but it can leave those you love feeling unnoticed, even neglected by you, so maybe make a promise to yourself to try and compromise where you can and remember to pay attention to the needs of others. You need to make sure you have time alone to recharge ready for the next battle but, again, others may experience this as a rejection, so take time to explain you just need to be quiet and with your own thoughts for a while.

Numerology

No. 7: Very analytical and detail-oriented, likes to observe and investigate things, and has a keen, inventive eye.

Tarot

The Moon: This is your personal planet, and in the Tarot deck one of the Major Arcana, symbolising that inner dreamy state of yours where you like to retreat in order to recharge and slowly simmer your next big idea. But the Moon can also represent an area in life where you're not quite seeing the big picture or everything that's going on. If there is something bothering you, don't ignore it – get to the bottom of it.

Famous birthdays

Rachel Weisz British actress
Piet Mondrian Dutch artist
E.L. James British writer

March 8th

Highly imaginative

You like nice things and feeling secure, so money – earning it and holding on to it – is important to you. This can make you seem less dreamy than many who share your Piscean sun sign. You have an excellent imagination coupled with a grounded work ethic, and you're not afraid of commitment or responsibility, so, with you, that success you crave is only a matter of time. You like to keep your cards close to your chest and your ambition is rooted in chasing both the recognition and remuneration you believe you deserve – you won't be shy about asking for a pay rise! In love, you'll unleash a secret romantic to reveal, once you meet the right person, a devoted and caring life partner.

Numerology

No. 8: Sees the big picture and aims for it, linked to abundance and material wealth, and uses financial success to give back to others.

Tarot

Ten of Pentacles: Pentacles represent the resources available to us, and in your case that means money, and lots of it. There's a large house in the background of this card, a happy couple conversing in front of it, and a wise, old, grandfatherly, white-haired man looking on with approval. You know what you want, you know how to get it and it's all there waiting for you to claim it as your birth right ...

Famous birthdays

Aidan Quinn American actor
Lester Holt American journalist and news anchor
Petra Kvitová Czech tennis player

March 9th

Energetic charmer

These two words hold a strong clue to the type of relationship you will thrive in, which is an age-gap relationship where what you bring to the party – whether you are the older or younger partner – is buckets of boundless enthusiasm and charm that kind of makes you seem ageless to those around you. Equally, these two words hold a clue to the type of work you'll excel in, which is anything where your ability to smooth troubled waters and persuade everyone the glass is half full will see you rising fast up the career ladder, whether that's a career in public relations, politics or the media. You love to cook and will make a stylish and beautiful home, wherever you live. In fact, you can't think of anything better than going that extra mile with thoughtful gifts and inspired entertaining, which, along with your kindness, may explain why you are so popular and have so many friends.

Numerology

No. 9: An old soul that looks to spiritual awareness to solve life's problems and likes to help others to do so in the same way.

Tarot

Three of Pentacles: Whatever career you choose, you are likely to gain some public recognition for your contribution which, although not your primary motivation, will be well deserved and should make you feel proud of all your hard work and achievements. You may be responsible for a change in the law or a change, for the better, in business practices. Whatever it is, there are awards and accolades coming your way.

Famous birthdays

Yuri Gagarin Russian cosmonaut
Samuel Barber American composer
Leland Stanford American industrialist and founder of Stanford University

March 10th

Deeply compassionate

With a strong need to withdraw and spend long periods of time reflecting and recharging, you can come across as a somewhat solitary figure who has decided they are better off living quietly alone. Actually, it's just your way of taking care of a deeply caring and sensitive nature which can be easily battered and bruised in the outside world. You are a true humanitarian and so may be working in any of the caring fields, such as medicine, social work, the peace corps or even forward-thinking organisations that use the arts to campaign for change for the better. You hate conflict and will often put the needs of others before your own, just to avoid any unpleasantness. You will thrive among family, friends and with a partner who understands just how sensitive you really are and knows that, for you, there is nothing of greater value than the giving and receiving of unconditional love.

Numerology

No. I: A powerful entity and results-oriented force, all about initiating action and getting things done.

Tarot

Six of Swords: This card depicts a boatman steering a vessel and its cargo of a shrouded woman and her child to a tree-lined oasis of a landscape in the far distance. On one side of the boat, the waters are choppy and on the other, still and smooth. For you, this card is about your ability to look the sorrows of the world squarely in the face and then work out some way those that are suffering can be helped to navigate towards a better and more peaceful life.

Famous birthdays

Sharon Stone American actress
Bix Beiderbecke American jazz musician
Olivia Wilde American actress and film-maker

March 11th

Enthusiastic leader

You make it look so easy – taking your team, colleagues and collaborators along with you, many of whom find being around you so uplifting and inspiring that they would willingly work for you for free! You are brilliant at spotting and encouraging people's full potential and don't have a discriminatory bone in your body: with you, when it comes to recruiting to expand the team, it's all about talent and potential. The only downside to being such a fantastic boss and one adored by all your workers, is that, sadly, this doesn't always translate to the same success in your personal life. Facebook? Reunions? Little trips down memory lane? None of this is for you because you live and thrive in the now. Yesterday has gone, tomorrow hasn't happened yet and you already know that all we have, which we can truly count on, is right now.

Numerology

No. 2: Shows resilience and power in gentleness, often provides the role of mediator, and linked to psychic abilities.

Tarot

The Chariot: How perfect; you're all go, go, go and your card depicts the mode of transport most likely to get you the most rapidly to your destination – your very own chariot, no less. And this is one drawn not by prancing horses in fine plumage but by one black and one white sphinx. What this card tells us is that you are able to walk a determined middle path between the polarities of light and dark, good and evil, and make your purposeful way through a well-lived life.

Famous birthdays

John Barrowman Scottish actor
Jenny Packham British fashion designer
Alex Kingston British actress

March 12th

Ageless entertainer

You are a gifted storyteller and born entertainer, able to communicate all your ideas both visually and verbally. You radiate charm and seem so easy-going that nobody would guess at the challenges you've faced and overcome or the deep courage and resilience underpinning your cheerful matter. People love being in your company but can start to find some of your more erratic behaviours a little off-putting. You're a born flirt – you'd flirt with the fridge if nobody else was home – so you're not going to appeal to the 'Steady Eddies' looking for a solid commitment. That said, if you find the right person, you will transfer some of that utter devotion you feel for family and friends to your love life and forge a long and lasting union.

Numerology

No. 3: Creative with the gift of imagination and an ability to communicate in writing, art or speech.

Tarot

The Sun: A card of warm, vibrant life that, like you, oozes vitality and charm, this is one of the Major Arcana cards which, in this case, speaks to us of freedom, hard-won success, abundance and a well-deserved final happiness over the choices you have made through life. Sunflowers, like those depicted on the card, track the movement of the Sun, turning their faces to its golden rays, and in the same way, you come alive when you release that same inner vitality and shine your light on others.

Famous birthdays

Marlon Jackson American singer
Liza Minnelli American actress and singer
Jack Kerouac American writer

March 13th

Spiritual seeker

Oh, to have been born in the 1970s (if you were, and on this day, then lucky you!). There's nothing that will get your heart racing faster than the smell of patchouli, a psychedelic kaftan, a one-way ticket to see the guru in the ashram in India and a travel bag packed with only a pair of rope sandals and a copy of the *Bhagavad Gita* – preferably in Sanskrit. You are the original, non-conforming 'love child' of no decade and all decades. You come and go with the wind and the tides, follow only those who share your spiritual beliefs and pretty much make the rules up as you go along. This will endear you to some and infuriate others, perhaps your parents in particular when you were first trying on this alternative lifestyle for size. You do actually have a latent and very serious psychic talent, but you may not find the right channel for it until later in life. You'll likely have – and leave – many lovers because you're never in one place long enough to truly settle down. Old age? Not a problem because you are never, ever going to grow old, on the inside at least.

Numerology

No. 4: Invested in the physical world, centred earth energy that is practical in application.

Tarot

Death: A sombre card and one of the Major Arcana, which simply reinforces that this is a message to be taken seriously. It is not a card that literally foreshadows death in the way we all fear it, more a card telling us that for something new to be born, something old has to die. You may already have learned this from your travels to the temples of Thailand and the holy ashrams of India. Nothing lasts forever. Everything will pass. Your job is simply to notice these changes, without forming an attachment, and try to accept graciously what comes and goes in your life.

Famous birthdays

William Macy American actor and director
Dana Delany American actress
Mikaela Shiffrin American alpine skier

March 14th

Perceptive empath

The trouble with being able to see the merit in multiple arguments and both sides of a dispute is that it can make you appear indecisive. You're not. You will definitely know if you want beans or peas, but you are not afraid to accept life is not made up of certainties and that often it will be difficult to determine the best course of action to take when the word 'best' itself is so open to subjective interpretation. You will not tolerate bigotry or unfairness, so you clearly have strong principles; you just struggle to decide on the single best course of action when there are so many to choose from. This can translate to your love life where you may struggle to commit to just one person. And you won't thrive in a big corporation where the rules may be rigid, with everyone expected to be and act exactly the same. An artistic calling and working with smaller teams will be more conducive for you and if you do get around to parenting, you'll excel because what some see as indecisive, others, especially your children, will experience as encouraging and non-judgemental.

Numerology

No. 5: Impulsive and restless by nature, spontaneous and likes to discover the world through the senses.

Tarot

Two of Pentacles: There you are, just as we said, weighing up all the options (in this case, pentacles) and taking so long to consider all the pros and cons of a decision that you may appear completely incapable of making one in this lifetime. You're not – and you will, but you won't be rushed or put in a position where you have to second guess yourself. The card shows a young man juggling two pentacles, one in each loop of the infinity sign. Is he (are you) destined to do this forever? Who knows ...?

Famous birthdays

Albert Einstein German theoretical physicist
Quincy Jones American music producer
Michael Caine British actor

March 15th

Natural diplomat

Artistic, creative, nurturing and wonderfully sociable, you'll enjoy a huge circle of good friends and acquaintances and be the first in the group that people turn to when there has been a falling out and some kind of mediation is needed. Your talent for bringing out the best in everyone you meet will work well for you in both your friendships and work circles, where you are always the one who'll first spot and start talking about the latest change in fashion and popular taste. You may act or write or paint or sing, make movies or design houses. Whatever career you choose, there's a secret fascination with the world of mystery and fantasy underpinning the often inspired choices you make. Where you lead, others will want to follow. You're a hopeless romantic and unwilling to live any length of time without a partner. If you don't have a partner right now, your preoccupation with finding love, and your focus on that, will be to the exclusion of everything else.

Numerology

No. 6: Empathic and nurturing, can problem-solve in an emotional and physical way, responsible and cares deeply about family and friends.

Tarot

The Hierophant: One of the more obscure of the Major Arcana cards in the Tarot deck, the Hierophant sits up high on a raised throne blessing the two men genuflecting at his feet. Is he blessing or is he delivering a mediated resolution to a dispute between the two men? You have been born with many blessings and you rarely feel more blessed yourself than when you are able to share your gifts to heal a rift between people.

Famous birthdays

will.i.am American rapper and songwriter
Ruth Bader Ginsburg American lawyer and judge
Gerda Wegener Danish illustrator and painter

March 16th

Pleasure seeker

Life's one long party for folk fortunate enough to be born on this day and what's even more fortunate for them is that they have a million ways to express and work that party gene to make a good living – from leading tour groups abroad to wedding planning, events organising, teaching or entertaining, which is just as well because this Piscean likes the lavish good life. They will often marry someone older and more established or someone with family money – just to make sure all those glittery things don't just fade away – and be entirely unapologetic for putting matters of finance on an equal footing with matters of the heart. Talking of the heart, with all this partying there will likely be more than a few broken hearts on both sides, but this is one fish who knows there'll be another one along soon – likely at the very next party which has been organised by guess who?

Numerology

No. 7: Very analytical and detail-oriented, likes to observe and investigate things, and has a keen, inventive eye.

Tarot

Seven of Swords: There's something of a ruthless streak in the story this card tells of a well-dressed young buck stealing away with five of the card's seven swords. Is it theft? You decide. He is definitely stealing away with something – but it could be they are his own swords and he simply wants to disappear in order to hold on to them, or they could be someone else's property and he's just getting a head start in the financial stakes. Why is he leaving two swords behind? Maybe he just can't carry them or maybe he has learned when enough is enough.

Famous birthdays

Jerry Lewis American comedian and actor
Lauren Graham American actress and author
Tim Hardaway Jr American basketball player

March 17th

Artistic communicator

You won't be signing up for the rigidity of a nine-to-five working day any time soon; in fact, you're unlikely to be signing up for anything and not least because you hate the idea of being pinned down by anything or anybody. You are so scared of having your wings clipped and feeling trapped, you've probably already mastered the art of 'fluid', even 'creative', communication, never quite saying 'yes' and never quite saying 'no' but leaving others to guess at your actual intention, which then allows you to stay fluid and change your mind as often as you like. You are inspired by beauty more than anything else and if you're not making beautiful, artistic things others will pay good money for, you'll be trading or dealing in them in some other way. Money is not an issue – abundance is heading your way – but settling down is. You just can't do it. In fact, the only way you'll sustain a long-term and meaningful relationship is to have one with someone who not only respects your independence and deep need for freedom, but also actively encourages it.

Numerology

No. 8: Sees the big picture and aims for it, linked to abundance and material wealth, and uses financial success to give back to others.

Tarot

The Hermit: Don't be too quick to make a literal interpretation of this card. Yes, we have a lone and cloaked figure stepping out by the light of a lantern into what? The night? A new life? Look more closely and you'll see that he is standing on top of a snow-covered hilltop. Perhaps he has had all the solitude and freedom he needs and is making his way back down the mountain pass to share his deep wisdom with the others who know you don't keep hold of love, or anything else that really matters, by tying it down to anything that does not have the fluidity to move and flow.

Famous birthdays

Rob Lowe American actor and director
Alexander McQueen British fashion designer
Kurt Russell American actor

March 18th

Positive peacekeeper

You're all about seeing the big picture and what needs to change to improve a situation, but you can get so carried away by your enthusiasm for the solutions under your nose that you gloss over the minor details which have the capacity to trip you up further down the road. Slow down and look at all the implications of implementing your humanitarian vision, and if you just can't do that, then appoint a good second-in-command who can because, as the saying goes, the devil is in the detail. One of the reasons you don't really like to get your hands dirty is that you hate conflict and will run a mile from the threat of even the mildest disagreement. Wanting to please all of the people all of the time – and keep the peace whatever the cost to them and to you – can backfire, make you seem indecisive and work against you in the long term. You need to learn to negotiate conflict both at work and at home. You'll probably favour a career in the arts where you will feel less compromised, and when choosing a life partner, make sure you don't hitch up with a drama king or queen; you need someone who values peace as much as you do.

Numerology

No. 9: An old soul that looks to spiritual awareness to solve life's problems and likes to help others to do so in the same way.

Tarot

The World: A positive card reinforcing your 'big picture' view of the world! You have the time, the energy, the talent and the vision to push through those progressive changes you want to see in the world. The woman we see dancing her way through life on this card is holding two candles, both burning at both ends. You have the same ability to keep running but make sure you're taking time to recharge and don't risk running on empty or you will start to struggle. Take a vacation, visit an art gallery – give yourself permission!

Famous birthdays

Luc Besson French director
Peter Jones British entrepreneur and businessman
Wilfred Owen British poet and soldier

March 19th

Poetic dreamer

Kind-hearted and generous to a fault, there's nothing that makes you happier than rushing to help someone in need. But you have a bit of a Jekyll and Hyde streak because on the other side of this dreamy, poetic and heroic nature is a super-strong will, a steely determination and, hiding as it does behind the dreaminess, an unexpected force to be reckoned with! Helping people, by the way, is one thing, telling them what to do and how to do it another; and if you persist with the latter – which is bossiness and not far from controlling – don't be surprised to find your calls being unreturned and parties or other social gatherings among people you consider close friends taking place without you. Your determination makes you brave and so you're probably an adventurous traveller with a secret wish to be a real explorer, and when it comes to relationships, you're equally brave, rushing headfirst into a union which may not be a good match. When you discover that it's not, you're at the door marked 'exit' without a backward glance or a second thought.

Numerology

No. 1: A powerful entity and results-oriented force, all about initiating action and getting things done.

Tarot

Queen of Cups: She's a dreamy queen, this one, but truth be told, quite secretive about just how deep her emotions run. This is a person who is going to hang on tight to the precious yarg she is depicted holding in this card – a sacred vessel full of ... what? That's the big mystery with this person, and there will be few with the talent and perseverance to break through the protective layers surrounding those emotions. But when they do, the rewards of a relationship with someone born on this day will be more than worth the trouble it has taken.

Famous birthdays

Julien McDonald Welsh fashion designer
Ashley Giles British cricket player
Tommy Cooper British comedian

March 20th

Multi-talented empath

Compassionate, empathic, imaginative, perceptive, tenacious ...
you have so many great qualities, we could probably run through
the entire A–Z and find one for all 26 letters of the alphabet,
by the end of which either your head will have swelled to such
an extent it is too large to pass through the door or you will be
making blushing protestations of denial. But you really are this
gifted. You tend to think the best of all those you meet and trust
everyone until they prove themselves untrustworthy. You might
just want to watch this naïve quality because it means you can
end up feeling burned when people take advantage and even
depressed when you work so hard and see so little real change for
the better in the world. It takes you a long time to recover from
these wounds, so when choosing a life partner, find someone
steady and stable who deserves your loving trust.

Numerology

No. 2: Shows resilience and power in gentleness, often provides the role of
mediator, and linked to psychic abilities.

Tarot

Nine of Swords: This is a card of immense and overwhelming sorrow which
is what you often feel when you bear witness to the ways of a callous world
that sees no reason to change, especially when making anything better
might mean making less dollar. People who suffer from quite serious
depression often draw this card and then despair that nothing will ever
change. Don't despair. If you suffer from depression, admit to it and get
the right help for you. In your case, this will probably be some kind of
talk therapy which will help you understand you're not responsible for
everything that's wrong with the world and it's not your responsibility to
try and put it all right again. You can only do your bit.

Famous birthdays

Spike Lee American director
Holly Hunter American actress
Ruby Rose Australian model and actress

March 21st

Tenacious trailblazer

It's not that you don't like words; in fact, you're rather good with them, but, with you, actions speak louder than words and so if it's progress you're after, it will be speedy action that's driving you on towards your work and life goals. Some appreciate your directness, others will find it a bit much but, with you, everyone knows exactly where they stand and why. You'll thrive in business or the military or any field where your natural leadership tendencies and leading by example will be welcomed, but watch that nasty temper or you could find yourself spending more of your downtime on your own than you might like or find healthy. Nobody likes a nasty verbal bashing or being intimidated into submission. Take care, too, not to alienate loved ones or potential mates with that Aries fire, which tends to dominate your softer Pisces core. You won't win true friends and influence people by bullying them, but you will earn their trust and loyalty by stopping to listen and learn. Sometimes, someone else might just have an answer you've not yet even thought about. And sometimes, when it comes to love, the person who's been telling you they are right for you might just be 'The One'.

Numerology

No. 3: Creative with the gift of imagination and an ability to communicate in writing, art or speech.

Tarot

Knight of Wands: If there was ever a card that encapsulates an incoming, fiery, Aries streak and a life based on motion and get up and go – rather than let's sit awhile and talk some more about it – it's this chap sitting astride a rearing stallion and brandishing a single wand of communication. What's he telling us? Or, shouting more like? He's telling us: 'Come on, let's go. There's no time to waste!'

Famous birthdays

Gary Oldman British actor
Russ Meyer American director
Timothy Dalton Welsh actor

March 22nd

Daredevil adventurer

And when we say 'daredevil', that will be both in and out of the bedroom. Sexually adventurous and attractive to both sexes, where you lead, others will follow, not knowing that you're only going to be in charge for as long as it feels like fun and that you'll be gone before anyone can even say 'the grass was greener'. You are a thrill seeker, so whether that means you end up working in the armed forces or jumping out of a plane for charity, you are always looking for the next adrenaline boost. Your boredom threshold is so low that you may work your way through multiple romantic partners and marriages and probably won't see anything wrong in dating (and stringing along) several people at the same time. The term FOMO (Fear of Missing Out) was probably invented for you, if not by you, but watch out all the bed-hopping and thrill seeking doesn't leave you finding yourself alone in old age pretending you much prefer your own company to anyone else's, because that's not true; you don't and are not a natural loner.

Numerology

No. 4: Invested in the physical world, centred earth energy that is practical in application.

Tarot

Three of Swords: Ouch! A heart-breaking card, with three swords plunging straight through the centre of a bright red heart, this tells you everything you need to know at one glance but the big question here is, whose heart is this? Is this showing you the damage you cause when you love 'em and leave 'em because your boredom threshold has been reached or is this the card warning that if you carry on acting in such a cavalier way, one day the tables will turn, and it will be your heart that's bleeding after a bruising. Food for thought, whichever way ...

Famous birthdays

Reese Witherspoon American actress
Andrew Lloyd Webber British composer and impresario
Stephen Sondheim American composer and lyricist

March 23rd

Clever analyst

So, if you need psychotherapy or analysis, what you want is someone paying close attention to every little flicker and flinch that will betray your real feelings about something, regardless of the words coming out of your mouth during your counselling session. What you don't need is someone welling up in sympathy when you tell a tragic tale of woe – you're not paying for sympathy but for guidance in finding ways to stop repeating the patterns that hurt you. These same analytical skills – an ability to watch closely and work out what is going on in someone's subconscious – would equip you well for a career in acting where you can bring some of those real-life observations you've made to your character portrayal. It's not that you don't care about others and their woes; you're just highly skilled at keeping your own emotions out of the picture. Be careful not to bring these same analytic skills to your personal relationships because it can make you seem critical and uncaring. In matters of love, engage the emotions and let your heart do the talking.

Numerology

No. 5: Impulsive and restless by nature, spontaneous and likes to discover the world through the senses.

Tarot

Two of Swords: We see a woman sitting on a moonlit beach, blindfolded and arms crossed defensively with her two swords raised to the heavens. She feels vulnerable because she cannot see which serves to enhance her other senses, especially her hearing and that mysterious sixth sense we all depend on for our intuition and survival. She is playing a waiting game and cannot make her next move until she has more information. This is a good maxim for you; develop all your senses, not just the ability to see, and then use that additional information to move forward in your life.

Famous birthdays

Joan Crawford American actress
Perez Hilton American blogger and media personality
Mo Farah British athlete

March 24th

Magnetic personality

What do magnets do? Draw things near and get them to stick, which is an excellent description of you and how you move through the external world. With charm in spades and more sensitivity to the feelings of others than most of your fiery fellow Arians, you're creative, imaginative and nurturing; a brilliant homemaker and host and someone who finds joy in the more artistic side of life. You don't like to be without a partner and so it's rare to find an adult singleton born on this day, and once you have mastered the art of maintaining a healthy level of independence within a loving and committed relationship, you'll finally feel complete and happy to make some of the compromises this is going to demand. You're happiest when life runs like clockwork and drama-free, so don't indulge those trying to knock you off your comfortable perch. Teach them to live and let live, just as you have learned to do.

Numerology
No. 6: Empathic and nurturing, can problem-solve in an emotional and physical way, responsible and cares deeply about family and friends.

Tarot
Six of Cups: There's a sweetness and nurturing quality to this highly emotional card where an older child is looking out for a younger sibling and showing them that no sorrow, especially those from childhood, will last forever and that even after the longest winter, the flowers will grow again. One of the most caring cards in the Tarot deck, this is a depiction of unconditional love and the return of better times, as signified here by the blooming white flowers of innocence and spring.

Famous birthdays
Steve McQueen American actor
Harry Houdini American-Hungarian illusionist
Alan Sugar British business magnate

March 25th

Kind protector

If there's one behaviour that makes your blood boil, it is bullying, and you've probably, even from childhood, been that one person with the courage to step in and stop the cruel taunting of someone who is unable to stand up properly for themselves. You simply cannot and will not tolerate that type of unkindness. If you work in an office, you'll be the one organising the workers' rights, or you may have decided to champion children and vulnerable families and opted for a career in social work. This quality – of wanting to put wrong things right again and stand up for those who cannot make their own voices heard – also makes you the perfect animal rights champion, so it's likely that if you don't work full-time as a campaigner trying hard to improve conditions for our four-legged and feathered friends, then you'll be doing this in your spare time on a voluntary basis. If you aren't already, you'll be the steady rock of your whole family and once you make that love match, you're not going anywhere else because you are committed for life.

Numerology

No. 7: Very analytical and detail-oriented, likes to observe and investigate things, and has a keen, inventive eye.

Tarot

Nine of Pentacles: There's a sense of calm order in this scene of a mature woman strolling through a paradise landscape with her favourite pet bird and taking in the last rays of a glorious sunny day. All is well in this world and not least because Pentacles, which represent resources, have been wisely used to create a more harmonious world order. The vineyard behind our lady is productive, the grapes ripening and ready to turn into wine, telling you that the good life – your reward for all the championing of those unable to fight for themselves – is waiting for you; you just have to find the time to slow down and pluck it out of the imaginary realms.

Famous birthdays

Elton John British singer-songwriter
Gloria Steinem American feminist
Sara Jessica Parker American actress and producer

March 26th

Energetic achiever

Quick-thinking and with an enviable clarity of vision, you have that fantastic ability to cut through the dross to the heart of a problem and identify a long-term and sustainable solution. You have no time for prevarication and will act fast once you have that solution in your sights, encouraging those you work or live with to follow your lead, ditch the dilly dallying and move confidently forward to achieve your personal and collective goals. Any type of public service will allow you to tune in to your strong and intuitive sense of right action, or you may be working in the arts and using your skills in that arena to ask ethical questions about right and wrong and demand answers. It's intense, this world view and this commitment to raising awareness and fighting for change, which means that however loved-up you may be, you will need to take regular time out. This means taking off on your own to marshal your thoughts, recharge your batteries and prepare for the next campaign calling out for your time and attention. You'd never label yourself as such, but you are, in essence, a committed activist who will work hard to support your chosen charities or causes.

Numerology

No. 8: Sees the big picture and aims for it, linked to abundance and material wealth, and uses financial success to give back to others.

Tarot

King of Swords: What do you need to cut through that dross we talked about? Well, a sharp sword wouldn't hurt, plus the training and knowledge to use it safely. The King of Swords represents a decisive leader who knows prevarication can cost valuable ground and that there are sometimes many surprising gains to be made by taking swift and uncomplicated steps towards your goals. This is an authoritative character who has all the life skills to clear the path ahead.

Famous birthdays

Keira Knightley British actress
Diana Ross American singer
Richard Dawkins British ethologist, evolutionary biologist and writer

March 27th

Budding celebrity

Fame is yours for the asking – if that's what you want, and even if not, you'll have the satisfaction of knowing this was entirely your choice. It doesn't matter what career you settle on because you really are the 'Special One' and if you do say yes to fame, then expect your rise to stardom to be dramatic, meteoric even. It's as if you have a direct line to the powers that be and understand that all you need to do is ask and you will receive. You'll simply be in the right place at the right time to get noticed by a casting agent if you're acting or an artist talent manager if you're singing; it's as if all you have to do is wait for the magic to happen and it will. You'll be spoilt for choice when it comes to dating and will likely be prone to falling head over heels in love in a heartbeat throughout your life, which can make things a bit tricky when you already have a spouse at home. It is as if you've been born with every golden opportunity anyone can think of at your feet. Your only job? To choose which of them you want to take.

Numerology

No. 9: An old soul that looks to spiritual awareness to solve life's problems and likes to help others to do so in the same way.

Tarot

The Magician: Working his magic for your happiness, the Magician is the most powerful of the Major Arcana cards, and in your case is doing his best to make the alchemy happen and bring you your heart's desires, even before you've thought to ask. There is an enormous responsibility that falls on those with celebrity status and public recognition, whatever their talents. How will you channel the Magician and use your voice to create a better world?

Famous birthdays

Mariah Carey American singer-songwriter
Quentin Tarantino American director
Gloria Swanson American actress

March 28th

Practical realist

With your ability to disengage the emotions and examine a problem or challenge in a cool, calm and collected manner, you are fantastic to have around in a crisis, making you well suited to a career in the police, the military or business, especially anything to do with finances. You are comfortable in your own skin and happy in your own company, but that somehow just makes other people want you around even more, so, from the outside, you seem to have a busy social life when sometimes all you really want is to go on a long coastal walk or kick back and listen to a classical music concert. Love is important in your life because while you come across as highly competent and self-confident, the truth is you are often secretly beset by an overwhelming sense of self-doubt and so need the support of loving friends and a devoted spouse to gently chide you through these rough patches. The more stable your home life and the more private your home, the more you can be yourself in private and take a break from feeling you have to prove your worth to everyone you meet.

Numerology

No. 1: A powerful entity and results-oriented force, all about initiating action and getting things done.

Tarot

Knight of Cups: Cool, calm and collected on the outside – just like the upright Knight of Cups depicted on this card – you are secretly often full of trepidation and self-doubt and so may be wary of any deep emotional involvement with anyone. Perhaps you've been badly hurt in love and have defaulted to picking fault with yourself to explain why you were betrayed or abandoned. But in this card, you are holding a large chalice out in front of you, which means you are ready to offer the whole of yourself up to a mate, and look at your horse – he knows instinctively how to take you forward, even when your steps on the ground would be stumbling.

Famous birthdays

Lady Gaga American singer-songwriter
Vince Vaughn American actor
Maxim Gorky Russian writer and political activist

March 29th

Fiery go-getter

Sometimes, when your birthday is on or near the cusp of your sun sign, your personality exhibits more of the key characteristics of the incoming sign than the outgoing one, but this is not the case with you. You are, quite simply, the epitome of Aries' fire energy. But, as with the life cycle of a fire that roars up into life and then dies back to its glowing and then dying embers, your energy comes in fits and starts. You may be all go one day and taking a duvet day the next. You're not as self-centred as others who share your sun sign and have learned to listen to and respect others, making you a good team player and someone who likes to share both the responsibility of taking on a task and then the credit for a job well done with all who helped make something happen. You are a passionate lover and caring partner but will likely take your time before making that big commitment because you know how long it takes to really get to know another person, and you're willing to give yourself and your potential life partner the time to build a good foundation of authentic love and trust.

Numerology

No. 2: Shows resilience and power in gentleness, often provides the role of mediator, and linked to psychic abilities.

Tarot

Two of Wands: You are interested in the world and in taking your time, not just to find the right partner but also to expand your understanding of the material and spiritual worlds. In this card, we see a well-to-do merchant standing on the terrace of his impressive home looking out over the sea to distant shores; in his hand he holds a globe, reiterating his interest in things outside his own internal psyche, including the unseen world and forces we can only see when we engage our psychic abilities. This is a card of well-deserved success – deserved because it is the result of respectful collaboration and a slow but sure progress through a long and well-lived life.

Famous birthdays

Elle Macpherson Australian model and businesswoman
Dora Carrington British artist and member of the Bloomsbury Group
Eugene McCarthy American politician

March 30th

Destiny shaper

You are one of those rare people whose words can and do make all the difference to others and who always knows just the right thing to say to help someone who may be struggling to find the courage to take their next step and stride out into the future that awaits them. You're so good at this you probably won't even remember what you actually said that made such a difference to the other person's life, but they will, and they'll be eternally grateful to you for it, too. It's not obvious at first glance that you are one of the 'Golden Ones' but it becomes apparent quite soon to those who spend time in your company that there is just something very special about you. You may not like or want the spotlight, and that's fine because if you do, it is yours for the taking, but you will be someone who gets things done. You are someone others turn to for advice and you are only too happy to give it with no thought of any kind of payback. And you have that extraordinary knack of making everyone fall just a little bit in love with you, even though when it comes to romance, you're an imaginative lover, but a little bit of a butterfly and really not that concerned with settling down with one person.

Numerology

No. 3: Creative with the gift of imagination and an ability to communicate in writing, art or speech.

Tarot

Six of Wands: Wands are all about communication, so the more, the merrier, and in this case, we see a young buck crowned in laurel riding with his cohorts into town in a procession that shouts: triumph! Whatever rewards lie ahead, he (you) has earned them. Some have not come without a struggle, making them all the more deserved. This rider knows he is entitled to his heart's desires – whatever those may be – and this is a feeling that, deep down, you share.

Famous birthdays

Vincent van Gogh Dutch Post-Impressionist artist
Celine Dion Canadian singer
Eric Clapton British singer-songwriter

March 31st

Flexible pragmatist

Getting the job done is more important to you than how you have to go about it and who you have to nag or push or persuade to bend to make it happen. This astute attitude and your ability to make things happen and remain pragmatic, without getting caught up in unnecessary dramas or unhelpful complications, makes you perfect for the business world, and nobody would be surprised to see you rise to the top in that world and claim the role of a captain of industry. You set your sights on a goal and work steadily to achieve it, taking into account the views and needs of others along the way, which makes you popular among work colleagues. That said, in your personal life there's a bit more of the 'my way or the highway' approach and prospective partners will likely run for the hills (and stay there) the first time they get a tongue-lashing for not going along with your idea of how things should be and witness the unleashing of what is truly a terrible temper. You need to work at getting and keeping that Arian tendency to explode in fury under control or you will find yourself living alone.

Numerology

No. 4: Invested in the physical world, centred earth energy that is practical in application.

Tarot

Strength: The message of this card is that strength comes in many forms and gentleness, including gentle persuasion, is one of them. You know just how strong you are: you don't need to put on a display to impress others. Lead by example and you will go in a direction that makes not only your heart happy, but also the hearts of those who trust and follow you.

Famous birthdays

Ewan McGregor Scottish actor
Christopher Walken American actor and director
Al Gore American politician and environmentalist

April 1st

Invincible warrior

Of course, nobody – and that includes you – is invincible, but for you this is such a strong self-belief that it is easy to convince others it must be true and their acceptance of this as a fact then feeds back into your own protestations that there's nothing too big, too onerous or too difficult for you to tackle with gusto. And for the most part, you're right. You can't abide inaction and have such strong opinions, all backed up by some impressive ideas and abilities, that there really is very little you won't find your way through, over or around. But this does not – repeat not – make you invincible. Your courage in the face of adversity is never in question but take care not to take so much on your shoulders that you fall and may then take some time getting back up on your feet. It's all 'go-go-go' with you, but a little humility goes a long way, so try to remember that; and maybe stop just long enough to listen to what others might have to say – none of us is ever too old or too wise to learn something new. You are an ardent lover and a great mate – until you get bored and then you'll be off to chase after the next seemingly unavailable person. This is not an attractive quality, so try and choose a mate who will keep your interest and try not to abandon those who have loved you.

Numerology
No. 1: A powerful entity and results-oriented force, all about initiating action and getting things done.

Tarot
Queen of Swords: This lady, just like you, does not suffer fools gladly and can cut through excuses with a single swoosh of her mighty sword. You'll admire her ability to do this, and spend your whole life honing your own ways of doing the same. She is intimidating, as are you when you are not practising the art of seduction. She's very clearly nobody's fool – and neither are you.

Famous birthdays
Otto von Bismarck German statesman
Debbie Reynolds American actress
Chris Evans British TV and radio presenter

April

April 2nd

Progressive thinker

It's not the thinking that's inherently wrong and the reason you may struggle to get others to pick up the baton and champion your cause, it's the way you sometimes push your ideas onto people instead of adopting a more subtle and collaborative approach, whereby you sow the seed of an idea and then help prepare the best ground for it to take hold and grow strong. Ramming the 'right thing' down people's throats is never the way to inspire them, so you are, at some point in your life, going to have to learn to temper the fire in your belly, learn the art of gentle persuasion and present yourself as more of an inspiring change-maker and less of a rabid crusader. You'll find the arts the best place to channel your energy and your vision for change; you certainly won't thrive in any rigid environment where nobody is particularly interested in your unique point of view. But if you accept that it may take time for people to catch on to your ideas, then all will be well in the end. You value the close bonds you form with family and friends, and are valued back by them, and in a romantic partnership, you are kind, caring and considerate.

Numerology

No. 2: Shows resilience and power in gentleness, often provides the role of mediator, and linked to psychic abilities.

Tarot

Eight of Wands: All the cards depicting wands speak to us of the need for good communication and of new ideas coming to the fore and gaining ground. This is an excellent card for you as your thinking really is progressive and may, at first, be challenging to some of those you need to help get your visionary ideas onto mainstream platforms. You have not one, not two, not three or four, but eight wands all working on your behalf and pointing in one single direction – the future.

Famous birthdays

Michael Fassbender Irish actor and racing driver
Hans Christian Anderson Danish writer
Marvin Gaye American singer-songwriter

April 3rd

Organised organiser

From the moment you picked up a pencil and wrote your very first word you have been writing To Do Lists. If something needs doing or someone needs to be persuaded to do it, then you're the person for the job. You're charming and flirty and fun and, underneath all that, deadly serious, not only about getting the job done but also making sure it's done to the best of everyone's ability, regardless of time and budget. You do not cut corners and don't expect others to, either. You know that tactful diplomacy is the most important arrow of communication in your quiver and people will be saying yes to you even before you've reached the end of your request. You are an asset at work where your organisational skills will be admired by all and a fantastic homemaker because you are there for the long haul and nothing is left to chance. Your partner and your children will feel the benefit of living such organised and tidy lives, which you know then frees you all up to have quality time together doing things you all enjoy, including, for you, writing or painting or theatre.

Numerology

No. 3: Creative with the gift of imagination and an ability to communicate in writing, art or speech.

Tarot

The Empress: You are the consummate work colleague, parent and partner, with the gift of knowing precisely which path to take and which choice to make to ensure life, yours and those of the people you love and care about, is as drama-free as it can be. Like the swan gliding gracefully across the millpond – the effort of paddling furiously to stay afloat remaining hidden below the surface of the water – you will work twice as hard as anyone else to achieve that same smooth sailing for yourself and your family.

Famous birthdays

Jane Goodall British primatologist and anthropologist
Marlon Brando American actor and director
Eddie Murphy American actor

April

April 4th

Big thinker

The phrase 'blue-sky thinking' was probably invented for you because when it comes to innovative ideas, you're always out front with yours and impatient to get them translated off the page and into action. It's that Aries impatience playing through all walks of your life; you wake up raring to go and can be guilty of throwing yourself at a project or a problem without properly researching the challenges first. But you mean well, people know that about you and so forgive you. If you've chosen to work in the arts, you'll soon be recognised for having the ability to blend business nous with an instinctive understanding of what the public wants – current fads and trends – and how best to deliver that to them. You'll also enjoy every second of channelling your Arian energy into the project in hand. In love, people may find you a bit confusing; part of you craves the stability of a safe and long-term relationship, while the other part doesn't want to relinquish your freedom and independence. It's tricky, and it's anyone's guess which part will win, and the outcome really depends on who you meet along the way.

Numerology

No. 4: Invested in the physical world, centred earth energy that is practical in application.

Tarot

Ace of Swords: All the ace cards in the Tarot deck tell us we're on the right path. Not only that, but there are unseen forces on our side urging us forward and supporting us along each step of the path we have chosen. Pentacles represent our resources, internal and external, and not just money. What could you mine deeper for the first time to help you implement some of those big ideas of yours? Who can you ask for help? What do you need to best prepare yourself before setting off along the path towards the distant mountains we see depicted in this card?

Famous birthdays

Maya Angelou American poet and civil rights activist
Graham Norton Irish comedian and TV show host
Karren Brady British businesswoman

April 5th

Motivated perfectionist

'Eyes on the prize' is the mantra that best applies to you. You're heading to the top and it's your perfectionist streak and dedicated attention to detail, as well as your commitment to being and giving of your very best at all times, that is going to propel you there. This will be a steadfast climb to the top. You are throwing everything you've got at this ambition to be the best of the best, and when you get there, you've no intention of releasing your grip. Fortunately, you like to play as hard as you work, so you have a good social network, you're fun to be around and you've a particular soft spot for children, which will make you a fantastic aunt or uncle if you don't get around to having any of your own. This could be the case because, giving as much as you do to your career aspirations, you are not always the most attuned partner or lover. In fact, you may find yourself on the receiving end of a Dear John discussion where you'll probably be shocked to learn just how neglected your romantic interest has been feeling. With your restless urge to conquer the next challenge, however, you may not really be all that bothered if (or how) they ditch you.

Numerology

No. 5: Impulsive and restless by nature, spontaneous and likes to discover the world through the senses.

Tarot

Seven of Wands: It's been a long old climb, but this card shows a fighting-fit young man staking his claim – literally – to the higher ground where he has already implanted six of his seven budding wands or sticks. He is so high up there's nothing else in the fore- or the far-ground. This is the pinnacle, and he wants everyone who follows to know he was here first because that's what is really important to him. There is a sense of triumph and completion about this card; he knew what he wanted, he worked hard to get it and now he is going to savour every second of his hard-won success. As will you.

Famous birthdays

Booker T. Washington American political advisor and orator
Bette Davis American actress
Colin Powell 65th United States Secretary of State

April 6th

Good Samaritan

Well, this is a little bit unexpected and unusual, because what we have here is a sentimental Aries who will do anything to avoid causing offence to others and feel badly about those they may need to step over and leave behind on their climb to the top of their career. You have a very strong sense of what's fair and just, and can come across as an idealist, and while you're happy to work as part of a team to realise your Good Samaritan goals, if you're totally honest with yourself, your preferred idea of being a team player really only appeals if that team has one particular person leading it: you! You have a good social network and get along well with most people you meet, but you gravitate towards those like-minds who relish the arts and feel inspired by beauty. You may not be the most ardent and passionate of the Aries lovers, but your life partner will feel appreciated due to your affectionate and warm-hearted good nature. And they will share your acclaimed desire to see more social justice in the world.

Numerology

No. 6: Empathic and nurturing, can problem-solve in an emotional and physical way, responsible and cares deeply about family and friends.

Tarot

Six of Cups: One of the most nurturing cards in the Tarot deck. We see an older boy offering a younger girl a loving cup full of hope and innocence restored – the cup takes the shape of a white flower. They could be brother and sister or just living in the same medieval village, but whatever their connection, he is being a Good Samaritan to someone weaker and more vulnerable than himself. Perhaps they share a story of an unhappy childhood or he has simply witnessed her suffering and sorrow. Whatever the truth of the narrative they share, he wants to make things better for her.

Famous birthdays

James Watson American biologist, geneticist and zoologist
Myleene Klass British singer
James Wade British darts player

April 7th

Enquiring researcher

Were you one of those children whose favourite word/question was why? Did you drive you parents mad asking for explanation after explanation in a bid to try and understand the world, the experiences you shared as a family and what you witnessed further afield on TV or in movies? You would be well suited to scientific research or investigative journalism – in fact, any career where asking your favourite word is always the starting point, whatever the expected end goal. You bring the perfect mix of logic, imagination and tenacity to any issue, question or challenge you are tussling with and you also bring a typical Arian enthusiasm to everything you embark upon, which helps inspire others to help you. Don't think you can get around every obstacle by simply battering your way through and keep that fiery Arian temper in check when your efforts to bulldoze through a problem fail. For the most part, you are pretty sunny and chilled – qualities that bode well for a happy and harmonious long-term relationship. Just make sure you're embarking on one of those with someone who knows better than to chain you down with endless restrictions and ground rules.

Numerology

No. 7: Very analytical and detail-oriented, likes to observe and investigate things, and has a keen, inventive eye.

Tarot

The High Priestess: It's not a term we hear much these days, but here is a lady best described as 'bookish'. She is seeking answers and digging deep into the spiritual scriptures to find them. The High Priestess is the female match to the Magician, but where he knows the 'How?' to make something happen, she starts a step before by knowing what needs to happen, where and when. Use your own strong intuition to find these same answers to the questions you will have about your own life.

Famous birthdays

Billie Holiday American jazz and swing singer
Francis Ford Coppola American director
Tim Peake British astronaut

April 8th

Competitive influencer

There is no second, third or fourth position in your work or social life; there's only number one and that's going to be you. And truth be told, you may not be all that squeamish about either how you get there, how you hold on to pole position or keep the potential competition back and at bay. Of course, this makes you the consummate sports professional – you have all the qualities and single-minded focus you need to reach and stay at the top of your chosen game, but you'll also stand out from the crowd if social media is your game and will relish the spotlight and platform bestowed upon you by having the title of influencer. If you're home-based and raising a family, yours will be the home everyone talks about; if you throw a party, everyone will want to come, even those who don't share your love of power, money and the status they bring. And if you've had to be a bit ruthless to grab the status you crave in your conscience-free world view, those rewards, some of which you'll be happy to share with those less fortunate, are more than worth it. You'll have to marry someone with the same values, which boil down to just one word that sums up your sun sign: me, me, me.

Numerology

No. 8: Sees the big picture and aims for it, linked to abundance and material wealth, and uses financial success to give back to others.

Tarot

The Devil: The human beings depicted on this card are chained below the devil's cloven feet, and in some ways, you may start to feel as you move through your life that you too have been chained to things (status) which may not turn out to be so important after all. Look closely and you will see these chains are really only loosely holding the humans in place, so the good news is you have the choice to break them and make a bid for a different kind of freedom any time you want.

Famous birthdays

Vivienne Westwood British fashion designer
Julian Lennon British singer and musician
Robin Wright American actress and director

April 9th

Efficient achiever

There's no sitting around daydreaming of lofty goals and visionary ideals; with you it's all about taking practical steps to achieve the next grounded goal and then the one that follows. You will do well in business or the military where order is key; you can't abide inefficiency and will run your home as expediently as your business or career. You like to keep busy, love to help others and will bring a methodical and determined approach to any task you agree to undertake. The only trouble is, you expect the same determined grit and focus from others and so can sometimes seem intolerant and domineering when they fail to deliver the same way you do. This can be a particular problem at home which, much as you might wish it otherwise, is not actually a military base. Take your foot off the gas and allow for a little more imperfection – you never know where, creatively, that might lead!

Numerology

No. 9: An old soul that looks to spiritual awareness to solve life's problems and likes to help others to do so in the same way.

Tarot

The Hanged Man: One of the Major Arcana cards, this is a difficult card that symbolises rigidity, leading to an inability to move up, down, left, right, forwards or backwards. In other words, it is a card warning you not to get so stuck in your ways you find yourself immobilised by any kind of change that might require you to adapt and move on. Being flexible is key to resilience in life and there will be times, however charmed or controlled a life you lead, when things happen that are outside your control. Hopefully, when this happens, you'll have allowed for some of that imperfection we talked about and so will have the resilience to cope with change.

Famous birthdays

Charles Baudelaire French poet
Nigel Slater British food writer and broadcaster
Marc Jacobs American fashion designer

April 10th

Action personified

You might be described by those who first meet you as a force of nature, and they'd be right: you can't abide inaction and appear to others to move so fast through life that you leave those watching your progress feeling dizzy with it all. You're a non-conformist, too, so will definitely be beating to the sound of your own drum. You're decisive and intuitive and not really bothered if others can't see your point of view or don't agree with a course of action you are hell-bent on taking. Mostly, people like you. You are sociable, can be quite kind and generous, but there is a hidden spiteful streak and woe betide anyone at the end of one of your tongue-lashings, because you won't stop short of the jugular – you'll be aiming right for it. You epitomise the fire energy of Aries and if things start feeling a bit quiet for your liking, you're not averse to stirring the pot. This doesn't make for the most harmonious of relationships, including marriage, and since you suffer from FOMO there's a good chance if things do turn dull, you'll be off to take someone else up on their offer of adventure and excitement.

Numerology

No. 1: A powerful entity and results-oriented force, all about initiating action and getting things done.

Tarot

Judgement: One of the Major Arcana cards, we see an angelic trumpeter literally blasting the dead up and out of their tombs to embrace life again and learn from their previous mistakes. When this card shows up in a tarot reading, it is a sign the querent (you) might need a sudden jolt out of their complacency and a nudge towards facing the truth of what's really going on below the surface in all aspects of their lives. Think of this as a 'Wake up!' call. And ask yourself which parts of your life are you sleepwalking through and why?

Famous birthdays

Omar Sharif Egyptian actor
Steven Seagal American actor and screenwriter
Daisy Ridley British actress

April 11th

Animal lover

Responsibility is not your thing, unless it is taking responsibility for an animal, in which case you'll be the first to say yes. But in all other aspects of life, it seems like you've decided there's really no appeal in growing up, so you're not going to. Clinging to this child-like essence means you 'get' kids and they get you. You're comfortable and happy around young people, in the same uncomplicated way you are around animals. It's the grown-ups you find less appealing, although truth be told, if you do ever decide to settle down with a life partner, you can probably see the sense in choosing someone who is older, has more life experience and is happy to do the 'grown-up' things for both of you. Success is easy for you because, whatever your apparent faults, you know yourself so well; you know the type of work environment in which you will thrive – an animal rescue sanctuary being an obvious one – and you're also smart enough to know you'll never have all the answers but can learn a lot from those who are ahead of you in the game of life. You're not great at handling criticism and can spiral into extreme depression, which doesn't match the scale of the perceived slight. Try and develop a thicker Arian skin.

Numerology

No. 2: Shows resilience and power in gentleness, often provides the role of mediator, and linked to psychic abilities.

Tarot

Wheel of Fortune: The success foretold by this card is written in the stars for you, but in another sense, we need to understand that your idea of success may not be a worldly one as in power, money and status. Running a well-funded animal sanctuary would be your idea of bliss, so there is something here about stepping out of one world and into another to feel fully aligned with the life path you have chosen. Use your hidden psychic intuition to find that path and step out onto it.

Famous birthdays

Jeremy Clarkson British TV presenter and journalist
Jennifer Esposito American actress
Joss Stone British singer-songwriter

April 12th

Lofty idealist

You believe you were born to do everything you can to create a more just, humane and compassionate world, and you have all the skills of persuasion to convince others to sign up for your cause. You are not really too concerned about making money, cannot stand idleness and can sometimes come across as a bit hoity-toity because you are all about the moral high ground, although in truth, if anyone deserves to set up camp there, it is you. You have a fierce wit and may even enter the world of comedy entertainment where, standing in the spotlight on stage during a live gig, you can use humour to highlight the injustices and indignities you want to see tackled. But as is the case with so many comedians, off-stage you may be something of a loner. Be careful this propensity doesn't tip into loneliness. You are immensely generous with all your resources towards those you are closest to, and although your love affairs (many) will be ardent, you're not too bothered about the convention of marriage. You know that being a lone wolf grants you a kind of freedom that a conventional relationship would only chip away at.

Numerology

No. 3: Creative with the gift of imagination and an ability to communicate in writing, art or speech.

Tarot

Two of Cups: You have everything you need to really connect with another human being but as we see from this card where a man and woman face each other to make a toast with the chalice each holds in their hand, there's a reluctance on your part to commit fully. The Cups in the Tarot deck represent emotion and what this card, with one of the parties stepping back or, equally, stepping forward more reluctantly, tells us is that you will always hold something back. Perhaps you need whatever it is you cannot give away for yourself and for the work you really came here to do.

Famous birthdays

David Letterman American TV presenter and producer
Tom Clancy American writer
Jacob Zuma South African politician

April 13th

Ambitious achiever

There isn't a frivolous bone in your body – you take life and everything you do so seriously that success for you is only a matter of time and sacrifice because you're not letting anything get in the way of your goals, including love. You're not chasing success for the limelight (although you're not averse to taking the glory); you want it for the security you believe it will provide. And the truth is, people respect you and your goals because those high standards you're setting ... you're setting those for yourself, as well as everyone else. You crave success and the status it brings, and you'll do anything to get it, including walking away from romance. Not for you a devil-may-care, let's-throw-caution-to-the-wind approach to matters of the heart; you're as serious about your love life as you are about your career, but if it comes to being forced to choose between the two, then the heart will always take second place to the head. Don't let your ambition cost everything you hold dear – there are some things we just can't get back when we ditch them for the bright lights of fame and fortune.

Numerology

No. 4: Invested in the physical world, centred earth energy that is practical in application.

Tarot

King of Swords: Thwack ... thwack ... that's the sound of the King's sword slicing decisively through all the obstacles in his path, including the ties that bind. There was nothing going to stop his meteoric rise to take his place on the Kingly Throne we see in this card, and he became adept at leaving behind anything that might have slowed him down, including pain and sorrow. The thing is, he got what his heart desired but, look, he is alone. Maybe heed this warning.

Famous birthdays

Garry Kasparov Russian chess grandmaster
Jacques Lacan French psychoanalyst and psychiatrist
Samuel Beckett Irish writer

April 14th

Creative genius

You know those people who can size up a dingy old dining room and a roll of gorgeous fabric and then transform said room into something so chic it looks as if it has cost a fortune? Of course you do, because this is you. You've got what others refer to as 'an eye', which to those without it seems like a divine blessing from the heavenly realms themselves. Whether it's clothes or furnishings or a camper van, you have the magic touch and when your work is done crowds will gather to admire it. If it's not obvious yet, you should be auditioning for one of the make-over reality TV shows because you'd ace it, or maybe you've found an outlet for your creative genius in garden design or high fashion retail or some other slot where looks are everything and gorgeousness pays. You don't just sparkle on the outside, you're also fun and spontaneous, and you've got that inner sparkle, too, so people really like being around you. Which is just as well, because you like to be appreciated. Choose a partner from among your admirers and don't ever let your mystery fade by telling anyone the secrets of your trade.

Numerology

No. 5: Impulsive and restless by nature, spontaneous and likes to discover the world through the senses.

Tarot

The Magician: If alchemy isn't already the name of your interior design business or lifestyle coaching website, it should be. Ask the Magician who can also whisk a little charm and glamour from thin air and, with the help of some smoke and mirrors, show people what they want to see, rather than what is actually there. You share this same gift, which you channel into your creativity. Treasure it. It's very rare.

Famous birthdays

Julie Christie British actress
Peter Capaldi Scottish actor and film-maker
Bobbi Brown American make-up artist and businesswoman

April 15th

Free thinker

If this is not already your job title, go see your boss and ask for it to be. As far as you are concerned, all your ideas are excellent – visionary even – and the thinking behind them is robust. However, others may think otherwise and challenge what they see as somewhat unusual ideas based not in reality, but in fantasy. When this happens, you will have to keep a lid on that Arian temper of yours because you do not like to be questioned, interrogated or crossed. The truth, as ever, probably lies somewhere in the middle. Many of your ideas are good, excellent even, but, like all blue-sky thinkers, you can get carried away with a notion that should really have stayed in your head. Try to adopt a little more patience so that you give others the chance to catch up with the originality of your ideas. You can be empathic when you want, so drop the 'my way or the highway' attitude in your romantic relationships, or it will be a fish supper for one for the rest of your life because nobody likes the idea of living with someone who only values their own freedom and expects everyone else to toe the party line.

Numerology

No. 6: Empathic and nurturing, can problem-solve in an emotional and physical way, responsible and cares deeply about family and friends.

Tarot

Knight of Swords: The movement captured in this image of the Knight of Swords brandishing his fiery weapons, as his horse bolts who knows where, is one of a fast-and-furious pace and if he weren't such an excellent horseman, this warrior rider would have fallen off his horse by the time they had reached the edge of the card. This is the classic 'rush past the good stuff and you'll look back and wish you'd stopped long enough to smell the roses, taste the coffee, remember why you were doing it all in the first place' message. Up to you if you want to hear it.

Famous birthdays

Emma Watson British actress
Nikita Khrushchev Russian politician
Emma Thompson British actress and screenwriter

April 16th

Spiritual seeker

You're not here for the material gains – you're here to delve deeply into as many traditions as you can to discover the Ancient Mysteries for yourself and live your life accordingly. You have a confident, even outgoing personality, but the core of you is a dreamier creature and much more engaged with your spiritual journey than any external challenges or prerequisites of success. With such an analytical and enquiring mind, you'd make a good detective, therapist or scientific researcher, and any career where you have the luxury of alone time to really think things through will suit you. You are a caring soul and will be the first to reach out to a friend in need or a colleague who is struggling with their workload, but you function best alone and won't sign up willingly to being part of a team effort. Solitude is important to you, as you need quiet to think things through, and you will seem reticent, even a bit moody, in new relationships. But if you do decide to give your heart and commit, you will be a loyal and steadfast life partner.

Numerology

No. 7: Very analytical and detail-oriented, likes to observe and investigate things, and has a keen, inventive eye.

Tarot

The Star: You may have already discovered that the healing arts often act as a doorway or portal to the deeper Ancient Mysteries, and with one foot on dry land and the other in a liquid pool of primordial matter, the naked woman depicted in this card is showing you that you, too, will need to keep one foot 'here' in order to be able to safely place one foot 'there' – wherever 'there' leads for you.

Famous birthdays

Charlie Chaplin American actor and film-maker
Pope Benedict XVI German former pope
Ellen Barkin American actress and producer

April 17th

Zealous campaigner

You want to see the world change for the better and you see yourself as a born champion of the underprivileged or abused, which means you'll likely choose a career such as politics, law or charity where you think you really can campaign for change. You have the dynamic and energetic personality needed to get others on board, so why is this sometimes such a challenge? It's because you can come across as too forceful and however worthy your cause, nobody wants to feel bullied, stigmatised or shamed into getting involved, so maybe lay off with the silent judgemental reproaches and try, instead, to perfect the art of inviting others to share the vision and help you make it happen – that way, it feels like a win-win for all. This may feel like lowering your standards and watering down your goals, but there's no point reaching for the stars if nobody's prepared to reach with you. This will also be good practice for your love life because, again, nobody likes feeling they are being judged and found to be wanting based on your impossibly high ideals.

Numerology

No. 8: Sees the big picture and aims for it, linked to abundance and material wealth, and uses financial success to give back to others.

Tarot

The Emperor: This is a man who has earned his reputation for wise counsel and who takes his responsibility – especially towards those less fortunate – very seriously. Play with the word Emperor and it's not too big a stretch to get to Empowered, which is the message for you with this card. The Emperor empowers you to step forward and make your mark in life, but also empowers you so that you can, in turn, empower others.

Famous birthdays

Victoria Beckham British fashion designer
J.P. Morgan American financier and banker
Sean Bean British actor

April 18th

Charismatic firecracker

If you're still playing the field – and even if you've left your flirting days behind – you already know you have 'It'. And when you have 'It' other people really like to be around you, in or out of the bedroom. 'It' has nothing to do with age, so it's likely you'll still be getting offers in your 80s and leaving a little trail of broken hearts in your wake, because you're really not all that bothered about being loved-up. You love your freedom. You don't suffer fools gladly and don't want to waste time training anyone to your way of thinking; you'd rather go home, read a good book and live out your days alone if the alternative means you'd have to make any kind of compromise. Uncompromising Aries. Pure Aries. Firecracker Aries. This is you. Your faith and/or other spiritual beliefs will move to centre stage as you age and it's likely you'll find a way to help others connect to theirs, too. This could see you involved in a community church or teaching yoga or even leading a shamanic quest somewhere in South America. You're forever young at heart; you know you've got 'It' and nobody is ever going to be able to take that away from you.

Numerology

No. 9: An old soul that looks to spiritual awareness to solve life's problems and likes to help others to do so in the same way.

Tarot

Six of Pentacles: With the Pentacles symbolising resources, in this card those resources are more spiritual than material and hard-won. We see a successful-looking man holding an old-fashioned weighing scale in his left hand. He is distributing something that looks like money but could be food or crystals to the two men begging on their knees before him. They are the disciples. He is the one dispensing whatever it is they most need. You share his motives, his generosity and his ability to share fairly that nourishment – earthly and divine – which is a privilege to share with others.

Famous birthdays

Kourtney Kardashian American media personality and businesswoman
David Tennant Scottish actor
Rosie Huntingdon-Whiteley British model and actress

April 19th

Chilled nature-lover

Not for you the bright city lights or demands of a career on the global stage – you're a nature-lover and so your dream home will be one surrounded by wildflowers and birdsong, in the countryside or as close as your circumstances will allow. You'll likely be a gifted grower yourself, which means you'd prioritise a garden over a second bathroom, and while vast sums of money may never come your way, you won't care, as long as you feel healthy and happy doing something you love. You don't have a materialistic bone in your body – or a mean one – so make sure you choose a like-minded mate who will also be happy muddling through, living from one pay cheque to the next and to swap a luxury lifestyle for one full of fun and the freedom to express your unique soul. You are generous to a fault and may find it hard to hang on to any little windfall that does come your way; you're more likely to give it away than stash it for a rainy day. Living a life that some might find a little precarious is not for everyone, but you have one of life's true luxuries and one that no amount of money can buy, which is going to bed at night and waking up in the morning feeling happy with your lot, even when it's not a lot!

Numerology

No. 1: A powerful entity and results-oriented force, all about initiating action and getting things done.

Tarot

Ace of Wands: If the ace cards bring us one clear message it is that, happily, we are already on the path our soul has chosen for us, so all we have to do is trust that and stick with it. Communication is an important tool for you, and in this card, we see the hand of Spirit passing you a sturdy and very fertile wand (budding stick), which is a sign that whatever ideas you want to share with the world, including those about your non-materialistic lifestyle, people will be only too happy to hear them.

Famous birthdays

Kate Hudson American actress
Maria Sharapova Russian tennis player
Ashley Judd American actress and political activist

April 20th

Driven perfectionist

If that sounds a little scary, take heed, because while we can all see the value of a job done well and to the best of our ability, those without your steely drive and determination may find you a little hypercritical and choose not to work with you again. It's true that the high standards you hold up for others are held even higher for yourself, but not everyone knows or appreciates that, so try and cultivate a little more empathy for others. If that's a stretch too far, then 'fake it 'til you make it'. You have everything you need, and more, to get to the top of your chosen career and would do well to think about being freelance and self-employed because that way, you won't have to bite your tongue when a sloppy colleague is cutting corners to get the job done. In truth, when you're fired up over something, people either love or loathe you, but as you mature, you'll develop those skills needed to be able to mediate through conflict and will be able to effortlessly inspire others with the way you negotiate and achieve the best outcome for all. You have a strong intuition, so just keep following those hunches, and in your private life look for those who can hold their own.

Numerology

No. 2: Shows resilience and power in gentleness, often provides the role of mediator, and linked to psychic abilities.

Tarot

The King of Swords: One of your big strengths lies in your capacity to somehow psychically 'see' the solution to a challenge or an obstacle, and so, in your case, the sword in this card represents your mental, emotional and psychic ability to take swift action and cut through the dross to what really matters. There's a butterfly above the King's head flying between two crescent moons, which tells us you can flit between the realms – between dreamtime and reality – without fear of losing your footing.

Famous birthdays

Jessica Lange American actress
Joan Miró Spanish painter, sculptor and ceramicist
Napoleon III First President of France

April 21st

Self-possessed motivator

Capable, efficient and self-disciplined, you're a shining example of the tenacity it takes to succeed without giving up life's pleasures, which, for you, revolve around your appreciation of the arts. You may even be the original sybarite, and you are most definitely an indulgent parent! Your ability to motivate others will be quickly noticed in any work environment and don't be surprised when offers to lead in some way soon follow. With your earthy grounded energy and reliable Taurean nature, you were born to teach or lead in some other way. Your hedonistic streak means you won't much like rigid rules, so be careful about the environment you work in – if you do settle on teaching, then look for positions in more progressive schools. You get enormous pleasure bringing happiness to others, which makes you an endearing friend and a worthy choice as a life partner. Just make sure you don't tip into trying to control everyone and everything, however pure your initial intent and motives.

Numerology
No. 3: Creative with the gift of imagination and an ability to communicate in writing, art or speech.

Tarot
Three of Wands: You are as steady as a rock or, in the case of this card, the three sturdy staffs surrounding the successful merchant we see looking contentedly out over the trading plains, where ships full of luxuries to be traded between civilisations sail back and forth. This is a person of whom we would say they have 'made it' in life. They have earned their position on the higher ground and with their love of life's little luxuries have enjoyed every step of the journey they have taken to get here.

Famous birthdays
Queen Elizabeth II Queen of the United Kingdom
Max Weber German sociologist, historian and political economist
Andie MacDowell American actress

April 22nd

Secret romantic

You keep your feelings buried quite deep, so it's possible your romantic nature is known to only a few and those are the few who have been lovers, past and present. With you, it really is a case of still waters running deep because, although you come across as cool, calm and collected, even in the face of calamity and crisis, you're actually highly emotional and as capable of dreaming big as anyone else. But you hate, absolutely hate, change and so although you're industrious and prepared to work towards those dreams, you'll balk at the challenge of big changes and find it hard to put your faith in anything you can't see or experience directly yourself. You like to think this makes you a down-to-earth realist, but sometimes it makes you a scaredy-cat. Find yourself a loving mate who appreciates your staunch and unswerving loyalty and devotion, then see if you can't find the courage sometimes to leap into the unknown with them. The rewards for that level of bravery are waiting.

Numerology

No. 4: Invested in the physical world, centred earth energy that is practical in application.

Tarot

Death: As we've already seen, this is not a card of doom or gloom, rather a card of the astonishing opportunities and new beginnings that lie in wait for you if you can find the courage that we've just talked about to let go of old ways/patterns/jobs/habits and throw yourself wholeheartedly into something new via the one thing you hate the most: change. But this card tells you, without a shadow of a doubt, that you can do it; you just have to believe in your ability to stay in motion, move forward in your life and, with love, leave behind anything that no longer serves you.

Famous birthdays

Vladimir Lenin Russian revolutionary and politician
J. Robert Oppenheimer American theoretical physicist
Vladimir Nabokov Russian-American writer

April 23rd

Engaged explorer

You may not actually leave the continent or even the sofa to set out on your 'travels', but you have such a good intellect and are engaged with and interested in so many things that nobody will tire of your company. You read voraciously, you stay up to date with politics and business matters and you are usually the best-informed person in the room whose opinion is always grounded in research and fact. Like all Taureans, you like your home comforts, so you're unlikely to pack a backpack and rough it to go exploring for real, but in your own way you're travelling the globe, each and every day, and you're a sucker for the feel of a good old-fashioned and bulky Sunday newspaper in your hands. You understand numbers in ways that bamboozle others and so may work in the financial sector in some way. People may 'switch off' when you tell them what you do for work (because they don't understand it), but they'll soon 'switch on' again if you've a romantic interest in them because you're a sensual and passionate lover who likes to make sure everyone has a very good time in bed. When you do decide to settle down your life partner will discover a huge and very kind heart lying behind that huge and very impressive intellect.

Numerology

No. 5: Impulsive and restless by nature, spontaneous and likes to discover the world through the senses.

Tarot

Ten of Cups: A joyous card, utterly joyous! The Cups represent our emotions and you've got so many here that you could afford to pass some to those with less. We see a happy couple and their children dancing under a rainbow and celebrating all that is good in their lives. Put simply, they are happy and, in this scene, taking the time to count their many blessings. If this is not you already, you can trust that one day it will be.

Famous birthdays

J.M.W. Turner British artist
Max Planck German theoretical physicist
Gigi Hadid American model

April 24th

Caring humanitarian

You are a deeply committed humanitarian and will be working in some way to improve the plight of others. One of your strengths is also one of your weaknesses, which is your refusal to quit. You care just as deeply about your family and friends as you do about your causes and this can cause tensions because you often feel split, especially when you recognise that you cannot give yourself wholeheartedly to both at the same time. You will need to learn to manage this internal tug and understand that the very fact you give everything you can every second of the day is already more than enough. If all this makes you sound a little bit worthy, you have an amazing sense of fun which means people will seek out your company for a good time. Don't ever let yourself lose this shining quality which brings a healthy balance to the proceedings as well as people who want to share your life.

Numerology

No. 6: Empathic and nurturing, can problem-solve in an emotional and physical way, responsible and cares deeply about family and friends.

Tarot

Four of Swords: There's no point glossing over the fact that this is a difficult card for many, but once we understand its underlying message and warning, the good news is we can do something about it. We see what appears to be an interred knight lying in the crypt of a church, signalling that if his earthly life is not already over, it is about to be. This is a card that asks us to recognise when we may be about to give up and need to take a step back from all the responsibilities we have accrued or had placed on us by others. In your case, this is a card that recognises that while you have admirable humanitarian goals, there may be times you feel overwhelmed by the sheer enormity of the task ahead. There will always be injustice and cruelty in the world and the day you accept this can feel like the day part of you has died. The fact is, this is the day you become more focused in your campaigning.

Famous birthdays

Barbara Streisand American singer and actress
Jean Paul Gaultier French fashion designer
Shirley MacLaine American actress, singer and activist

April 25th

Music-loving optimist

You share your birthday with many well-known musicians, including the singer Ella Fitzgerald, and Taurus rules the throat, so it's likely that music is not only a passion of yours, but perhaps also the artistic arena you work in. You enjoy and appreciate all artistic endeavours, but music is your main 'thing'. Ever the optimist, you're much more adventurous than many who share your sun sign, making travel another important part of your life and something you will want your life partner to feel just as passionately about as you. You're charming, witty and intelligent, so there won't be any shortage of people hoping to be considered for that role, but make sure you choose someone who understands and maybe even shares your tendency to get bored and your need for a regular change of scenery, or you will end up at loggerheads. Freedom and independence are your favourite two words, and you have the wisdom to understand that what life is really about is the journey, not the destination. This understanding underpins your natural curiosity and will keep you engaged with life all the way through to old age.

Numerology

No. 7: Very analytical and detail-oriented, likes to observe and investigate things, and has a keen, inventive eye.

Tarot

Three of Pentacles: There's a very good chance that whatever artistic endeavour you are involved with, but particularly if it is music, you will end up being recognised for your talents and contribution to the genre of your choice. If you've gone into composing, you will be composing for blockbusters, not TV ads, and while you won't actively seek the celebrity limelight, you could end up as a household name and someone known for their talent, rather than just the fact they've been on TV.

Famous birthdays

Renée Zellweger American actress
Ella Fitzgerald American jazz singer
Al Pacino American actor and film-maker

April 26th

Careful planner

Not for you the 'close your eyes, take a leap and hope for the best approach' to either work or your personal life; you are a planner and that means a careful examination of all the facts and figures, outcomes, potential disasters and likely successes long before you agree to take any kind of action. You will do well whatever your chosen career and will be very well suited to management, where your ability to plan and ensure the smooth running of any project will reassure both the workforce who follow your lead and the stakeholders looking for their return. If you have a fault – and, like the rest of us, I'm afraid you do – it is that you can become way too controlling and utterly dismissive of anyone who is not prepared to do things your way. Nobody likes a boss who thinks they are running a dictatorship, so you are going to need to learn to embrace a more collaborative approach and consider the thoughts, feelings and ideas of others when you're busy planning. Whatever path you choose you will do well, well enough to give back both money and your time. Just make sure you don't confuse confidence with arrogance, and you will easily keep all the balls in the air and all your 'big picture' dreams on track.

Numerology

No. 8: Sees the 'big picture' and aims for it, linked to abundance and material wealth, and uses financial success to give back to others.

Tarot

Strength: It takes strength to step into any kind of managerial or leadership role and to sustain it, but this card is not talking about the strength of force, rather the strength it takes to calm a lion using gentle powers of persuasion. We see a gentle maiden closing the lion's mouth. She is not afraid to silence his roar but is reassuring him that all will be well and by respecting his strength into the bargain. This is the strength you can develop as you navigate your way through the world.

Famous birthdays

Melania Trump Former First Lady of the United States
Ludwig Wittgenstein Austrian philosopher
Carol Burnett American actress and comedian

April 27th

Inspiring philanthropist

An ideal mix of idealistic dreamer and characteristic Taurean steadiness, you have a magnetism that draws people to you and holds them there because what you promise is what you deliver, and so you really are someone who holds true to their word. You're all about action and have good business acumen, so if you want success, it's yours for the taking, although you're really more interested in campaigning to make the world a better place than you are in raking in big money for its own sake. If you do amass a fortune, you'll set up some sort of charitable foundation to make sure it is channelled into good works. You bring this same charming idealism into your personal relationships but be careful your high ideals don't mean you are constantly feeling disappointed and let down. Nobody can live up to your ideals of flawless perfection – including, and especially, you! Try to accept the good with the bad and focus instead on the long-term humanitarian goals you can achieve with someone like-minded and just as committed by your side. If you need the inspiration of some role models to help you imagine this rewarding way of life, look no further than Bill and Melinda Gates.

Numerology

No. 9: An old soul that looks to spiritual awareness to solve life's problems and likes to help others to do so in the same way.

Tarot

The Lovers: An especially important card for you because if you get this part of your life right for you, everything else will just fall into place. It may be that you don't meet your perfect soulmate until you have a little of life, including perhaps a first marriage, tucked under your belt. Don't see this as a negative; understand that it takes the time it takes to mature a happy marriage and a philanthropist pair to perfection. Now that should be music to your ears.

Famous birthdays

Jenna Coleman British actress
Tess Daly British TV presenter
Darcey Bussell British ballerina

April 28th

Inspiring role-model

There are some – particularly those born on this day – who will never have to compromise or yield to get what they want because everyone else will yield to them. There's no denying your physical attractiveness, but there's something else: the something we call charisma or 'It'. You were born with 'It', so you've never had to try hard to get other people to do your bidding, and even when you're in danger of becoming a little overbearing, people will still admire your gusto and clarity of vision. The fact is, you really do have courage running through every fibre of your body and it is as if people just know that about you. You inspire others to find their courage and, when they do, win their lifelong loyalty. You could be a devastatingly effective politician or decide to become an actor and use your profile to highlight issues of unfairness. Whatever path you choose, it won't be long before you're being asked to write books and give TED talks to share your inspiring vision. You love sex (and success), which may cause problems when it becomes clear commitment comes secondary with you; there's just too much life to see, too much to get done and too many people to meet to ever settle down and say: 'That's it, I'm done.'

Numerology

No. I: A powerful entity and results-oriented force, all about initiating action and getting things done.

Tarot

Ace of Cups: It's as if the Holy Spirit or another faith's equivalent is actually dive-bombing down to Earth to tell you that anything you want and need to get the job done is yours for the taking. The card shows a dove diving headfirst into a large golden chalice supported by the hand of Spirit. The elixir of life spilling from our Holy Grail signifies an overflowing of abundance, which in your life translates to charm, looks, riches, personality, charisma and heart. You are the whole package, and more.

Famous birthdays

Terry Pratchett British writer
Penélope Cruz Spanish actress and model
Melanie Martinez American singer-songwriter

April 29th

Passionate enabler

You are grounded and pragmatic, but these strengths belie a strongly creative side that is also keen to problem-solve and move forward towards the best solution. You have a very strong nurturing side which will always find a creative outlet in both your work and personal life; and your appreciation of beauty takes in all things, from art to food. Your people skills are second to none and, coupled with your ability to balance serious responsibility with a sense of fun, this makes you a great friend, an excellent workmate, a kind, caring and steadfast life partner and a nurturing parent who won't be afraid to let their child fail to learn as long as you are there, behind them, to quietly help them back to their feet. But all these people qualities will mean nothing unless you're prepared to graft and, at heart, this is the secret to any success you achieve in life. Like the stalwart Taurus you are, hard work lies behind your success in life, although it's only in looking back that you can see how hard you've worked to get to where you are. Be sure, however, that people don't exploit this and ride on the back of your hard work to promote themselves.

Numerology

No. 2: Shows resilience and power in gentleness, often provides the role of mediator, and linked to psychic abilities.

Tarot

The Empress: One of the Major Arcana, this is a powerful card signifying initiative and action. You, just like our Empress, exert a powerfully feminine influence in all that you do; an influence that is both creative and highly protective of those you love and the things you care about. She is, in so many ways, the queen of womanhood, wise beyond her years and a nurturing mother to all – including and especially original ideas – she creates and gives birth to.

Famous birthdays

Michelle Pfeiffer American actress and producer
Daniel Day-Lewis British actor
Duke Ellington American composer and pianist

April 30th

Multi-talented optimist

You're an optimist because you have no doubt – none whatsoever – that you won't be able to use your many skills to make the world a better and fairer place for all to share. You are the keystone species in all your networks, both work and personal. People look to you for guidance and encouragement and value your dependability and light touch, which can make a task seem less daunting. You're not a team player – you're a born leader – but you excel at getting people on board and so your real forte is putting a dream team together. You are calm in a crisis and there's not much that can throw you off balance, and since people really do value you, there's a strong chance you will become well-known through your work and contribution via the career you've chosen – this may very well be social work or teaching or campaigning or writing. You're a gifted parent and, as in work, the keystone species that everyone in the family depends on in your private life. Pick a life partner who understands that, for you, work comes first, and build a strong union that can accommodate your need to use all your fantastic skills for the greater good.

Numerology

No. 3: Creative with the gift of imagination and an ability to communicate in writing, art or speech.

Tarot

Ace of Wands: What did we say about those communication skills of yours? All of the ace cards in the Tarot deck tell us that we're on the right path and supported by the unseen 'helping hand' of Spirit and our ancestors. The suit of Wands represents all forms of communication, with the Ace of Wands being the pinnacle. This card not only denotes a strong affinity for writing, but also having a reputation for this skill, so it may be that you are, or will become known as, a campaigning journalist or an insightful novelist, screenwriter or poet.

Famous birthdays

Nicolas Hulot French journalist and environmental activist
Cloris Leachman American actress and comedian
Travis Scott American rapper and singer-songwriter

May 1st

Patiently persistent

You're the embodiment of two of the key Taurean traits –
patience and persistence. If the race is between the tortoise and
the hare you know who you'll be backing and who's going to win
through sheer bloody-minded determination to get to the end
of whatever it is that lies ahead. You're not particularly bothered
by the good opinion or otherwise of others and once you've set
your course of action, there's very little that will knock you off
course. Stability is important to you – in both your work and home
lives – but you have a deeply romantic nature, so can be prone
to being swept off your feet, Disney-style, for entirely the wrong
type of person with which to build a stable and meaningful life.
One of your key strengths is the ability to recognise and grasp
opportunities that come your way, so don't be surprised if this gift
doesn't propel you to the top of whatever work you've chosen to
commit to. When you give 100 per cent to all your projects and
all your people all of the time, there's a risk of draining your own
batteries, so make sure you take that holiday allowance, find ways
to take it down a couple of notches and find out for yourself what
it feels like to let go of the reins a little and really relax. We call
this 'downtime'!

Numerology

No. 1: A powerful entity and results-oriented force, all about initiating action
and getting things done.

Tarot

Ten of Pentacles: It may not seem like the flashiest card in the Tarot deck, but
this card is telling you that you can have it all, if you make the right choices:
the rewarding and stimulating work, a happy and committed relationship
with someone who is also in it for the long haul, a beautiful home, and more
than enough money to achieve the security that has always been important
to you. Slow but sure wins the race, whichever race you choose.

Famous birthdays

Wes Anderson American director
Joanna Lumley British actress, presenter and activist
Calamity Jane American frontiers woman

May 2nd

Peace-loving pacifier

You're always going to be the peacemaker in the room and people will bring their conflicts to your door, looking for advice and solutions that may not have occurred to them. Often, you'll just know the right answer and right direction for someone to take; it's as if the fairies have whispered it in your ear! Talking of ears, there's a good chance you are very musical, perhaps even making your living playing, singing or composing. If it's not your primary career, then it's likely to be an important pastime and something you cherish, along with making others feel strong emotions through sharing your music and songs. You feel things very deeply and that's not something you want everyone to know, so sometimes you'll find it easier to write a song or a poem than to talk honestly about your own feelings. This can make you a bit tricky to really get to know, but for those who persevere you are a thoughtful, loyal friend and a kind and loving life partner.

Numerology

No. 2: Shows resilience and power in gentleness, often provides the role of mediator, and linked to psychic abilities.

Tarot

The World: It really is your oyster, particularly if you take your talents, whether musical or for peacekeeping, onto the global stage. You know who you are and what you want, and don't do well being put into this category or that. The freedom to think your own thoughts and be your own person is crucial for you, and once you can do that, there's a sense, both externally and internally, that the world is yours for the asking and the taking.

Famous birthdays

David Suchet British actor
Catherine the Great Russian Empress
David Beckham British footballer

May 3rd

Perceptive analyst

Governed by your head before your heart, you are an acute observer of people with a natural ability to work out what is really motivating them and what's not being said, which means you'll probably end up working in a field related to, if not in, psychology or psychiatry. If you choose a scientific path, it will be the researching of human behaviours that interests you and, with your gift for communication, you may end up writing books or sharing your knowledge via other platforms, including documentary film-making or some form of broadcasting. You're highly sociable but because you can so easily detach your emotions, you may struggle to commit to one of them yourself. The pragmatic part of you just won't want to take the leap of faith that falling in love and bonding with another person requires. Once you do form a strong attachment, you're a steady and caring mate, but it can take you some time to get there and so you may not really settle down until later life. Expect to have a good time getting there because you are fun to be around.

Numerology

No. 3: Creative with the gift of imagination and an ability to communicate in writing, art or speech.

Tarot

Nine of Cups: With this card, we see a middle-aged merchant sitting with his arms defensively crossed in front of the nine cups (emotions) that he is protecting. He may as well have a stamp on his forehead carrying the warning: this far but no further! I can hear you thinking, fair enough. Like you, this chap is not giving his feelings to the first passer-by. He is a little more discerning than that. But, again like you, he risks ending up without the fulfilment of a mutually loving relationship unless he unfolds those arms and lets himself go enough to explore what that might look like with a potential mate.

Famous birthdays

Bing Crosby American singer and actor
James Brown American singer-songwriter
Rob Brydon Welsh actor and comedian

May 4th

Cool customer

You're nobody's fool, which you, more than most, will take as the highest compliment anyone could pay you. You are kind-hearted and can be very sympathetic to the plight of others, but you're not going to risk being made to look a fool and that can sometimes make you seem somewhat remote and offhand in your dealings with others. The truth is, once convinced of a real need, you'll be the first in line offering a helping hand and advice, but not the mug who thinks throwing money at a problem will make it go away. You're more than happy to work slowly and surely towards the goals and ambitions you set for yourself and since you are such a good judge of people and their needs, there's a seat at the top table of the business world with your name on it if that's the route you take. Plus, if you do, you'll balance the demands of this cut-throat work with your love of the arts and nature. You are an emotional bull, but those emotions often lie buried under several layers of insecurities. If someone can access them – and the real you – they'll find a true romantic and loving, loyal mate.

Numerology

No. 4: Invested in the physical world, centred earth energy that is practical in application.

Tarot

Page of Wands: He cuts rather a romantic figure, the young man we see standing tall alongside his sturdy staff (wand) in this card. He is, like you, sure-footed and knows all he has to do is keep putting one foot in front of the other, and surely good things will come. And they will. This is a card that says you can expect good things as long as you keep your head (which you will) and don't allow yourself to be distracted away from your goals.

Famous birthdays

Audrey Hepburn British actress and humanitarian
Graham Swift British writer
Will Arnett Canadian actor and comedian

May 5th

Ambitious motivator

You're a natural seller which means you can easily recruit others to your way of thinking, and fortunately most of your thinking is concerned with making the world a happier place for everyone living in it. You could sell anything to anyone, so may be literally working in retail or using those same skills to sell a political message to an electorate; whatever route you're taking, just take care that you're not always on transmit and never on receive because it can make you seem overly domineering and controlling. One of your skills lies in your ability to meticulously organise the details and sweat the small stuff many would be tempted to gloss over. Add to this your seemingly boundless energy and enthusiasm for the things you believe in and it's not hard to see why where you lead, others will happily follow. Take care your powers of persuasion, in work and at home, don't become your powers of manipulation. Nobody likes to think or feel they've had the wool pulled over their eyes and your ambitions are so lofty there is no way you can achieve them on your own.

Numerology

No. 5: Impulsive and restless by nature, spontaneous and likes to discover the world through the senses.

Tarot

King of Wands: This is your card, no doubt. Our King of Wands has the Midas touch – he can work with and inspire all who cross his path, from the least to the most privileged, and as we've seen, sell ice to the Inuits if that's what is required. He, like you, has mastered the art of seducing someone into his way of thinking. Just make sure that when you harness this gift and use it, you are doing so for the greater good of humanity, and not your own ego.

Famous birthdays

Michael Palin British comedian and actor
Adele British singer-songwriter
Karl Marx German philosopher and economist

May 6th

Sociable networker

You live for relationships, at work, at home and in your downtime. If someone's throwing a dinner party that nobody wants to miss out on, it will be you because you have impeccably good taste and the cash to splash to make sure there's the best of everything on the table. It's not about impressing people, it's about showing them you care and, when it comes right down to it, success in life is as much about who you know (who can help put opportunities your way) as it is about talent and hard work. You will be successful whatever path you choose because you are a people-pleaser and would rather be lost in a crowd – although the thought of you being lost anywhere is highly unlikely – than spending time alone. You're a born diplomat and like to work collaboratively, which will make you an excellent boss, as well as the peacemaker at home.

Numerology

No. 6: Empathic and nurturing, can problem-solve in an emotional and physical way, responsible and cares deeply about family and friends.

Tarot

Ace of Swords: There's not much that's more effective at moving obstacles out of your path than a metaphorical sword and this one is being handed to you by the unseen forces of Spirit and your ancestors, so you can be sure you will only be putting it to good and rightful use. Put simply, you can carve the path ahead to wherever you want to go, knowing that everyone who can root for you will be doing so. You love people; they love you.

Famous birthdays

George Clooney American actor
Orson Welles American actor and director
Rudolph Valentino Italian actor

May 7th

Spiritual guru

OK, I'm not saying you are a spiritual guru already, but I am saying you have all those qualities that could put you on that path where your understanding of the Ancient Mysteries or religious truths behind the dogmas could mean you become some kind of spiritual, religious or political leader. If you don't become an actual leader, then you will be someone who shares their thoughts and discoveries on matters unseen with a wider audience than the captive one at home. Talking of home, this may be the one area of your life where, ironically, you find it difficult to practise the loving kindness you preach – it is as if you are so wrapped up in your search for the deeper and more spiritual meaning of life that you've no time, energy or inclination to engage with the less esoteric matters closer to home. But this does not give your personal relationships the solid foundation they need to thrive. Perhaps you don't care overly. You have a sense you were born to work on a bigger stage than any of the ones we can see and if that's where your life is taking you, then you are perfectly aligned with your soul's purpose.

Numerology

No. 7: Very analytical and detail-oriented, likes to observe and investigate things and has a keen, inventive eye.

Tarot

Temperance: We see an angelic being pouring the knowledge of life between two chalices in a card that is full of biblical resonance. It looks like a priestly undertaking, an act of communion, an understanding of the deeper mysteries of life – everything that defines who you truly are and what you came here to do, which is to research and then share those mysteries with your fellow-seekers. You may not seek it out initially but fear not because this card tells us it will find you.

Famous birthdays

Gary Cooper American actor
Johannes Brahms German composer and pianist
Robert Browning British poet and playwright

May 8th

Outspoken realist

What would you call a spade? Some might say shovel, others favour the term digger, but with you, a spade is always a spade. You will be the person in the room prepared to say what everyone else is skirting around to tell it like it is, and you'll do so with a deft touch and a dollop of humour that means you can get away with saying what others might just be thinking. It makes you seem bold and confident in the working setting, which you are, and these qualities, coupled with your outspokenness, will likely see you skyrocket to the top echelons of whatever field you have chosen to work in: business, the law, science or the arts. You have a strong sense of fairness and will speak up for those you perceive have no voice, but when it comes to affairs of the heart, you're a little mousier and a whole lot quieter. Where's all that bullish confidence now? You struggle to initiate romance, which leaves you dependent on the other party to make that first move, but if they do, and it all works out, you will be the steadiest and most loyal of loving and committed life partners.

Numerology

No. 8: Sees the big picture and aims for it, linked to abundance and material wealth, and uses financial success to give back to others.

Tarot

Three of Pentacles: You're not aiming for public success, but it's coming your way because this card is all about being recognised on some kind of public stage for a life well-lived and a job well done. If we wanted to use an old-fashioned word for what is to come it would be 'glory'. When it does come knocking at the door, enjoy it. You will have worked hard for it and will have deserved every accolade coming your way ...

Famous birthdays

Harry S. Truman 33rd President of the United States
Ricky Nelson American singer-songwriter
Sir David Attenborough British naturalist and broadcaster

May 9th

Explosive firecracker

You will feel justified every time you lose your ferocious temper because you won't be losing it over the little things – it will be matters related to the highest of moral grounds and matters pertaining to the most serious questions of life and death that fan the flames of temper. You are a fearsome and fiery champion of the underdog and will work in some way to try and redress the balance between the worlds of the haves and have-nots. You may be a lawyer or a judge or a politician or a campaigning activist. The quality you need to work on as you work your way through your goals is that of compassion; not for those undervalued and underprivileged, but for those trying their best to help you to change the status quo yet sometimes (oft times) failing to live up to your lofty ideals. Nobody is perfect. If you don't start to understand that all relationships are built on imperfection and that there is joy to be had from learning about one another, then you will be a singleton for most of your adult life and, if you are not careful, an increasingly cantankerous and irascible one.

Numerology

No. 9: An old soul that looks to spiritual awareness to solve life's problems and likes to help others to do so in the same way.

Tarot

Eight of Pentacles: Pentacles in the Tarot deck represent resources, including money, and here we see a diligent young man working hard to amass some savings and make his way in the world. He represents what it is that you really want for all who share this planet, namely the opportunity to work and provide for family and each other, as well as to go to bed at night feeling the satisfaction of a good day's work and the pride in oneself for having achieved that. It's not really any more complicated than that, is it? You just want to make sure everyone has an equal chance to make their way in the world and avoid falling, through no fault of their own, into the abyss.

Famous birthdays

Albert Finney British actor
Billy Joel American musician and singer-songwriter
J.M. Barrie Scottish writer

May 10th

Impulsive go-getter

The interesting question with you is go-getter of what? You're a highly motivated self-starter and so the answer to that question is whatever it is that appeals right now because there is nothing you relish more than to throw yourself at and into a new project. You're happy to be a pioneer over new terrain and blast a way through to new horizons but prefer to launch from a stable home base. Once you've secured one of those, there really is no stopping you. Whether you're chasing life in the fast lane of politics or the slower pace of a crafting potter, you'll make a splash without seeming to break a sweat and will very likely find yourself as an influencer. Make the most of this and the platforms that give you a voice to help change the world for the better. In your private life, choose a partner who is not threatened by all the glitz that goes along with having thousands of social media followers. You're savvy enough to know these people are not your friends but if you can share your passions and do your bit to help us all live more harmoniously together, you'll be happy.

Numerology

No. I: A powerful entity and results-oriented force, all about initiating action and getting things done.

Tarot

The Fool: He's nothing if not impulsive, this one, stepping out towards a cliff edge with his little dancing dog following faithfully at his heels. Or maybe the dog is not dancing but jumping up as a warning not to step any closer to the edge. In this card, the Fool represents that part of us which craves new beginnings, and the dog is our instinct; he may be small, but he knows when and how to keep us safe. Enjoy the adventures but remember that for you, whatever you do and wherever you go, the grass can never be greener than the place you choose to water it – this, for you, will always be your home.

Famous birthdays

Fred Astaire American dancer and actor
Bono Irish singer-songwriter
Sid Vicious British bassist and vocalist

May 11th

Artistic trendsetter

Artistic with a capital 'A', you're a one-off original when it comes to what you think, how you live and what you wear. If you know the rules – and you probably don't – they won't be relevant to you because you have absolutely zero interest in fitting in or following the herd. Ruled by the Moon, you are highly sensitive, so much so that you will sometimes take offence where none was intended and waste a lot of time brooding over imagined slights. The artist Salvador Dali shares your birthday, which should tell you that you really do see the world in such a unique way it may be difficult for some to understand your vision or preferred way of living. You won't waste your breath trying to explain yourself but will just move on to the next canvas/person. Be careful that you don't end up ploughing too lonely a furrow as you age. It may not seem so, but the wise man and woman know there's a great deal to be learned from the Buddhist mantra: *chop wood, carry water*. In other words, there may be more artistic depth to the everyday banalities than at first appears.

Numerology

No. 2: Shows resilience and power in gentleness, often provides the role of mediator, and linked to psychic abilities.

Tarot

The Moon: Look closely at the image here, which may reflect – as the Moon reflects the Sun's light – how you feel. There's not one but two dogs howling at a frowning moon, with a scorpion in the foreground pulling itself out of the water and up onto the riverbank. Great art often emerges from great pain and you are likely no stranger to the creative impulse that follows tragedy in either your life or that of someone you care deeply about. Channel your grief and confusion into your art and share some of those universal truths with other souls who have suffered, for whatever reasons, too.

Famous birthdays

Salvador Dalí Spanish surrealist artist
Irving Berlin American composer and lyricist
Natasha Richardson British actress

May 12th

Wise philosopher

You are naturally eloquent, what makes your philosophising so appealing to others is the healthy dose of wit you throw into the mix. Whatever career you've chosen, whether politics, broadcasting, sport or scientific research, you will be outstanding at it. As with all Taureans, home and the security it brings is important to you, but you also have a very strong restless streak, so it is going to be a challenge trying to balance your need for stability with your urge to throw caution to the wind, give everything away and travel the world with nothing but the smallest backpack to slow you down. This constant vacillation between staying put and taking off makes it seem to others that you blow hot and cold emotionally, and if you were being honest about yourself, you'd probably have to admit that's true and a tad unfair on those you embark on a relationship with. Maybe try an alternative to the 'norm' such as living in different countries or hooking up with a travel writer – that way, you won't be home together long enough for either of you to get itchy feet.

Numerology

No. 3: Creative with the gift of imagination and an ability to communicate in writing, art or speech.

Tarot

Knight of Cups: If there's one person who's going places it's this dashing Knight of Cups who's sitting ramrod-straight on his trusty steed and heading into his future in a straight line: no distractions, no diversions. The Cups represent our deepest emotions and the fact that our knight is holding just one tells us he would give his (your) heart to the right person but will have to break the habit of moving on as soon as it starts to feel real with someone. Moving on is a great way of protecting your heart, but by doing so, you are missing out on the very great joy of loving, and being loved in return.

Famous birthdays

Gabriel Byrne Irish actor and director
Katharine Hepburn American actress
Dante Gabriel Rossetti British Pre-Raphaelite artist

May 13th

Positive charmer

We never really know what's going on behind closed doors in someone else's life but the impression you leave is that, for you, life is just one long skip through the daisies and that nothing ever really throws you off balance. That's not true, of course, because you are only human, and life will throw challenges your way. But you have the light touch of someone who can shrug off most things, shake themselves down, pick themselves up and go on choosing to see the glass as being half full. Good for you. Why not see the positive wherever you can find it? Your enthusiasm for life is infectious and you won't be travelling towards any of your dreams and goals alone. You're really great company and an excellent team player so, for as long as your interest is engaged, you're reliable, supportive and really good to have around. That's not the case if and when you give in to the urge to swap all that security and dependability for the excitement of something or someone new. In fact, if you sometimes don't resist this frequent urge, you'll risk getting a bad reputation for being flighty, which, when you are committed, could not be further from the truth.

Numerology

No. 4: Invested in the physical world, centred earth energy that is practical in application.

Tarot

The Empress: She, like you, has an abundance of charm and can take her pick of the summer harvest goodies that surround her. The Sun shines on this lady as it shines on you and there's not a cloud or anything else looming to spoil this picture of a golden day at the end of a long summer. This is how you see life and good for you because you're right, life is and can be good a lot of the time and for many of us. Just don't forget those who through no fault of their own have had more struggles. A little compassion, especially when you have so much to be grateful for, can go a very long way.

Famous birthdays

Harvey Keitel American actor
Stevie Wonder American singer-songwriter
Joe Louis American boxer

May

May 14th

Independent self-starter

Ask for help? You wouldn't know how as you have independence flowing through every blood vessel in your body. Throw in a good dose of Taurean stubbornness and sometimes you don't ask for help even when you should. Luckily for you, those who grow to love you will know precisely when to step in. You have great insight and may be the person whose ideas for creating a better future really do help change the world. You believe in yourself and your abilities and thanks to your sociable nature, you are someone other people like to be around. But for all your progressive thinking at work, at home you may be a little bit of a stick in the mud. Stability is important to you and you do not like change. However, that independent spirit can mean you go back and forth quite a bit before making a commitment. While this can cost you dear, and you may lose some potential mates because you've dilly-dallied, when you do take the leap you will do so with all your heart and make someone a fantastic life partner.

Numerology

No. 5: Impulsive and restless by nature, spontaneous and likes to discover the world through the senses.

Tarot

King of Cups: You know that bloke who everyone likes, the one who can always think his way out of any problem, large or small? Well, that's the King of Cups and the way others see *you*. This card depicts what people used to call a 'decent chap' or a 'fine fellow'; caring and sensitive and nice to be around. The throne, in the image on this card, appears to be gliding across some pretty choppy seas, but he (and the single cup he is holding) remain steady and upright and seem utterly unfazed by the turbulence. With a gaze fixed firmly on the future you know exactly where you're heading, how to get there and what is waiting for you. The King of Cups is, like you, very sure of himself and his place in the world.

Famous birthdays

Cate Blanchett Australian actress and producer
Tim Roth British actor and director
George Lucas American director

May 15th

Wisdom seeker

Some may wonder at your preference for solitude, but you are far from alone when you have your head buried in the books that have been written about the Ancient Mysteries. You have a deep thirst for esoteric learning, and understand that you, along with all the other mortals on the planet, are simply passing through. You have an enormous empathy and compassion for others, and this only grows with age. You will likely work in the caring professions or may choose a clear spiritual path where you can bring your wisdom to the fore and share it with others through teaching or writing. Whatever you take on, you will always do it to the very best of your ability. You can appear, especially as a young adult, as something of a dreamer when you get that far-away look that signals you are tussling with life's bigger questions, but if and when you need to take practical action to implement an idea, you will, and the 'look' will pass until the next time. There's nothing flaky or alternative about you because you put in the time to acquire the knowledge that will help you to better understand your soul's purpose.

Numerology

No. 6: Empathic and nurturing, can problem-solve in an emotional and physical way, responsible and cares deeply about family and friends.

Tarot

The Lovers: This is the card that can symbolise a great earthly love or simply reflect your love of the esoteric, as is shown in this image by the winged one showering her blessings on the mortals below. You will already know which interpretation applies to you and, indeed, it could so easily be both. You are blessed, you know you are blessed, you feel you are blessed. So, your only job really is to stay on track, keep studying, share your wisdom and give thanks for the many wonderful blessings that have already been (and have yet to be) heaped on your wise old head.

Famous birthdays

Mike Oldfield British musician
Pierre Curie French physicist and Nobel Prize winner
Brian Eno British musician and record producer

May 16th

Devoted lover

Although you have so many endearing qualities, the one you will most likely be known for is your ability to fall madly in love at the drop of a hat. You are an absolute sucker for romance, but don't let the packaging bedazzle you so much you forget to examine the contents. Spend some time thinking about what kind of person will be a good match for you and don't jump in with all the might of a crashing bull every time someone catches your eye. Romance does not pay the bills! Happily, whatever you choose to do, you are likely to be very successful, especially if you do anything creative like writing, drama or music. You may be very psychic and if you're not, it's probably only because that's not what you call those intuitive hunches you have had and followed all your life. You will be interested in the Dark Arts because you have an enquiring mind and none of the fear that would stop others from lifting the lid to look into that particular cauldron of mixed delights. As you shape up and into your own spiritual path, it may be that you gather some followers; lucky for them that you are an authentic and honourable person who can slot very comfortably into the driving seat but who also knows when to shift to the passenger's side and give someone else a chance to drive.

Numerology

No. 7: Very analytical and detail-oriented, likes to observe and investigate things, and has a keen, inventive eye.

Tarot

Ten of Pentacles: This is the card of your (romantic) dreams. We see a loved-up couple gazing deeply into each other's eyes, lost in their romance and oblivious to both the white-haired wise old man who is looking on and the two faithful white hounds sitting at his feet. This is your sort of love – truly, madly, deeply – and your challenge, at some point, will be finding and then sharing deeper ways of sustaining it over a long lifetime.

Famous birthdays

Pierce Brosnan Irish actor
Henry Fonda American actor and director
Liberace American pianist and singer

May 17th

Ambitious campaigner

It's hard to avoid failure when you set your sights so impossibly high. For this reason, one of your biggest challenges is going to be learning to be more realistic about your humanitarian and campaigning goals; otherwise, you're going to end up feeling very dispirited. You are far more interested in improving the lot of others than your own but, at some point, you are going to learn that no amount of sheer willpower is enough to remove the stubborn obstacles in your path. Set your sights a little lower and build, over time, to the goals on a grander scale that fire your determination. You are caring and creative, and so may find a good career fit working with a charity whose causes you support and deploying the arts to raise awareness of what needs to change and why. You are a people-pleaser so would also enjoy working as a festival organiser or even financial advisor; anything where you can go home at the end of a day feeling you've made a positive difference to someone's life. As a mate, you understand the value of a stable and loving home life and have no problem making or keeping a strong commitment to your chosen partner.

Numerology

No. 8: Sees the big picture and aims for it, linked to abundance and material wealth, and uses financial success to give back to others.

Tarot

The Tower: This card represents the collapse of your ambitious plans, but only if you don't scale them back to a more realistic level. There's a fire raging from the top of this building and we see those who can throwing themselves out of the windows to either safety or death. It's a risky strategy and one you would do well to heed. Stop throwing yourself and your energies either into the inferno of inevitable failure, or out of one disaster and straight into another. Instead, set yourself some more realistic humanitarian goals and then use your prodigious energy and innovative ways of thinking to achieve them.

Famous birthdays

Bill Paxton American actor and director
Dennis Hopper American actor
Enya Irish singer-songwriter

May 18th

Fearless fighter

Your commitment to fairness and justice for all is such that you are never afraid to speak out where you see wrong action and to urge change for the better. And since you're afraid of nothing, it's probably an understatement to call you fearless. Prejudice, discrimination and any form of injustice will not be tolerated in your world view and you'll likely be using your talents in the creative arts to make this clear to anyone prepared to listen. You can feel hurt, disappointed and despondent when others don't jump to join your cause or seem to care much that there is so much inequity in the world. A stable and loving home life will go a long way to offsetting your struggle to understand those with less empathy, so make sure you choose a partner who is in it for the long haul with you. This shouldn't be too hard since you're a deeply romantic and loving partner who relishes the intimacy of a committed and close long-term partnership. You are an unusual blend of creativity, spirituality and idealism; this is a rare and special mix, so take care not to burn through all your resources by taking on the cares of the whole world but forgetting to take care of yourself!

Numerology

No. 9: An old soul that looks to spiritual awareness to solve life's problems and likes to help others to do so in the same way.

Tarot

The Hermit: This card warns of those times when the challenge of getting people to care more about each other just feels impossible and overwhelming; these are the times when you will withdraw – like the Hermit – to a safe space, first to lick your wounds and then to regroup your energies ready for the second charge. Use this important time productively because the Hermit holding out his lantern to light our way in the dark has much to teach the collective. But in your heart, you already know this.

Famous birthdays

Tsar Nicholas II Last Emperor Russia
Bertrand Russell British polymath
Frank Capra Italian director

May 19th

Lucky winner

We often – almost always – link these two words: Lucky Winner. But what if your wins have nothing to do with the luck of the draw and everything to do with those psychic powers that you work so hard to bury and hide? How did you know to back that particular horse or choose those lottery numbers? Luck? There may be a bit of that going on, but that doesn't explain why so many wins come so effortlessly your way. Of course, there's no way you're going to reveal your secret methods. As a steady Taurean you'd be way too embarrassed to even talk about the 'unseen', but you know full well that you are able to predict the outcome of things you have no insider knowledge about. Love and sex are important to you, so it's likely you've saved the very best of your psychic skills to help you choose a partner who can match your passionate nature. You love to be swept off your feet, will move heaven and earth and use more than a little of that magical fairy dust to make your chosen mate feel the same way!

Numerology

No. 1: A powerful entity and results-oriented force, all about initiating action and getting things done.

Tarot

Wheel of Fortune: They say fortune favours the brave, so maybe the fact you will have more than your share of good fortune through life is your reward for having the confidence and courage to be yourself and listen to your psychic intuition. When it comes to the big decisions – what job to go for, who to marry, what numbers to choose to win the jackpot – it has never let you down and it never will. Fortunes, as you know, come and go and someone's fortune can go up and down. You will be able to weather all the changes ahead because fundamentally you know you are lucky, and that luck won't be gone from your side for long.

Famous birthdays

Ho Chi Minh Vietnamese revolutionary Communist leader
Grace Jones Jamaican singer-songwriter and record producer
Pete Townshend British guitarist

May 20th

Quick-witted researcher

It may seem that you move so quickly and with so much energy from subject to subject, person to person and place to place that your engagement with them could only be superficial, but nothing could be further from the truth. You have a huge appetite for new experiences and people, and you will leave others (exhausted) in your wake as you move with the speed of lightning from one topic to another, digging deep to learn as much as you can before you move on to learn more. Clever, curious, practical – and sometimes a little mercurial – you simply have the ability to process new information at three times the speed of everyone else! You may work in the arts and, if not, you will be a huge supporter of them and other humanitarian and philosophical ideals. And while you may never quite make a commitment to just one lifetime partner, you will have your share of romantic adventures and probably take the view that the ties you form with family and long-standing friends give you all the emotional support you need. Plus, you like having the freedom to explore whatever catches your imagination next, without having to accommodate someone else.

Numerology

No. 2: Shows resilience and power in gentleness, often provides the role of mediator, and linked to psychic abilities.

Tarot

The Star: The healing card of the Tarot deck and one of the Major Arcana. You work in your own way to right wrongs and heal those who cross your path, both two- and four-legged. You may not think of yourself as a healer, but that's where your extraordinary gift lies; you will be doing it without thinking about it. Make sure you do whatever is necessary to take the same kind of care of yourself. Yours is a rare gift; one that some people call *joie de vivre* – this is both inspiring and a pleasure for others to be around.

Famous birthdays

James Stewart American actor
Cher American singer and actress
Honoré de Balzac French writer

May 21st

Stubborn idealist

There's not much that can knock you off course once you've made up your mind to put a plan into action and so you can't really be surprised to learn others find you stubborn, if not downright obstinate. Happily, for you, time usually shows them that you are almost always right to stick to your guns, especially if you are working in the worlds of either finance or technical innovation. You're not scared to stick your neck out and it's a rare day that you're not proven right and well worth listening to and trusting the next time you propose an ingenious idea that nobody has thought of before. You are hugely sociable and will go to great lengths to make sure things are in place so that everyone can have a good time. There's nothing you like more than to chill with family and friends, and you enjoy supporting the arts and even dabbling yourself. If you do withdraw it's because you are focused on the task in hand and not because want to isolate yourself. Make sure those who love you understand that and try, perhaps, to tone down the obsessive need to show people you know what you're talking about and are always right!

Numerology

No. 3: Creative with the gift of imagination and an ability to communicate in writing, art or speech.

Tarot

The Hanged Man: Sometimes, when we become so fixed to our beliefs that we can't hear a thing anyone else has to say, we can end up, metaphorically, just like the Hanged Man, suspended upside down with no way of moving forwards, backwards or sideways. He's in a bind, and one that he put himself in. Turn this same card the other way around and, this time, he appears suspended in mid-air with a veritable golden halo around his head. Try it; turn yourself upside down or inside out and see what gems you can find when you don't hold on so stubbornly to a fixed belief. It's called growth.

Famous birthdays

Princess Stéphanie of Belgium Crown Princess of Austria
Noel Fielding British comedian
Mark Cavendish Professional cyclist from the Isle of Man

May 22nd

Persuasive charmer

Teaching, advertising, public relations, broadcasting, journalism, marketing or promotions – you will likely be working in one of these fields, where you can use your superb communication skills to help people decide what to buy, what to think, who to vote for and where to spend their hard-earned cash. You're a born leader with the ability to inspire others to live up to their full potential. Underneath that charming, sociable and quick-witted nature of yours, there's a core of steely determination which can shock those who come across your ability to harness a single-minded focus for the first time; it seems to be at odds with the chilled and laid-back way you present yourself. But you're a Gemini so, expect the unexpected ... Your focus is so entirely on your mental efforts that you don't give feelings much of a chance to get in the way. This can make it hard for you to work out what you want and what is going to make you happy. One clear outcome of this attitude is that you will choose a partner based not on love and romance, but on the basis that you have enough shared interests to enjoy each other's company and still like and want to spend time with each other when the physical attraction has waned. Ever the pragmatist ...

Numerology

No. 4: Invested in the physical world, centred earth energy that is practical in application.

Tarot

Queen of Wands: The Wands in the Tarot deck are all about communication and not surprisingly, given your gift with words and writing, here you are, represented by the Queen of this attribute. This is one lady with her head firmly screwed on, and just to reinforce her sense of place and purpose, we see her familiar – a little black cat – sitting at her feet, representing her agile and quick-witted mind.

Famous birthdays

Laurence Olivier British actor and director
Arthur Conan Doyle British writer and physician
Naomi Campbell British model and businesswoman

May 23rd

Naturally curious

You're a bit of a mixed bag – open-minded and easy-going one minute, stubborn and inflexible the next. You're not the easiest to work out! That said, people actually like being around you, which is really thanks to the fact that you instinctively know how to get along well with everyone. You may have chosen a career in teaching, either through the written word, or speaking or broadcasting, as you have a natural curiosity about the world and how it works and a great affinity with language, written or spoken. When it comes to intimate relationships, you're more interested in companionship and mutual interests than in any fiery passion which may burn itself out. You're wary of showing your vulnerabilities and will work hard to get your guard up until you feel comfortable in letting it down. You'll likely be an experienced traveller who, rather than idling away your free time on the beach, will be off climbing mountains and visiting temples and learning as much as you can about different cultures and lost civilisations – knowledge which is likely to form the basis of your next TV programme, book or after-dinner speech!

Numerology

No. 5: Impulsive and restless by nature, spontaneous and likes to discover the world through the senses.

Tarot

Queen of Swords: If there is one card that is all about being decisive, even if that means decisively changing your mind and opinion, it is our Queen of Swords. Quick-witted and changeable, she is governed by air, so she may be here, close by, one minute and vanished the next. This can be how some people will experience you. Others will be amazed as they watch you slash through old ideas and old ways of thinking with your shiny sword to open up pathways to innovation and the evolution of our collective consciousness.

Famous birthdays

Joan Collins British actress
Robert Moog American engineer and pioneer of electronic music
Drew Carey American actor and comedian

May

May 24th

Resourceful catalyst

You're one of those people who can just make things happen. Where others get mired in the sticky details or seemingly immovable obstacles, you have that uncanny ability to pinpoint what can be changed – especially when it is simply someone else's attitude which may be responsible for the blockage – and then go about changing it. You are an excellent communicator which helps smooth these interactions and there's a good chance you'll be using these skills to sell something or market something else or change people's hearts and minds through politics. Family will be important to you and the challenge here will be to give others the space to explore their own thoughts and ideas, instead of imposing yours on them all the time. You'll find this hard, but it's important to work on this because nobody wants an over-controlling partner or parent. Also, watch your tongue when your temper threatens. Words can be very wounding, and you can use your same excellent communication skills to strike where it hurts with an acerbic and hurtful word or two that may take someone on the receiving end a long time to forgive and forget!

Numerology

No. 6: Empathic and nurturing, can problem-solve in an emotional and physical way, responsible and cares deeply about family and friends.

Tarot

The Devil: This card is about control, but a control that could so easily be slipped away from. The two humans, male and female, depicted in this card at the feet of the devil are only loosely bound to his dominion and it wouldn't take much for them to slip away back towards the light. For you, the message is two-fold: watch out that you are not becoming too controlling of others or of yourself. Sometimes our best discoveries are made in making our mistakes, in having the courage to admit we have been wrong and in opening ourselves to new possibilities and ideas.

Famous birthdays

Kristin Scott Thomas British actress
Bob Dylan American singer-songwriter
Priscilla Presley American businesswoman and actress

May 25th

Moral leader

There are no shades of grey in your world; there is right and then there is wrong. According to your moral code, we all know the difference and anyone maintaining there are any shades in between is kidding themselves, probably to try and feel better about a questionable choice they have made or are about to make. In your personal life you won't think twice about punishing any transgression of the moral code by simply cutting off all ties and cutting the transgressor out of your life for good. In work, you're as open-minded as the next but only to those ideas and plans that dovetail with your moral code and ethical ideology. You have great leadership skills and will happily carry the baton for your team, but you recognise there is no 'I' in team and nor do you want there to be. You are happy to lead all involved to success and may decide to use your skills and strong sense of honour to work for charity, as a campaigner or in politics somewhat left of centre! You have an enormous sensitivity towards the suffering of others and will do all within your power not only to champion the cause of the downhearted and downtrodden but also to actively change their circumstances for the better.

Numerology

No. 7: Very analytical and detail-oriented, likes to observe and investigate things, and has a keen, inventive eye.

Tarot

The Emperor: One of the Major Arcana cards, our Emperor sits proud on his throne and with his long, white beard appears to be the epitome of wisdom. This is a mature man who has already lived much of his life and learned to accept responsibility for his choices along the way. And, like you, he has a strong moral code and sense of natural justice and honour which others look to for guidance and the reassurance that choosing to be the 'good guy' is always the right choice, even when it feels like losing.

Famous birthdays

Ian McKellen British actor
Paul Weller British singer-songwriter
Mike Myers Canadian actor and comedian

May

May 26th

Nonconforming seeker

Not for you the tried-and-trusted ways of conformity, whether applied to work or play. You like to see yourself as the Lone Wolf. You won't want to commit to one job or life partner, there's just too much to see, learn and experience before you decide you've done enough to hang up your boots. You have a natural affinity with the performing arts and will relish the spotlight if it comes your way, but you will also use your profile to inspire others to support worthwhile causes. When you're on form, you'll feel and be seen as someone who is dynamic and inspirational, but be careful that you don't unleash a degree of bossiness and – worse – hypocrisy, which means you're insisting on keeping your own freedom and autonomy while demanding that others give up theirs. If you've gone into scientific research or academia, it won't be long before you're leading the project or running the department; your natural assertiveness will equip you well for those roles. In private, you can be a bit impulsive, but you are generous with your success and will want to share any good fortune that comes your way with others.

Numerology

No. 8: Sees the big picture and aims for it, linked to abundance and material wealth, and uses financial success to give back to others.

Tarot

Page of Pentacles: Sometimes the feeling that the grass is greener is the reason you flip and appear to make impulsive decisions, especially in your private life. Intellectually, you know this isn't true and that you have everything you need to move forward on the right path for you, but in case you are having one of those impulsive urges, stop to take a look at the Page of Pentacles who has shown up to tell you not to risk it all for a mad moment. You'll find other ways to create that sense of being unshackled without having to give everything up.

Famous birthdays

Helena Bonham Carter British actress
John Wayne American actor
Peter Cushing British actor

May 27th

Progressive humanitarian

You wake up every morning energised by the thought of a new day that you can use to help the rest of humanity in some way. You have a confidence that is both attractive and reassuring to others and you'll do anything to get your 'message' about the importance of caring for others to the ears of those who can help raise the funds to improve social justice and those who can pass legislation that insists on it. You are respected for your humanitarian visions and will be known as someone devoted to the cause and their work. You may have chosen to train as a doctor or gone into the diplomatic service; whatever the route, your goal of eradicating human suffering will remain unchanged. You'll have no trouble attracting a mate, but you may struggle if there is any suggestion you may be wrong about anything; you're not good with criticism, however well-intentioned, and tend to put your beliefs above everyone else's. This can make you seem controlling. Keep an eye on this and rein it in when you see the signs that others will recognise as red flags to be avoided.

Numerology

No. 9: An old soul that looks to spiritual awareness to solve life's problems and likes to help others to do so in the same way.

Tarot

Six of Swords: We see a boatman pushing a punt carrying a shrouded woman and her young child away from the choppy waters on the right to the calmer seas on the left. Sometimes, this card speaks to the querent represented by the woman or even the child, both of whom are leaving their sorrows behind them, but in your case, we are looking more closely at the boatman who is in charge and steering their collective direction of travel. His gaze is fixed firmly on that brighter future; he has the skills to navigate these difficult waters and take his vulnerable passengers safely to their happier destination. This is what you can, and maybe already do, for others in need of a helping hand.

Famous birthdays

Jamie Oliver British chef, restauranteur and TV personality
Christopher Lee British actor
Henry Kissinger American politician and diplomat

May

May 28th

Forward thinker

Those who scoff today at your forward-thinking ideas will be the very same people accepting them as 'normal' practice and thinking in years to come, so all you have to do is find the right platform from which to share your vision, bide your time and step forward for the credit when everyone can finally see the sense in what you are saying. This is going to be easier said than done because you are a sensitive soul and don't always do well with criticism, however well-meaning or ill-informed. Try to resist the urge to withdraw from the world to lick your wounds because, as all those who have taken this path before you will attest, coming back to the world is often a slower, harder and longer slog than leaving it behind. You'll be drawn to the creative arts and if it's the stage or movie industry that's calling your name, you'll most likely be behind the camera calling 'Action!'. You would also thrive working as an artist or inventor; anything where you get to drive yourself to your destination and find a way, en route, to work on your progressive ideas. You are kind and loyal and appreciate those qualities in your family, friends and partner.

Numerology

No. 1: A powerful entity and results-oriented force, all about initiating action and getting things done.

Tarot

Judgement: With an angelic figure blasting the sounds of a loud bugle at the waking dead, this card represents the idea of a wake-up or clarion call to those who need a sharp kick up the butt. In your case, you're not one of those sleeping 'dead', rather you're the one sounding the alarm and issuing a warning to all of mankind. Perhaps you are a climate change campaigner or a spokesperson for social justice whose warnings to date have been ignored; but don't give up ... your time, or rather the time when your message will be heard, will come!

Famous birthdays

Kylie Minogue Australian singer-songwriter and actress
Ian Fleming British writer
Thomas Moore Irish poet and lyricist

May 29th

Chilled dude

When the charisma has been doled out by the shedload, the recipients (in this case you) can sometimes sit back on their laurels thinking that it's fine for others to do all the work. I'm not saying you're lazy; maybe just a tad languid. You're pretty happy to go with the flow until something – usually something at work – fires your imagination and then the other twin kicks into action. There is a real hidden strength behind your usual 'take-it-or-leave-it' attitude because the most powerful person in the room in any transaction is the one who cares the least about the cost to themselves of any bold decision or action. This person will always be you. And if you've chosen a corporate career you will leave others spinning on the spot with your astonishing *chutzpah* and success! It won't be long before word of your reputation for inspired problem-solving, conflict resolution and action spreads. With your growing success comes a growing generosity of spirit and you'll be happy to share your good fortune with those you love. When choosing a life partner, if you can be bothered to do that, choose someone who values their own independence. If anyone actually lives up to the title 'dude', it's you.

Numerology
No. 2: Shows resilience and power in gentleness, often provides the role of mediator, and linked to psychic abilities.

Tarot
Three of Cups: Success is coming your way, albeit so effortlessly there will be those struck by envy who may think that you don't really deserve it. But they're not part of the party of friends depicted by this card, raising their glasses (chalices) to a job well done and a successful outcome for all. It's a card of modest celebration – nothing too onerous, which, as we've seen, would not be your style. Just chilled and genuine with those who understand you toasting and sharing in your success.

Famous birthdays
Bob Hope British-American actor and comedian
John F. Kennedy 35th President of the United States
Rupert Everett British actor and writer

May 30th

Lively entertainer

If anyone can keep multiple balls in the air, it's you. But there's also a chance you might actually run off to the circus, because you are a born entertainer. You're a bundle of nervous Gemini energy flitting from one subject or activity to the next and back again all in the space of a single breath. If you have a totem power animal, it's the butterfly, because you can flit with the best of them, alighting here one minute and over there the next. The right partner for you will be someone who likes their own space and freedom as much as you and who enjoys your company because you are interested in and eloquent on the subject of so many different things. The word 'routine' strikes fear into your heart and the second you think that may be what lies in wait for you, you'll be off. Yours is a sparkling, easy-going personality that others find impossible to resist, even when a little red flag pops up in their mind with the word 'shallow' written large on an imaginary banner. If you are shallow, you're unapologetic about it – there's just so much you want to do, see and say that there's really no time at all for standing still.

Numerology

No. 3: Creative with the gift of imagination and an ability to communicate in writing, art or speech.

Tarot

The Fool: In days of old the word fool did not mean silly or idiotic or even foolish; it was used to describe the character who entertained the King and the courtiers with tales of myth and fantasy, staying at court just a night or two before moving on with his little companion dog to seek out pastures and adventures new. He is, like you, a born entertainer; happy to sing for his supper, never staying in one place long enough for the grass to grow under his feet, and happiest when making others happy with his tales of what lies beyond the boundaries that restrict most earthly mortals.

Famous birthdays

Jennifer Ellison British actress and TV personality
Howard Hawks American director and screenwriter
Harry Enfield British comedian and actor

May

May 31st

Mercurial visionary

It's not that you are inconsistent; you are very consistent when you've made up your mind, but you may make up your mind in opposite directions several times a day! Perhaps you are championing good old-fashioned values at breakfast, but by lunch, you'll have kicked those views into the long grass and be espousing the benefits of more alternative lifestyles. It is as if your Gemini twins sit, in their views, at opposite ends of the spectrum. This can make it hard for those around you to feel they know you or what you really think. What this characteristic does give you is the ability to see all sides of an issue or a disagreement, and so you may be the one people can rely on to find an ingenious resolution that will keep all parties happy. But this flip-flopping of yours includes flip-flopping between enormous optimism and terrible pessimism, and for anyone wanting to share your life, either as a friend or a life partner, it can sometimes feel as if it is just too hard to keep up with you. That said, you are generous with your time, attention, love and loyalty in relationships, just as long as you're not made to feel trapped and suffocated.

Numerology

No. 4: Invested in the physical world, centred earth energy that is practical in application.

Tarot

King of Wands: The Wands represent our vitality, and this royal is passionate about getting his message across. Enthusiasm is an attractive quality, but when you enthuse about one point of view just as much as the opposite, people will feel they don't know where they stand with you. It's not true, but with a nature as mercurial as yours, you can see why you may have an uphill battle persuading people otherwise.

Famous birthdays

Clint Eastwood American actor and director
Colin Farrell Irish actor
Walt Whitman American poet, essayist and journalist

June 1st

Instinctive investigator

To say you find other people and their behaviours intriguing would be a serious understatement. Finding out what makes someone tick fascinates your Gemini mind. But much as you love digging into the lives of others, you are likely to be guarded about your own. In fact, this wariness about revealing too much of the 'real' you could explain your interest in discovering more about others. It's a brilliant way of deflecting the attention away from yourself. You also have a very low boredom threshold and are quite capable of juggling lots of balls and being interested in lots of things all at the same time. This makes you good company, but there is also merit in choosing just one topic to research and explore. You're also disinclined to relish the idea of settling down with one person (remember that boredom threshold?), so may have a series of important relationships over your lifetime. Family and friends could be almost more important to you than finding a life partner, and the bonds you make and keep with these are likely to be very strong.

Numerology

No. 1: A powerful entity and results-oriented force, all about initiating action and getting things done.

Tarot

Two of Swords: Here a blindfolded woman sits at the edge of the seashore, arms crossed defensively over her chest and a sword raised and pointing to the heavens in each hand. In the background, there's a distant golden shore, and in the sky the sliver of a crescent moon. There's something quite mystical about the whole image, which tells us there is much to be gained from turning our gaze inwards and discovering our own intuition. You know that guarded feeling of the arms crossed saying 'This far and no further', but it may be that you have to adopt this stance to find the safe space you need to look inwards.

Famous birthdays

Morgan Freeman American actor and director
Marilyn Monroe American actress
Alanis Morissette Canadian singer-songwriter

June 2nd

Incurable romantic

Who doesn't love the idea of falling truly, madly, deeply in love? The trouble is when it is the 'idea' of being in love that is all-consuming, rather than the reality. And, since you love a party and enjoy flirting, you know, deep down, that you're on pretty shaky ground when you throw yourself into the next grand passion. Then it's probably only a matter of time before reality bites and you have to see the affair for what it is. Reckless and charming, you enjoy connecting people along the way, making you a great networker both socially and in your professional life. You may come across as a bit of a social butterfly and will probably think that's a compliment. In truth you will flit from one experience to the next in your search for truth and life experience. There will come a time when you feel that your flirting days are done and that's when you'll be ready for the person who really can be your one-and-only, but it's possible you'll have broken quite a few hearts along the way. Your greatest strength lies in your ability to adjust quickly to both people and events, and that characteristic will carry you through your whole life.

Numerology

No. 2: Shows resilience and power in gentleness, often provides the role of mediator, and linked to psychic abilities.

Tarot

Four of Wands: After all your flirting and party nights and flitting from one topic (and one person) to another, there is the prospect of the most joyous of unions waiting for you once you do decide to take love and life a little more seriously. We see a very happy, garlanded couple celebrating their union with family and friends in the background and a big party taking place outside the city walls to mark the occasion. Everyone is happy because your union is one of those that gives the rest of us the hope that the same thing can happen for us.

Famous birthdays

Thomas Hardy British writer
Dana Carvey American actor and comedian
Dominic Cooper British actor

June

June 3rd

Exuberant optimist

When the party invites go out, the name on the top of the pile is always yours. People love having you around and not least because you have the knack of making any event more fun for everyone. You're also likely to have strong leadership skills and will do well working in politics, teaching, the military, medicine or the church – anywhere you can inspire others to follow. You won't be chasing the limelight, however, but it will probably come your way because you have the sort of qualities people admire. Don't be surprised if you get further along in life and find you even become a household name. Your powers of persuasion are strong, and you have such an engaging sense of humour that most of the people you meet think of you as the one who really can lift everyone's spirits. This can all be a little head-turning so take care that you don't fall into the trap of muddling leadership with bossiness; a good leader creates the space for others to feel safe in speaking out and sharing their opinions and views. In your private life, you'll bring both humour and adventure into your home while making sure everyone in the family feels loved, cherished and supported.

Numerology

No. 3: Creative with the gift of imagination and an ability to communicate in writing, art or speech.

Tarot

King of Pentacles: The Pentacles represent our resources, internal and external (including money). Here we see a very successful self-made man sitting comfortably in the midst of an abundance of gifts that have been used well throughout his life. Like you, he is kind and generous and someone everyone wants to have and be around. There's a twinkle in his eye that suggests a good sense of fun, an appreciation for a good joke and a love of making people laugh and feel better about what is going on around them.

Famous birthdays

Tony Curtis American actor
Allen Ginsburg American writer
Rafael Nadal Spanish tennis player

June 4th

Caring influencer

Your enthusiasm for the world of ideas and expanding not only your own consciousness but that of all those around you is infectious. Using social media probably comes naturally to you, and you're unlikely to have a problem reaching the numbers of followers that can make you an influencer. If this is where you excel, you'll use the considerable communication skills that come naturally to many Geminis to the greater good. You may move into one of the caring professions or pick up the baton of the committed activist, using your growing influence to inspire others to also support the humanitarian causes you champion. You're ruled by Mercury, the planet of communication, but this can sometimes make you seem a little unpredictable and changeable. It's not that your commitment to the cause has wavered, it's more that your focus has shifted. You will have a deep and genuine love for the people you care for, but if you are honest with yourself, your work and career take the top slot in your life. Not many partners will tolerate this so be careful you don't set up home with someone who is going to need more than you are willing to give.

Numerology

No. 4: Invested in the physical world, centred earth energy that is practical in application.

Tarot

Three of Pentacles: This is the card of public recognition, primarily accolades to come for your work achievements rather than any accident of your birth. It tells us that your desire to make a difference to the world – and to inspire and influence others to take up the baton and do their bit – is being acknowledged, along with the sacrifices you have made in your private life in order for you to stay at the coalface and raise awareness of the issues we should all be thinking about. Take a moment to allow yourself a pat on the back for a job well done ...

Famous birthdays

Angelina Jolie American actress and humanitarian
Bruce Dern American actor
Rosalind Russell American actress

June 5th

Idiosyncratic visionary

There's a fine line between genius and lunacy so it's important to think through some of your more visionary ideas quite carefully before steaming ahead. An ability to communicate your ideas is one of your key strengths. Sometimes some of your more extravagant notions really are 'out there' and you may need to be meticulous in your planning. Happily, time will often prove you were right all along, but it's probably best to choose a career path that can accommodate your left-brain thinking. The creative arts, for example, or even scientific research, since sometimes the wilder the hypothesis, the more visionary the outcome can be. In your personal relationships you can be prone to occasional neediness which some may find off-putting, but this is really just a sign of your creative sensitivity. You may need the sort of reassurance that others can find draining, especially if you constantly place your needs ahead of theirs. Be aware of this trait and work towards a greater thoughtfulness, so you can also provide the support to your partner that you expect to receive.

Numerology

No. 5: Impulsive and restless by nature, spontaneous and likes to discover the world through the senses.

Tarot

Ace of Swords: At your very best, you have the ability to slice through any and all objections to more visionary ideas and convince others they will work, so this card, which encapsulates the power of the single sword at your disposal, reinforces the idea that you are (usually) on the right track with your thinking. The hand we see holding the sword is the mighty hand of Spirit upholding you and your ideas; trust this invisible support, even when the going gets tough and the obstacles in your path seem insurmountable. You have come here with the gift of being an original thinker and will be helped behind the scenes to find ways to use that gift for the greater good.

Famous birthdays

Mark Wahlberg American actor and producer
Laurie Anderson American avant-garde artist and musician
Federico García Lorca Spanish poet

June 6th

Deceptively original

The phrase 'still waters run deep' could have been created with you in mind, because on first meeting there's little suggestion that behind a mild-mannered public face you have a razor-sharp mind and an intellectual curiosity which often makes you seek out radical ideas. With a likely leaning towards lateral thinking and the courage to forge your own path, you can come across as unexpected and highly individual. With these character traits you might want to consider pursuing a career where you are your own boss. You'll need a partner who won't flinch from your originality, one who will celebrate and cherish what makes you stand out from the herd. Because there's a tendency to hide the full extent of your intellect, this can sometimes make you come across as a little insecure. Just remember we can't make meaningful change in the world without upsetting some folk along the way. Not everyone is going to want to embrace your ideas, although plenty will.

Numerology

No. 6: Empathic and nurturing, can problem-solve in an emotional and physical way, responsible and cares deeply about family and friends.

Tarot

The Hermit: You may be very happily ensconced in the bosom of a large, loving family and have built a huge network of friends and acquaintances with whom you like to socialise, but this is still the card that will speak on a deeper level to you. What we see here is a lone soul, shrouded in a cloak of mystery himself, but with the ability to light the way ahead for others. It may be, of course, that you have chosen a solitary life or may be in a current phase of solitude. The important thing is to understand that this has nothing to do with loneliness; rather this is a character who recognises the power inherent in getting to know our true selves, finding our wisdom, and then sharing that with the wider world once we are ready to emerge back into that energy.

Famous birthdays

Alexander Pushkin Russian writer
Alexandra Feodorovna Last Empress of Russia
Steve Vai American guitarist

June 7th

Skilled multi-tasker

There's not a lot of stopping to smell the roses in your world because you have an innate tendency to be constantly on the go. It takes serious downtime for your brain to stop whirring, and you actively enjoy having several plates spinning all at once, finding this keeps you on your intellectual toes. You may also be drawn to the Ancient Mysteries and could have psychic abilities that you might choose to develop. Plus, with your willingness to learn and easy-going and friendly manner, you may find a role in the healing arts. When it comes to love, you're a sapiophile, which means you have a tendency to fall for someone's mind rather than their physical attributes and you expect them to be the same. This bodes well for a long-term commitment because when physical passions fade, mental ones just get stronger as you discover more about yourselves. You can sometimes come across as a little emotionally reserved because you don't always trust your own feelings, but you can overcome this by learning to slow down, tune in and trust your own inner wisdom, which will guide you along the path you have chosen.

Numerology

No. 7: Very analytical and detail-oriented, likes to observe and investigate things, and has a keen, inventive eye.

Tarot

Two of Pentacles: Here we see a young showman juggling two pentacles inside the sign for infinity. That mystical sign denotes your strong interest in all things 'other', including psychic studies, the occult and the Ancient Mystery schools. The juggling we already know you're capable of, but with this card there is a sense of an eternal back-and-forth which is not always going to produce any forward motion. Take care not to get stuck in a pattern of vacillation, chopping and changing your position, but combine learned experience with study because this is the best way to realise your destiny.

Famous birthdays

Liam Neeson Irish actor
Dean Martin American singer and actor
Prince American singer-songwriter

June 8th

Formidable analyst

You have a tendency to live in your head and love intellectual stimulation, which means boredom is your biggest fear and you will do almost anything to avoid anything you find tedious. Unfortunately, this can include those who may not share your passion for knowledge. You could do well in areas of more scientific research and exploration, but whatever career path you choose, you will need a certain amount of freedom. You have more than your fair share of charm so won't have any problems attracting friends or a partner. You're likely to be a steadfast and loyal lover – as long as you don't start to feel your freedom is being threatened. Your ruling planet is Mercury, the planet of communication, so when you do find The One, you expect to tell the world, in your own unique way. In your teens and early twenties, you were probably the original rebel without a cause and it's possible this resistance to authority figures will remain with you throughout your life so, again, choose your life partner and your career path wisely.

Numerology

No. 8: Sees the big picture and aims for it, linked to abundance and material wealth, and uses financial success to give back to others.

Tarot

Ace of Wands: Where do they come from, those flashes of genius you've had your whole life? Those 'aha!' moments which propel you, even if only momentarily, into some other realm where your vision of the future unfurls, showing you what path to take and what choices to make in order for you to realise your dreams and goals? In the Rider-Waite Tarot deck the Wands denote communication skills and there are none finer than those depicted by the ace. You will, literally, ace your way through life, as long as you resist the urge to belittle others who are not your intellectual match. Instead of snarling, try killing those you find irritating with kindness.

Famous birthdays

Nancy Sinatra American singer and actress
Kanye West American rapper and record producer
Tim Berners-Lee British computer scientist and inventor of the World Wide Web

June 9th

Coolly rational

If ever there was a Gemini who embodied the dual personality of the twins – light and dark, kind and cruel, cautious and impetuous – you may be looking at him or her in the mirror. For others, it's less easy to spot the shifts in attitude, and what appears to them to be two entirely different sides to the same person can sometimes create tension. What you seem to struggle with is consistency. You are perfectly capable of all the emotions that attract others to you, including kindness, empathy and thoughtfulness. The problem is sustaining any of these attributes, because sometimes there's a tendency to show an opposite emotion. You probably struggle with such a mercurial nature, but your saving grace may be an ability to change tack, making you brilliantly decisive in a crisis and immensely brave in the face of adversity. This makes you a good life partner for someone who sees these gear-switching qualities as positives and can weather the changes. Channel this changeable nature of yours into work that requires you to be clear-sighted and decisive.

Numerology

No. 9: An old soul that looks to spiritual awareness to solve life's problems and likes to help others to do so in the same way.

Tarot

The Magician: It can sometimes feel to others like a sleight of hand, this extraordinary business of one twin showing up and then, with no prior warning, the complete and total opposite other character, but if, like the Magician, you learn to work with it, then this ability to use all facets of your personality to explore a wider and more honest range of human emotions, and channel those into your work or find ways to help others do the same, can become a real asset. It may be that you find your way to the healing arts either as a skilled practitioner, able to withstand the worst anyone can throw at you in the therapy room, or as an advocate.

Famous birthdays

Michael J. Fox American actor
Johnny Depp American actor
Les Paul American guitarist and inventor

June 10th

Fearless adventurer

You see life as an enormous adventure. You sometimes appear to be constantly in motion, literally and metaphorically, and even as you age, people will think of you as full of energy and young at heart. You're such a good communicator that any career that utilises this will suit you, including the law, politics, journalism, broadcasting, teaching, acting or sales. Whatever you choose, these communication skills will help you achieve your ambition, even if you may also have to learn to temper your fearlessness occasionally with a little caution. In love you can be generous and affectionate, but you will need this to be reciprocated because, although it's seldom obvious to others, you can sometimes yearn for reassurance, especially when you're exhausted yourself. Your partner will need to appreciate the fact that while you are eager to share all your ideas with them when it suits you, you sometimes need to go off and think things through alone. This tendency to take time out on your own could lead to arguments, so it's important to remember how this can appear to others.

Numerology

No. 1: A powerful entity and results-oriented force, all about initiating action and getting things done.

Tarot

Strength: One of the Major Arcana cards, Strength speaks to us of those qualities we draw on to navigate our way through the life that unfolds for us. One of your strengths will be an ability to easily communicate your thoughts, ideas, visions and plans, but another is your total belief in yourself as someone who has much to give to society to help create a better world for everyone. You are less sure of yourself in personal relationships but when striding out into a new adventure you are fearless and strong, because at some deep level, you know you have whatever is needed to keep yourself safe and come home all the richer and wiser for your experience.

Famous birthdays

Elizabeth Hurley British actress
Judy Garland American singer and actress
Robert Maxwell Czech-British media mogul

June 11th

Inspired thinker

You're one of the more emotional Geminis, more likely to be following your heart than your head through life. You may also be a born diplomat, because you hate conflict and will do everything in your power to avoid anything that could escalate into a heated dispute. You like harmony and having beautiful surroundings in which you can find peace, probably organising your living arrangements to ensure a tranquil home life. You may also find that you have a strongly intuitive streak, which could touch on the psychic because you've created the right environment for communication to function on many levels. Once you start to trust these flashes of truth, inspiration or guidance, you will find you're able to explore new ideas that could be surprising, even to those without this gift. But try and trust those hunches because they will serve you well in business and in your personal life. In love, you need a partner who matches you intellectually, and you know passion fades, so finding someone interesting as well as attractive is likely to be very important to you in the most meaningful relationships of your life.

Numerology

No. 2: Shows resilience and power in gentleness, often provides the role of mediator, and linked to psychic abilities.

Tarot

Seven of Cups: This card denotes the importance of learning that it's the things we cannot see, taste, touch or buy – namely, love and a feeling of being connected to and with something bigger than ourselves – that matter most in life. Cups are all about our emotions and with seven of them shown here, each one filled to the brim with all the temptations of a material life, the only one you are interested in is the one filled with a sense of the other. Some call it faith; some use the word spirituality. You'll have your own word for, and understanding of, what it is and what it means in your life.

Famous birthdays

Gene Wilder American actor and comedian
Hugh Laurie British comedian
Richard Strauss German composer, pianist and violinist

June

June 12th

Smooth operator

It can sometimes be a bit of a cliché, but those that have the gift of the gab can occasionally be the smoothest of operators. You are likely to be one of the chattier Geminis with the ability to talk your way in and out of any situation. You love to engage in banter, tend to make friends easily, are always outgoing and often eager to please. You are fun-loving with a natural gift for seeing the funny side, but be careful that you don't end up cast as the clown in your social group, which could make it difficult to get taken seriously when you wish to be. There may be a whisper of the word dilettante in your wake, as you're interested (superficially) in everything, but not always very keen on knuckling down to dig any deeper. Your perfect job will be anything that allows you to drop in, explore your surroundings, share your findings and then move on. You were born to embrace diversity, change, travel and adventure, all of which makes you an excellent friend, but not always the most steadfast of partners since you bore easily and may also struggle to commit to anyone until you meet your match, when you find the jigsaw pieces fit.

Numerology

No. 3: Creative with the gift of imagination and an ability to communicate in writing, art or speech.

Tarot

Three of Swords: We see a broken heart here, bleeding after being pierced by three sharp swords. So, the question here is whose heart is this? Yours? Or someone you've left in your wake as you moved on to the next adventure? Try and take more care with the feelings of others, or it may just be that you meet your mercurial Gemini match one day and it will be your heart, not someone else's, left in tatters on the floor. If that ever happens, remember grief is a fantastic catalyst for change and growth, and rest assured that you'll emerge as a bigger person the other side of a broken heart.

Famous birthdays

George H.W. Bush 41st President of the United States
Anne Frank German-Dutch diarist
David Rockefeller American banker

June 13th

Enriching empath

Like many air signs, you have that uncanny ability to see what isn't immediately visible to others and to hear the unspoken, which can be a burden until you learn to trust this ability to work out what is really going on and what needs to change to create a better society in which to live. If this sounds like you, trust your ability to feel comfortable with this and live at ease with this spiritual force. Whatever it is and wherever it leads, it is very much of the air and not earthbound. You are likely to be a deeply compassionate soul and naturally empathic, so your path in life may well have some humanitarian mission at the heart of your ambition and goals. As long as you don't become emotionally overwhelmed, something that many empaths have to be aware of, your compassion means you're able to accept others, warts and all, without wanting to change or mould them. The other side of what can sometimes be a rather intense focus to life is that when you relax, you're easy to be around and capable of prioritising your personal relationships, working hard to help support your family and those you love.

Numerology

No. 4: Invested in the physical world, centred earth energy that is practical in application.

Tarot

The Sun: To those who love you and whom you love in return, it will make complete sense that this is your birthday card. You bring such warmth and positive energy to your relationships that others can't help but bask in the glow of your loving vibes. Being around you is uplifting in the same way we all feel better when the Sun breaks through and we get to bask in its gentle warmth and nourishing rays. This is a lovely card for a person with more than their fair share of lovely qualities.

Famous birthdays

Malcolm McDowell British actor
Mary-Kate Olsen American fashion designer and actress
William Butler Yeats Irish poet

June 14th

Gregarious leader

Like all Geminis, your ruling planet is Mercury, and today's birthdays show an enquiring and discriminating take on life. There's also a tendency to mentally take things apart and put them back together again, which will probably resonate with you because you have an impressive ability to assess a situation, dismantle what no longer has purpose and reassemble that which you wish to keep. This decisive aspect of your nature will impress many but take care you don't come across as arrogant – it may appear that you have such a determined self-belief, there's no space for anyone else's point of view. Good leadership is about being able to collaborate, not simply impose your will on other people. You may also come across as a bit blunt but, in your defence, that's because once you have set your mind on something, you tend not to waste any time in working out ways to achieve it. Some of the skills that might work well for you in the business world, including being direct, may not go down so well in your personal relationships. If necessary, you may need to temper that no-compromise attitude in order to build the loving relationship you aspire to.

Numerology

No. 5: Impulsive and restless by nature, spontaneous and likes to discover the world through the senses.

Tarot

The Emperor: This card, one of the Major Arcana, shows a mature and regal man sitting on a throne which represents all the authority he has earned for living his life in the truth of his own integrity. Did he make some enemies along the way? Probably, because he was not someone who would compromise his own values. But, like you, he also makes the most of the adventure of this life, and where he (you) can, also helped others along the way. This card shouts 'Respect!'

Famous birthdays

Donald Trump 45th President of the United States
Steffi Graf German tennis player
Will Patton American actor

June 15th

Ethereal outlier

You are an interesting mix with a bit of a twin aspect, inspired by nature, the arts and the mystery of the spiritual world on one hand and also a cool-headed scientific rationalist on the other. You may feel the tension of this duality and manage it by veering more on the side of the spiritual. Add to the mix something of a solitary nature or preference for your own company, and it's easy to see why you may come across as something of a loner, following your own path and rules. On the surface you have a friendly and sociable nature, but deeper down, you can mistrust feelings, your own and those of others, and may find this challenge extends to your romantic life. It may take you a little effort, but because you probably also want the love and security of a long-term relationship, you may need to strike a balance to achieve this. As you are likely to be something of a thinker when it comes to problem-solving, turning to writing, philosophy, the media or science to work through your ideas comes naturally.

Numerology

No. 6: Empathic and nurturing, can problem-solve in an emotional and physical way, responsible and cares deeply about family and friends.

Tarot

The Hermit: At first glance this can seem a sad card. One of the Major Arcana, it depicts a man whose hooded cloak represents an aura of mystery, but whose bright lantern held high represents a way to illuminate the path, and this can be shared with others who find their way to the solitary space he occupies. It can be tempting to feel sorry for solitary figures and wonder how they appear to have ended up alone. But this misses the point that solitude introduces us to the one person we can always rely on – ourselves. If you use occasional solitary times to think things through and recharge your batteries, you will find yourself at peace and happier to share yourself with others.

Famous birthdays

Courteney Cox American actress
Ice Cube American rapper
Helen Hunt American actress

June 16th

Thoughtful introvert

Given the choice, many might say they would choose to be extrovert rather than introvert, but being something of an observer, this sits quite comfortably for you. You've probably already realised that your own thoughts are often more interesting than those of others and may have little interest in spending time impressing others with a show of extrovert behaviour that you consider rather empty. As a result, you can come across as rather serious. With a strong personal code of ethics, you tend to care deeply about issues like social justice and fairness. Since you are likely to have the ability to think about the necessity for short-term actions to achieve long-term goals, you are likely to be well suited to the business world. Once you have made your money, you will have no qualms in spending it to help make things better for those less fortunate. You are a loyal and steadfast partner whose preference will probably be to make one union that lasts a lifetime.

Numerology

No. 7: Very analytical and detail-oriented, likes to observe and investigate things, and has a keen, inventive eye.

Tarot

Knight of Swords: Cool, calm and collected on the outside (you), but racing with the wind on the inside (our knight), this card speaks to that busy mind of yours, which is always figuring the odds, highlighting the best short-term course of action for the best long-term results and slicing your way (with the sword) through obstacles to create a better world for those less fortunate. The sense we have of the character depicted by this card is that once a decision has been carefully thought through and made, there will be no stopping its progress.

Famous birthdays

Geronimo Mexican Apache leader and medicine man
Gustav V former King of Sweden
Enoch Powell British politician

June

June 17th

Solitary change-maker

For many born on this day, there's a tussle between liking the good life and wanting all the material rewards and knowing that you can't buy what really matters in life. This is the dual aspect, again, of Gemini, and it can take time to work out that feeling connected to something meaningful doesn't automatically lie in material possession but must be balanced emotionally. This is also the birthday of a change-maker. Sometimes to achieve change, it's necessary to forge a solitary path in order to harness all your imagination, vision and energy. The good news is that you are entirely comfortable about making what sacrifice might be required in the short term, to achieve the greater good. Those you love will recognise your commitment to creating a better world, but take care you don't inadvertently sacrifice them in your pursuit of this dream. There is also likely to be a strong streak of kindness running through you which can help protect from this, making you both a tender lover and very caring parent.

Numerology

No. 8: Sees the big picture and aims for it, linked to abundance and material wealth, and uses financial success to give back to others.

Tarot

Six of Pentacles: This card suggests that you are likely to achieve considerable material success over your working life, which is something of an irony since money has never been your god or goal. Happily, what this financial security will allow you to do is invest in the worthy projects you believe in. In this card, we see an older merchant with balancing scales in one hand and a pile of gold coins in the other which he is dispensing to the two men kneeling before him. Today we might interpret this as two app developers looking for venture capital to develop an app that will benefit others in some way, receiving the necessary investment to do so.

Famous birthdays

Venus Williams American tennis player
Igor Stravinsky Russian composer and pianist
Barry Manilow American singer-songwriter

June 18th

Gregarious optimist

Glass half full or half empty? With you, it's always half full, which makes you an uplifting person to be around. You're probably determined to squeeze the very last drop of joy from each day as well as being encouraging and supportive of others. You are so authentically convincing in your enthusiasm for whatever you turn your attention to that you could easily make a name for yourself as a talented actor, or you might head off into business or down the road of scientific research where, equally, you may blaze such a trail that you become known for it. Your preference may be to bring your high energy into teamwork because of your gregarious nature, rather than pursuing solo goals, and you have a highly original and quirky sense of fun which helps stop the task in hand from becoming too burdensome for you or your team. In love, when you finally do settle down (and this may take a while), you are both affectionate and considerate of your partner's feelings. You are also likely to be a committed and involved parent but may need to take a step back and let your kids discover things for themselves rather than constantly corralling their interests.

Numerology

No. 9: An old soul that looks to spiritual awareness to solve life's problems and likes to help others to do so in the same way.

Tarot

Three of Pentacles: This is the card that denotes public recognition and accolades and awards for work done, so well has it inspired, encouraged and supported others. You haven't set out to seek the limelight but when it comes your way, open the door, open your arms and embrace it, because you have earned all the praise being heaped on you . As you move into old age, you will, quite naturally, step back from the hurly-burly of the world and discover the deep-seated spiritual 'motor' that has driven your passions and your success.

Famous birthdays

Isabella Rossellini Italian actress
Paul McCartney British member of The Beatles
Jeanette MacDonald American singer and actress

June

June 19th

Freedom-loving dynamo

There's something about your energy and the way you engage with life that is reminiscent of the elusiveness of the Scarlett Pimpernel ... They seek him here; they seek him there [...] That damned elusive pimpernel ... It's not that you are deliberately avoiding people, it's probably just that you are busy living your life. You are also likely to love exploring new horizons – often the more dramatic the destination, the better – enjoying the adventure of new experiences, and meeting new people. Intellectual stimulation is important to you, and you may even be something of an adrenaline junkie. You love deep conversations, too, so if you do settle down long enough in one place to get a job, it will likely use communications in some form or another. And while you like the idea of being in love, when push comes to shove (and it will), you're not giving up your freedom without being entirely convinced. An ideal partner is likely to be one who also enjoys the journey as much as the destination, with lots of adventures along the way.

Numerology

No. 1: A powerful entity and results-oriented force, all about initiating action and getting things done.

Tarot

Seven of Swords: We see the figure of a young man depicted here who actually looks like a real chancer. He is stealing away in broad daylight with five of the seven swords, leaving two remaining upright in the ground to protect the city he is leaving behind. He is in a rush – a feeling that will be familiar to you – and making his big escape from the old and dull routine into his exciting future. Except what about those five swords? Do they belong to him or is he stealing away with booty that is not his to run off with? Is this the lovable rogue we know as the Scarlet Pimpernel? It's always as well to be aware of our more elusive traits and how they appear to others.

Famous birthdays

Kathleen Turner American actress
Boris Johnson British prime minister
Paula Abdul American singer-songwriter

June 20th

People-pleaser

Although it can sometimes have a bad reputation, your willingness to please others may stem from being an inveterate peacemaker, which makes you liked by everyone you meet. Throw in the bonus of being a witty conversationalist and someone who is interested in so many things, and you can be sure there's never a dull moment around you when you have your public face on. Probably very literate and with a feeling for words, you might be drawn to a life as a writer, actor, musician or some kind of artist. You also probably have an intuitive – almost psychic – sense of what we might call 'the mood of the people', so if you go into any form of public service you'll also do well because that ability can put you one step ahead of the pack. You are far more willing to compromise than many Geminis, again the peacemaker, and so will find it easier than other more independent types to opt for the security and support of a long-term, loving relationship. The only red flag could be that you are so anxious to keep the peace, maintain harmony and avoid rocking the boat, that your default position could be to put the needs of others before your own. While this might work most of the time, in the longer term it could backfire and cause unnecessary drama, because all relationships should be built on an equal respect for the needs of each person.

Numerology

No. 2: Shows resilience and power in gentleness, often provides the role of mediator, and linked to psychic abilities.

Tarot

King of Wands: When this man speaks, people listen. He could sell ice to Inuits, so we can see that he definitely has the gift of the gab. The trick here is to work out how best to use it for the greater good rather than to sell something people don't need or already own. There is an air of the seductive around you. Just make sure you're using it wisely and don't find yourself with a reputation for being a wee bit slippery with all that fast-talking.

Famous birthdays

Nicole Kidman Australian actress
John Goodman American actor
Errol Flynn Australian-American actor

June 21st

Radical revolutionary

Not for you the time-worn motifs and beliefs that everyone else is happy to settle for. Instead, you have a desire for truth and will seek this out in your dealings with the world. In times gone by, you would probably have been the first to sign up for the next crusade and more than happy to march your troops across far-flung lands in search of some version of the Holy Grail. You are likely to demonstrate those excellent leadership qualities, especially when under pressure, so whether you are now leading the way in science or politics or teaching, your team will be happy to follow you. Be aware that a commitment to your truth can sometimes make you a tad dictatorial, which could easily alienate some of your team. You are also likely to have a playful, sensuous streak and are not above using seduction to get your own way. Be aware of a need to adjust your charm offensive when necessary, because there's a definite time and place for seduction, and this needs to be respected. Once you settle down you are a loyal and loving partner who is likely to enjoy investing in domestic harmony, even though your tendency to flirt with others may sometimes rankle.

Numerology

No. 3: Creative with the gift of imagination and an ability to communicate in writing, art or speech.

Tarot

The World: This card represents a veritable goddess with the world at both her feet and her fingertips. This is a creature whose power lies in the truth and if you allow her, she will lead you to yours so that you can truly live by those values and not those being imposed on the rest of society as a way of controlling the herd. This is a card of celebration because all your hard work will pay off and you will find meaningful ways of communicating those truths once you find them.

Famous birthdays

Juliette Lewis American actress
Jane Russell American actress
Prince William Duke of Cambridge

June 22nd

Romantic idealist

Not for you the path of the hermit or the lone ranger – you came here to find true love with your soulmate from other lifetimes and you are not leaving without it. This quest for a loving relationship is important to all those under the sign of Cancer, but with you it's a primary consideration. You are likely to be committed to the idea that navigating the ups and downs of life with someone who you love and also trust is the best way. But it may be the case that you are more romantic than realistic and unwilling to accept that even the grandest of passions either eventually settles or burns itself out, leaving nothing but glowing embers to remind those lovers of its once fiery flame. It may be important to recalibrate and make a little space for the mundane because nobody – including you – can be the Romeo to someone's Juliet (or vice versa) all day, every day. A bit of realism will help you to see that a little compromise may be necessary but, if life does disappoint, maybe channel that romance into other creative areas – that way, you can live out all your fantasies without the risk of being disappointed by reality.

Numerology
No. 4: Invested in the physical world, centred earth energy that is practical in application.

Tarot
Four of Wands: This is the card of the ultimate romance, a blissful romantic union between two souls who have found each other in this lifetime. The just-married couple we see depicted clearly have eyes only for each other as they slip away from their own wedding party to dance under a bough of red roses. Romantic? You bet. And this card very much chimes out that which may influence you on your life journey: the search for a soulmate.

Famous birthdays
Meryl Streep American actress
Kris Kristofferson American singer-songwriter and actor
Cyndi Lauper American singer-songwriter

June 23rd

Impassioned philosopher

Like many Cancerians your head longs for the security of a safe and secure loving home, while your heart keeps urging you to break free, roam the world and make a pact with excitement and the adrenaline of adventure and the unknown. As you mature, it's likely you'll relieve this tension by finding a partner who is an excellent intellectual companion and one who can tolerate a more unconventional union with you. When it comes to politics, you are an idealist and one who feels strongly about social justice and supporting the community. This idealism could take you into a career in politics (local or otherwise) or political research, the law, education, medicine, government or journalism. Whatever you choose, it will be important to you to have the freedom to explore philosophical ideas and share them with your network or audience, which is likely to be wide-ranging and extend across the globe. When it comes to your own social life, however, you tend to have a wide range of acquaintances but only a handful of true friends for whom you would move heaven and earth.

Numerology

No. 5: Impulsive and restless by nature, spontaneous and likes to discover the world through the senses.

Tarot

The Magician: The charisma, charm or magnetism of the Magician, one of the Major Arcana cards, is something you are likely to share, and this is probably also the most powerful card in the Tarot deck. All four suits are depicted in this card: the Sword, the Wand, the Cup and the Pentacle, indicating that the Magician has everything he needs at his disposal to bring about change. This may be the case for you, too, and your task will be to find the best way to do this, without sacrificing your ideas and ideals.

Famous birthdays

Frances McDormand American actress and producer
Edward VIII Former King of the United Kingdom
Alan Turing British mathematician and computer scientist

June 24th

Nurturing diplomat

A tad more worldly and ambitious than many of those born under this sign, you still have the Cancerian attachment to home as a place to retreat to. And with your strong appreciation of all things harmonious and domestic, you may even work in one of the fields related to homemaking, perhaps as an architect, interior designer or running a specialist homewares store. You're also likely to be good with people, with a strongly intuitive streak, able to bring out the best in others and to negotiate a diplomatic resolution to confrontation. In work, you like to share your creativity, perhaps through teaching, writing or in the arts in some form. There may be a marked tendency to fall in love with the ideas of love, which may be difficult to match up to an actual person, but if you can retain a sense of realism and not let your heart rule your head, then it's likely you will make a very successful commitment to the person that is right for you. Either way, your domestic life will be important and from where you derive your security.

Numerology

No. 6: Empathic and nurturing, can problem-solve in an emotional and physical way, responsible and cares deeply about family and friends.

Tarot

Nine of Pentacles: Everything about this card speaks to us of a serene kind of beauty, depicting an elegant and beautifully dressed woman completely at ease with herself and her surroundings. The Pentacles represent our resources, including financial, and our lady appears to be strolling through a healthy vineyard with the red grapes ripening in the glorious golden sun of late summer. It is a pleasing aesthetic and a scene of deep contentment which represents what many of us seek to achieve and you in particular.

Famous birthdays

Jeff Beck British guitarist
Lionel Messi Argentinian footballer
Juan Manuel Fangio Argentinian F1 racing driver

June 25th

Intuitive idealist

There may be a tendency to let your heart rule your head, and not just in your love affairs, as this can sometimes catch you out in the world of work where it might mean you sometimes come across as a little bit unpredictable. Or moody. That's not entirely surprising with the Moon as your ruler, waxing and waning and often rather emotionally led, but it can be confusing to those trying to get to know you better. Bear in mind that it's not always obvious to others what you're thinking. You may also have a need for approval, which reflects a very deep sensitivity that needs to find a healthy path between your emotional and intellectual responses. This is not a criticism but a gentle suggestion to stop beating yourself up when it feels as if you can't make a decision. Instead, list the pros and cons and then sleep on it, to help your focus. You also like to be around younger people, so may work in a field related to teaching or childcare. If you have your own children, you're likely to be a very loving parent, but this can extend to godchildren, nephews and nieces, too.

Numerology

No. 7: Very analytical and detail-oriented, likes to observe and investigate things, and has a keen, inventive eye.

Tarot

The Moon: Another of the Major Arcana cards, the Moon often hints at obfuscation because it's not always easy to see it, which could reflect how you deal with your emotional life and what you keep hidden. This card can also suggest some kind of internal struggle to regulate our emotions, which is worth being aware of and may require you to seek more balance in life.

Famous birthdays

Antoni Gaudí Spanish architect
George Orwell British writer
Carly Simon American singer-songwriter

June 26th

Congenial charmer

Being described in this way reflects your ability to manage your emotions, as you may use your charm to deflect scrutiny the moment you are asked to reveal your true feelings. It is not that you are being deceptive or disingenuous, but you're likely to have an intuitive streak about others, and particularly about those you might not entirely trust. You probably have a strong self-reliant streak, too, so it's unlikely to be a problem for you to beat a retreat. The only problem is that without ever risking vulnerability, you may not get the emotional support you need when you need it, and may feel hurt as a consequence, especially as you're likely to be available to those who need yours. Try to be a little more open and it may yield its own reward, allowing others to care for you in a similar way. You're also probably savvy with your finances and savings, another self-preservation trait, and are likely to do well on whichever career path you choose. Just try to remember to give yourself the same kind of consideration you give to others and ask for help when you need it.

Numerology

No. 8: Sees the big picture and aims for it, linked to abundance and material wealth, and uses financial success to give back to others.

Tarot

Five of Pentacles: The Pentacles represent our resources – material, emotional and spiritual – and five (as in the number on this card) is a pretty healthy pile. So why do we see what looks like a poverty-stricken, cold and hungry woman in this card, battling through the snow with someone younger limping behind on crutches? This is not about financial problems but about the internal hardship you have a tendency to inflict on yourself by refusing to be as kind and compassionate towards your own vulnerabilities as you are towards those revealed by others.

Famous birthdays

Chris Isaak American musician
Ariana Grande American singer-songwriter
Chris O'Donnell American actor

June

June 27th

Fierce protector

You're likely to have a strong sense of justice and feeling for the underdog, and this could influence many of the decisions you make in life, from the work you do to the people you love. Nobody will ever have to teach you right from wrong, either, because knowing the difference between the two is part of what gets you out of bed every day. Seeking to protect the exploited and downtrodden may well form part of whatever career interests you have because you are unlikely to be the silent type where you see something is wrong. You don't think it is someone else's job to stop injustices and other cruelties, but something that needs to be addressed now, and you are up to the job. Charity begins at home, though, so you are likely to forge a strong loving relationship that supports you in your work. But you could also be as uncompromising in your personal as your work life, and not everyone will appreciate your commitment to your work. This won't be a huge concern, however, because at heart you believe that you will find love and possibly through your work.

Numerology

No. 9: An old soul that looks to spiritual awareness to solve life's problems and likes to help others to do so in the same way.

Tarot

Six of Cups: This card depicts an older child giving a young girl a chalice full of pure white flowers and it is often the card that appears when there has been some childhood upset or bereavement. It may be that you had some difficult experiences in childhood which helped forge your compassionate activism and, on some deeper level, you understand that however hard those trials, they have given you strength to take on the task without fear of any sorrow you may encounter.

Famous birthdays

Tobey Maguire American actor
Isabelle Adjani French actress and singer
India de Beaufort British actress and singer-songwriter

June 28th

Good listener

The world needs more people like you – generous, kind and quick to help others and supporting their dreams and goals however you can. You are also likely to be a brilliant organiser and have such a charming personality that people will be offering to help without even realising they are giving up their weekend or handing over a chunk of their pay packet to a good cause. When it comes to careers, those in the caring professions or charity work may well fuel your interest. You may well have the gift of optimism, making everyone feel happy, and you may also love to travel and learn about new places and new cultures. If you have a fault, it could be that you are a bit undiscerning when it comes to protecting your heart, falling in love fast and deep, without much concern for its immediate consequences. All this could be avoided if you just slowed down long enough to ask if this really is someone you can trust, travel with, live with and love for a very long time? It's as well to ask these questions before getting in too deep, as this can save a lot of heartbreak later for all concerned.

Numerology

No. I: A powerful entity and results-oriented force, all about initiating action and getting things done.

Tarot

Three of Cups: This is a card depicting great celebrations, where chalices are raised to collectively toast an achievement. The Cups themselves represent our emotions, and this is a happy card where the three, who have helped and supported each other, are equal (they each have one cup) and sharing one of those magical moments which make life worth living.

Famous birthdays

John Cusack American actor, screenwriter and political activist
Kathy Bates American actress and director
Jean-Jacques Rousseau Swiss philosopher and writer

June 29th

Amiable peacekeeper

That intuition, which provides the gift of knowing how others are going to react, may be something you've had since childhood and all you have done since then is hone that useful skill. It means you can usually predict outcomes with considerable accuracy, either working to avoid unpleasantness or to persuade others to work together harmoniously in the first place. You may appear to be naturally good at this, so you may have found your way into work as a mediator or in some kind of peace-keeping role. You could give the impression that nothing is ever too much trouble, but, if anyone starts taking you for granted or abusing your good nature, they could then see your self-protective Cancerian streak come to the fore. This shadow side can come across as quite abrupt, so it's as well to be aware of this so you don't alienate people who might find this sudden change difficult. In all probability you will create a family of your own, because you prefer not to make life's journey alone, and when you find the partner you want to share your life with you are often a very romantic, responsive and affectionate lover.

Numerology

No. 2: Shows resilience and power in gentleness, often provides the role of mediator, and linked to psychic abilities.

Tarot

The High Priestess: This card is the female match to the Magician, and where he tells us what needs to be done the High Priestess knows how to do what needs to be done, which some might argue is a more useful attribute since it means you can get started. This is quite a powerful card because the Priestess is depicted with her books of learning and sacred symbols, which she has earned the right to use. It is a card of innate and learned wisdom and having the courage to apply that wisdom, too.

Famous birthdays

Gary Busey American actor
Little Eva American singer
Nicole Scherzinger American singer and TV personality

June

June 30th

Excellent teacher

A willingness to share and impart what you have learned is core to your personality, which is curious by nature. You may not be working as a teacher per se, but you would probably excel if you chose that career path in one form or another. Even if you don't, you're likely to enjoy learning new facts, skills or abilities throughout your life and your natural willingness to learn will probably make you an excellent student. You may also have a typical Cancerian shrewdness with money matters, allowing you to travel and meet a wide range of people with whom to exchange ideas. These skills also lend themselves to journalism or reportage. Acting or politics, which could also give you something of a stage, may also attract you, while your sensitive side is well-protected, so you are unlikely to shy away from debate. Like many Cancerians, however, you may have an idealised view of romantic love and could get quite despondent about relationships if reality kicks in too soon.

Numerology

No. 3: Creative with the gift of imagination and an ability to communicate in writing, art or speech.

Tarot

The Knight of Pentacles: Like the knight, you want to know what lies over the horizon. He has everything he needs to make his decision and is just waiting for it to become clear, which is very useful to remember when you are in a similar position and perhaps need to temper some of your romantic illusions.

Famous birthdays

Susan Hayward American actress
Rupert Graves British actor
Cheryl British singer and TV personality

July 1st

Adventurous go-getter

You know what you want and you're smart enough to know how to work to get there, and with this combination of graft and ingenuity, there's not much that's going to stop you. You are more assertive than many of those who share your Cancer sun sign and the combination of an adventurous spirit, a shrewd intellect and an insightful mind makes you a force to be reckoned with. Your public persona is usually equable, self-contained and friendly, although getting close to you isn't always easy and protecting your more sensitive side could make you appear rather emotionally detached. This may also be linked to the fact that yours is a creative temperament, but when you retreat internally to focus, you could unintentionally alienate people. You are nurturing and empathic in your personal relationships, but sometimes there's a tension between your need to be free and that yearning for a stable home. Bear in mind that a sound domestic set-up actually gives you the security to come and go, and then you can relax a little and focus on the pleasures of life.

Numerology

No. 1: A powerful entity and results-oriented force, all about initiating action and getting things done.

Tarot

Page of Wands: This card represents communication and the Page of Wands, being younger and less experienced than his royal counterparts, the King, Queen and Knight, suggests someone eager to get his or her message out to the wider world and initiate those changes needed to make it a better place for all. The page is alone and surveying the landscape, considering the new green shoots emerging on his wand and weighing up its potential for growth. The ground he stands on is level and stable, so there are no nasty surprises lurking to trip him up. He just has to decide what he wants, where he wants it, and head that way.

Famous birthdays

Diana, Princess of Wales former member of the British royal family
Liv Tyler American actress
Dan Aykroyd Canadian actor and comedian

July 2nd

Gracious host

Socialising is top of your 'To Do' list and so important to you that you'll chose a career that allows you to mix and mingle. You enjoy the good things in life and being surrounded by beautiful things, so you may choose to work in interior design, antiquities or areas that will also bring you into contact with the financially well-to-do. Financial resources and what these can confer are important to you, so you'll work hard to accrue your own and, even better, join forces with someone who'll help you both be comfortably set for life. You are naturally gregarious, and people are easily drawn to you, but when it comes to choosing a life partner, you've got your sights set on your soulmate, and nothing less will do. Your intuition is strong, and you may also have a strong psychic streak, so when 'The One' does finally show up, you will recognise them instantly and – at least for you – it's likely to be love at first sight. This can possibly make you a little intense, so it's worth being aware of this and allowing the object of your affection to come to a similar conclusion in their own time.

Numerology

No. 2: Shows resilience and power in gentleness, often provides the role of mediator, and linked to psychic abilities.

Tarot

Judgement: This card depicts a winged creature blasting a trumpet over the graves of the dead and shocking them back to life and this world. It's a metaphor for a wake-up call and tends to show up in the readings of those who have become complacent or are effectively sleepwalking through life and missing all the good bits. You won't, initially, think this applies to you, but it does because your fixation on the good times and things that pass – including money and power – may mean you neglect some of your other gifts. Be careful not to go through life without exploring how you can use the gifts money cannot buy, particularly to help and support those less fortunate.

Famous birthdays

Olav V Former King of Norway
Hermann Hesse German writer and artist
Imelda Marcos Former First Lady of the Philippines

July 3rd

Astute analyst

Led by your head rather than your heart, you could give the impression that you've transcended earthly emotions, which might result in you seeming a little cool in your relations with others. This is handy if you're working with people in a field that requires you to be professionally detached but could cause you problems in your personal relationships. You can make your intuition and ability to analyse work for, rather than against, you and this could lead you into areas of psychology or people management, even in leadership positions. Intimate relationships, however, may be something of a leap of faith for you because of a tendency to over-analyse every nuance that *could* cause relationship issues down the line. Park this approach when you are dating and maybe accept that true love means accepting the whole of somebody. Happily, that cuts both ways, which means you can be more honest about some of your vulnerabilities, too. This is a subtle internal negotiation but relying on your intuition alone isn't enough, as you also have to weigh up tangible evidence. So, learn to confide in those you trust and allow the magic that can occur between two people unfold.

Numerology

No. 3: Creative with the gift of imagination and an ability to communicate in writing, art or speech.

Tarot

Five of Swords: This card shows some kind of skirmish that has taken place between the three male figures depicted; the victor over the other two has not one but three swords in his possession. He has three swords because he has engaged in combat to take them, but the question here is why, when one sword would be sufficient, has he felt the need to fight so hard? Does this ring any bells? Think about dropping the swords (defences) and letting those who care about you see who you really are, instead of fighting them off.

Famous birthdays

Tom Cruise American actor and producer
Julian Assange Australian publisher and founder of WikiLeaks
Vince Clarke British musician and songwriter

July 4th

Community champion

You have absolutely zero interest in going it alone and live for the community you are part of, or manage to form, in whatever situation you find yourself in. You live by the creed that there is no 'I' in the word team and will work three times as hard as anyone else to help your team reach its joint goals, particularly when it comes to your commitment to your family. Because of this, career success where it involves teamwork is highly likely and you are always happiest when working towards the benefit of your community, whatever that means to you. Think about your work/life balance, though, because this commitment to the team and focus on its success could encourage workaholism, and you may have to press pause to rectify this. You may also need to learn to say no when necessary to avoid being taken advantage of, as others may consider you a soft touch. It's important for your own health and well-being to set reasonable boundaries and while you set the bar so high for yourself, also ensure that others measure up. The purpose of those in a team is to share responsibilities, not to shoulder it all.

Numerology

No. 4: Invested in the physical world, centred earth energy that is practical in application.

Tarot

Ten of Pentacles: This is the card of a successful and happy life, one in which the success has been earned through hard work and good values. It is also a family card as we see a happy couple celebrating an established love with a wise old man looking on approvingly. In many ways, this is the life everyone yearns for and you have no problem doing the work to make this possible, more than earning every scrap of happiness and joy that comes your way.

Famous birthdays

Stephen Boyd Irish actor
Gertrude Lawrence British actress
Giuseppe Garibaldi Italian politician who contributed to Italian unification

July 5th

Cool dude

Have you been here before? You're likely to be one of those people who exudes effortless 'cool', from the way you dress to what you think, how you furnish your home, the music you play and the people you party with. For you, life is too short to be toeing any corporate party line, so you'll have to find a way to make your living on a more independent or even freelance basis, but, as you can clearly do a lot with not much (money), the ups and downs of that lifestyle won't give you too many sleepless nights. Your cool status won't diminish with age because it has nothing to do with what you do or don't do in the outside world and everything to do with being confident enough to show who you really are and what you really care about. And while you're quite happy to live quietly alone or with your loved ones, being quiet does not equate with being shy because when the party lights turn on, so do you. If you could bottle and sell this extraordinary quality of yours, one that you just take for granted, you would be wealthy indeed. People are drawn to you, in part because they can't shake the notion you have a secret or know something about life that might benefit them, too.

Numerology

No. 5: Impulsive and restless by nature, spontaneous and likes to discover the world through the senses.

Tarot

The Empress: Like you, this star-crowned person has charisma/charm/grace by the bucketful. Everything about and around her is luxuriant: the trees, the crops, the golden sun behind her. She has no need to try and impress or reach for more because she has more than enough and knows it. Independently spirited, if this character had been born in more modern times, she'd be headlining the main stage at rock festivals anywhere, but only if she felt like it.

Famous birthdays

Paul Smith British fashion designer
Jean Cocteau French poet and playwright
Georges Pompidou French politician

July 6th

Family focused

The family is probably the most important thing in your world, whether that is the immediate family, the extended family, the work 'family' or your idea of the world as one big family. You prefer not to be alone, so there's no way family won't be a huge part of your life as soon as you meet the person you plan to create one with. On the surface, you are pretty chilled and easy-going, but this public face masks a deeply rooted drive to succeed, to be the best and recognised as such, basking in the glory of your success. This hidden streak may seem at odds with the sweet nature you present, but your mettle comes from a steely core. You're likely to have a strongly artistic leaning and may find yourself working in music, arts or entertainment in some way. There is a good chance you'll acquire some sort of public recognition, which will please you, but even if you hit the big time, you'll find the time for family. In love you are a real romantic looking for your fairy-tale ending and when you've found it, you'll do everything in your power to keep the magic alive.

Numerology

No. 6: Empathic and nurturing, can problem-solve in an emotional and physical way, responsible and cares deeply about family and friends.

Tarot

The Chariot: One of the Major Arcana cards, there is only one direction of choice when you are in the driving position of this chariot and that is forwards. This suggests that you may not travel at any great speed, but you don't need to rush as you will travel, throughout life, in a straight and direct line towards the goal on which you've set your sights. There's always room for family passengers in the seats behind you, and with a chariot being pulled by one black and one white Sphinx, the symbology shows the significance of steering a careful course on a middle path, and not being swayed to the left or to the right.

Famous birthdays

Sylvester Stallone American actor and director
Janet Leigh American actress
Nancy Reagan American actress and former First Lady of the United States

July

July 7th

Private pragmatist

You have plenty of the Cancerian charm that draws people like a magnet, but you are essentially a very private person, so what they see is barely a hint of what lies beneath. Your pragmatism helps pave the work path for success and people like and trust you. There's a chance some will be envious of that strong streak of self-belief you rely on as you navigate your way to achieving your own goals and dreams. With your sensitive side there's a chance you could find yourself working in the creative industries, and music might be your first love, followed by the stage, movies and painting. A big part of your private persona is your ability to commit deeply to your partner, from whom you get as much emotional support as you give. Kinship and friendship are both important to you, but it's helpful if you can keep the private part of your life away from your public persona, and protecting this may be second nature to you. You are an original thinker and capable of great innovation, but you need to watch that you don't accidentally flip into being entirely unrealistic about what you can hope to achieve.

Numerology

No. 7: Very analytical and detail-oriented, likes to observe and investigate things, and has a keen, inventive eye.

Tarot

Five of Wands: The Wands represent communication, both with others and ourselves, and in your case, this card speaks of the internal tussles you may undergo as part of your unique creative process, arguing with yourself about the way in which this reaches expression. As part of your engagement with the wider world, this card warns that there may be ongoing struggles with those who deem your goals unrealistic and fanciful and who are, as a result, unwilling to invest their time, money or energy in helping you to realise them.

Famous birthdays

Ringo Starr British member of The Beatles
Jeremy Kyle British TV presenter and journalist
Shelley Duvall American actress

July 8th

Practical thinker

Both ambitious and tenacious, you are likely to have a strength of will that beggars belief, and there will be times you are so determined that you could possibly cross the line into ruthlessness. This could make you well suited to the business world, which doesn't suffer fools gladly, but what really fires you up is the notion of a company with all its cogs working together like a well-oiled machine. You may have a hugely practical streak and ability to focus on details, which ensures there's nothing down the line that could trip you or your workforce up. Everything you suggest or do is supported by sound reasoning and solid research. You're unlikely to be a gambler, either with your own welfare or that of others, and as you progress through life your steady leadership will earn respect. In your personal life, your practicality may make you appear over-emphatic, but you're not a bully and so will stop short of actually imposing your desires on others. You're sensitive to your partner's needs and know that progress is more likely as a result of willing co-operation.

Numerology

No. 8: Sees the big picture and aims for it, linked to abundance and material wealth, and uses financial success to give back to others.

Tarot

King of Cups: The Cups represent emotions, reiterating the sensitivity you have to the feelings of others, and suggests a degree of empathy that will serve you well in both your business and professional life. Beneath the calm exterior you like to present to the world, you are more emotional than others may realise, and when your heart engages, you will do anything you can to help that person, that family, that community.

Famous birthdays

Angelica Houston American actress and director
Kevin Bacon American actor
Giuliana Benetton Italian co-founder of the United Colours of Benetton

July 9th

Spiritual guru

You may not recognise yourself in this description but that will be because you may not have yet stepped onto that path or, if you are older, you looked the other way when it was offered. There's nothing inherently wrong with that; the important thing is that you have all the qualities – including a strong psychic gift – that would make you a fine spiritual leader of some sort, should you so choose. You may, instead, work as a healer or carer in some other capacity. You're unlikely to look for work in financial services or other fields that don't engage your heart or your considerable powers of intuition. Growing up you may have felt that you were somehow 'different' in some way, but as you mature, you'll learn to appreciate that in order to change things for the better it can be necessary to stand outside the herd. You'll look for these same qualities in a life partner – someone who understands the value of a connection with something deeper than materialism and someone who accepts you as the inspiring spiritual seeker you are or could so easily become.

Numerology

No. 9: An old soul that looks to spiritual awareness to solve life's problems and likes to help others to do so in the same way.

Tarot

Strength: This card denotes a strength or fortitude that probably lies in your deep connection to something beyond the mind and body, which some may call spirit or soul. There's a quiet determination that enables you to stand your ground in whatever sphere you might choose and you're unlikely to argue with anyone about any of this because, as far as you're concerned, this is the basis of the connection we all have to each other. You may even have found this through a conventional faith or through more alternative practices like yoga or shamanism.

Famous birthdays

Tom Hanks American actor
Kelly McGillis American actress
David Hockney British artist

July 10th

Pioneering change-maker

Some people will do anything to avoid change but that's unlikely to be you, and this immediately sets you apart from most of those sharing your sun sign. Home is still important to you and, at the end of the day, you'll opt for the security of a settled home life. But outside the home, you're willing to push against the *status quo,* question traditional ways of doing things and find more innovative solutions to obstacles that could stop others mid-track. You have a strong artistic streak coupled with something of an emotional response to things both at home and at work. All this adds up to a need to express yourself creatively, perhaps through writing or the arts, so please don't limit yourself to a career (in the corporate world, for example) that would not comfortably allow for this. You are discerning in both your friendships and romantic liaisons. You will take your time to make new friends and to start dating, but once you find a like-minded tribe and the person you want to share your life with, you'll have no problem committing and setting up a secure and stable home with a busy and happy social life.

Numerology

No. 1: A powerful entity and results-oriented force, all about initiating action and getting things done.

Tarot

Ace of Cups: The Cups represent strong emotions, and this card suggests someone whose powerful emotions are never far from the surface. This goes some way to explaining why you may be prone to, or find yourself suppressing, occasional emotional outbursts, usually as a result of frustration either with yourself or others. But the advantage to having this kind of nature is that it allows you to connect in a more meaningful way with yourself, with others and with what really matters; and this is what makes it imperative that you find ways to express and share this knowledge.

Famous birthdays

Jessica Simpson American singer and actress
Marcel Proust French novelist
Carl Orff German composer

July 11th

Tactful peacemaker

You're highly sensitive to the moods of others, but you will possibly use this ability to read the mood in the room to actively avoid discord and confrontation, going out of your way – a very long way out of your way – to avoid any kind of unpleasantness. There's possibly something of the observer about you, as you prefer to see rather than be seen, especially emotionally. People are drawn to your easy-going nature but may struggle with your lack of engagement, not understanding that this is a protective measure that's often seen in Cancerians. In romantic relationships you may have a tendency to project what you want, rather than what you actually get, onto another, which could make you unrealistic about them. Take a tip from more grounded sun signs and use your learned experience to help guide you.

Numerology

No. 2: Shows resilience and power in gentleness, often provides the role of mediator, and linked to psychic abilities.

Tarot

Knight of Wands: This represents a youthful desire to communicate and can suggest a rather unrealistic and over-romanticised view of life. Sometimes this desire for a perfect, everlasting love reflects deep-seated feelings of insecurity and unworthiness, requiring passion to hide a low self-esteem. Your life lesson might be about dropping the façade just enough to show your vulnerable side, and this may help ensure a more realistic and enduring connection with someone.

Famous birthdays

Suzanne Vega American singer-songwriter
Yul Brynner Russian actor
Giorgio Armani Italian fashion designer

July 12th

Empathic cheerleader

You probably have such a genuine interest in helping others progress towards their goals that you are already working in the field of personal development or human resources. This type of work will suit your ability to comfortably switch from empathic to hard-nosed, in order to nudge someone into taking action for their own good. People are likely to trust and depend on you, seek you out for your guidance and advice and look to you for leadership. Your integrity shines through all your dealings, which is why there's so much trust and respect for your opinion. Plus, you're not afraid to take on the establishment when you think something is wrong and needs correcting. In your private life you are likely to be protective and encouraging of those you love and care about, maybe even over-protective. You want to see everyone reach their potential, but you may need to take care sometimes that you don't overstep the boundary between caring and interfering, because however well-intentioned, this could sometimes backfire. It's also important for others to learn self-reliance, which they may not be able to do if they are constantly shielded from learning for themselves how to manage life.

Numerology

No. 3: Creative with the gift of imagination and an ability to communicate in writing, art or speech.

Tarot

King of Cups: This card suggests someone brimming with emotional intelligence and who is so attuned to the feelings of others that he can almost predict how someone is going to react, long before they know themselves. This card is all about having an empathic and caring nature, but also warns that there may be times in your life when you become too emotionally involved, which can then cloud your usually excellent judgement skills.

Famous birthdays

Anna Friel British actress
Christine McVie British singer-songwriter
Henry David Thoreau American naturalist and essayist

July 13th

Pragmatic counsellor

You may have been born with a tendency to mistrust those 'glass half full' people who insist on looking on the bright side, and you may find it difficult to understand how they can remain so cheerfully positive given the news you read. There's no point asking you to be anything other than pragmatic about life, but you could temper an anxiety by also opening up a little to what is good in the world, engaging with nature on a walk, for example, which will help feed your soul. There's a survival instinct connected to a pessimistic view, and the upside is that you're usually well-prepared and have probably created a secure home to which to retreat. It may take a conscious effort to manage negative thoughts, but it is possible. It may also be that, with your sensitivity, in doing this for yourself you become able to support and help others, perhaps through work as a counsellor. When looking for a life partner, it may be worth consciously looking for someone who welcomes the security you can provide while challenging your more negative thoughts. This will help reinforce your confidence and activate your more positive side.

Numerology

No. 4: Invested in the physical world, centred earth energy that is practical in application.

Tarot

Eight of Wands: This is a dynamic card that suggests you need to stop procrastinating, put worries aside and start whatever it is you have always dreamed of doing. The Wands represent communication, so the more the merrier and, in this case, they are all pointing to a far horizon beyond a body of water. Water represents your emotional life, so the message here is to dive in, resurface with whatever it is you need from your unconscious to make your dreams come true, pack your bag, pick up your pen, buy that rundown old vineyard or do whatever it takes to make that happen.

Famous birthdays

Harrison Ford American actor
Patrick Stewart British actor
Eric Portman British actor

July 14th

Independent thinker

There are times you'd like to just ditch that Cancer shell and stride out, unprotected, into the great blue yonder and take your chances along with the rest of us who don't have the luxury of a hard, safe shell to retreat into. The key thing to note with this is that, although you probably would like to do this, there's no suggestion you actually will. You do have an internal freedom versus security tussle and can feel restless wanting to know where the grass might be greener, but for those born on this date, stability and security will probably win out in the long term, so you may as well know that and alleviate this internal tension, freeing up your energy. Find a soulmate, fall in love, settle down and create the home you need to come back to after all your forays into the wider world. You are probably blessed with a social conscience, too, so are likely to choose a career that reflects that, working perhaps as a teacher, social worker, campaigner, counsellor or even faith leader. If you do head down the business route, you will do equally well since you have a pretty shrewd head on your shoulders.

Numerology

No. 5: Impulsive and restless by nature, spontaneous and likes to discover the world through the senses.

Tarot

Three of Pentacles: This card speaks to us of the resources we have (internal and external), how we use them and how others see us as a result of the choices we make. In your case, this card denotes your humanitarian spirit and social conscience and suggests you will likely put as much, if not more, back into society as you ever take out. There's a strong sense of civic activity and duty underpinning this card, so this might also include local or national politics in some way.

Famous birthdays

Ingmar Bergman Swedish director and screenwriter
Gustav Klimt Austrian artist
Woody Guthrie American singer-songwriter

July 15th

Worker bee

If there's something that needs to be done, the worker bee is the one we all turn to, not least because they take on much that others don't want to do, and then do it with incredibly good grace. You will be a key member of your chosen community in both your home and work life, taking what you see as your responsibility towards others very seriously. You're not afraid of hard work and bring an easy charm to every situation, which makes you a pleasure to have and be around. Fascinated by what makes people tick, you are likely to choose work that allows you to use your exceptional powers of observation and analysis, which, coupled with your worker-bee tendencies, makes it inevitable that you'll rise to your personal pinnacle of whatever career you choose. Personal relationships may prove a bit trickier because you've a tendency to over-romanticise things, wanting an idyllic love affair which may not weather the storms should they occur. Remember to keep your dreams grounded in real life, otherwise when trouble strikes, you may opt to disappear and look for someone else with whom to perpetuate the myth.

Numerology

No. 6: Empathic and nurturing, can problem-solve in an emotional and physical way, responsible and cares deeply about family and friends.

Tarot

The Star: One of the Major Arcana, this is the card of healing. So, the question you need to ask is: What might need healing in your life? We have something of a clue in looking at your romantic nature and desire to live a fairy-tale life. You know those couples who always say, '*We never argue*'? This may be because they both have so many defences, they never reveal their true selves to each other. And then, if they finally do ... bam! The whole fairy-tale collapses. This card suggests you reflect on what might need addressing to ensure a more realistic take on life.

Famous birthdays

Forest Whitaker American actor
Brigitte Nielsen Danish actress
Rembrandt Dutch artist

July 16th

Sympathetic carer

You are easy-going, sociable and very friendly, and other people find themselves drawn to your energy, which works well for you because you are not a solo crab. You like to live and work with others and are likely to enjoy being surrounded by like-minded people who care about you as much as you care about them. You have great practical skills, so may choose a career which involves something being built or created, or you may take your easy-going and entertaining manner a stage further and try out as a stand-up comedian, even if only for fun. In matters of family and love, you are a great partner, sibling, son or daughter, and friend: affectionate, caring and actually very entertaining. You have what they call in the trade 'funny bones', love to make other people smile and recognise that we all feel better for a good belly laugh at some ridiculous situation or another we may find ourselves in. Your ruling planet is the Moon, so your innate sensitivity needs to be considered, too. Be careful you don't use your *joie de vivre* as a defence against your own sadness when this happens, looking out for others and then neglecting your own needs. It's not a weakness to let others help you when you need it.

Numerology

No. 7: Very analytical and detail-oriented, likes to observe and investigate things, and has a keen, inventive eye.

Tarot

Queen of Cups: The Queen of Cups sits quietly on her throne, looking at the precious vessel she is holding in her hands. This may represent the way you might sometimes isolate yourself, keeping your deepest emotions securely contained and hiding them behind your all-round, nice guy/girl persona. You may sometimes be too considerate of others, hiding your real feelings, which could make you difficult to get to know. Share a little more and risk getting the support you need.

Famous birthdays

Ginger Rogers American dancer and actress
Barbara Stanwyck American actress
Roald Amundsen Norwegian polar explorer

July 17th

Quiet achiever

You are probably known for your ironic wit but only by those that get past your highly reserved demeanour. Possibly prone to sometimes feeling a little nervous and insecure, you may be like a hedgehog, a bit prickly on the outside – especially if feeling under attack – but soft and defenceless on the inside, all of which makes for quite a complex character. With you, what you see is not exactly what you get. There's probably a steely determination to succeed, and beneath that shy exterior is a tenacious determination to be recognised and praised for your talents and contributions. You are actually very capable of handling responsibility and so will quickly advance up through the ranks of management if you've chosen a career in business, where you are likely to be a shrewd executive who is able to drive a hard bargain if needed. Your witty side may take some time and confidence to develop, but it's definitely there. When it comes to love, you'll take your time to commit, but when you do you will expect the same lifelong devotion in return and may wobble and retreat if you don't feel it's there.

Numerology

No. 8: Sees the big picture and aims for it, linked to abundance and material wealth, and uses financial success to give back to others.

Tarot

The World: One of the Major Arcana, this card tells of external success in the world, which is something you feel is important. With a shrewd and instinctive sense of the world, all you have to do is keep at it, keep believing in yourself, and trust that the world will deliver the right opportunity at the right time and that when it does, you will be the perfect candidate for it.

Famous birthdays

Donald Sutherland Canadian actor
James Cagney American actor and dancer
Camilla, Duchess of Cornwall Member of British royal family

July 18th

Team player

Camaraderie is your buzz word and if there's not a team in play, whatever the task, you're unlikely to be signing up until there is. It's not that you can't tolerate solitude or working alone, but you prefer not to. You'll probably look to join social groups outside the office, too. Sports are likely to be part of your life because you're never happier than when you're part of something bigger. It is all about solidarity and fraternity and being a member of a group, so you may be drawn to a career in the military or you may become some kind of community campaigner or organiser. Once you sign on to a cause, you give it 100 per cent. As a result, you can come across as a little narrow-minded since you find it hard to make space for more diverse views. You can be a little impulsive, rushing headlong into new teams or joint ventures, which can cause problems at home if you haven't stopped to consult anyone else. Your partner may feel you spread yourself too thinly and ask you to make more time to spend at home.

Numerology

No. 9: An old soul that looks to spiritual awareness to solve life's problems and likes to help others to do so in the same way.

Tarot

Temperance: One of the powerful Major Arcana cards, here is a figure pouring water for the pool of life between two golden chalices, in an attempt to ensure there is the same volume of liquid in each. This is about carefully balancing between this and that, now and then, before and after, yesterday and tomorrow, lost and found, love and hate. For you, this card speaks of finding an emotional (water) balance between giving yourself to the outside world and keeping something back for yourself and your family. It asks that you learn to regulate your emotions and practise discernment.

Famous birthdays

Nelson Mandela South African civil rights leader
Richard Branson British entrepreneur and businessman
Hunter S. Thompson American journalist and author

July

July 19th

Astute advisor

While some crave the limelight and all the public plaudits that make them a household name, you are someone who probably understands that true power often sits in a quiet corner where the real work gets done. You're likely to have the patient skills of a researcher and can dig up the answers to any conundrum with ease. Happily, what you are asked to find is unlikely to make any difference to you, as your only motivation is to get to the truth of the matter and use it wisely. This inclination is a powerful one, as there will be some who may possibly underestimate you, but the fact is that you are painstaking and discreet and really only care about getting the best job done and by the best people for the job. You may gravitate towards a role as advisor, whether this is in national politics or local advice centres, as there's likely to be quite an intuitive side to you, too. You will need to ensure you make time for your own personal life, or you could lose out on that, and this would be a shame because it is important to you. When you look for a partner, find someone who won't curb your independence or restrict your ethical stance, someone who is likely to share your own standards in life.

Numerology

No. 1: A powerful entity and results-oriented force, all about initiating action and getting things done.

Tarot

The Wheel of Fortune: With talents like these, in the past you might have been recruited (and been tempted) to sign up with the secret service and work as a spy, although nobody would ever have guessed it such is your ability to disarm. The spinning Wheel of Fortune is always a fortuitous card and it speaks to us of a change in fortunes, always for the better and always beyond perhaps your wildest dreams. But to reap this reward it's often necessary to buckle up, as it can be something of a rollercoaster ride.

Famous birthdays

Brian May British guitarist
Edgar Degas French Impressionist artist
Benedict Cumberbatch British actor

July 20th

Infectious optimist

There's likely to be so much optimism and zest for life that there's never a dull moment when you are around. Because of this, people are likely to gravitate towards you and since you enjoy the role of organiser, it's often a win-win for everyone. You are naturally drawn to the more creative and artistic side of life, but whatever career you choose, your sunny nature, thirst for knowledge and practical skills all combine to ensure the likelihood of success. You relish being part of a team and have the ability to deliver constructive criticism in a way that someone can accept without feeling undermined or wounded, which is a wonderful gift in a manager. These same traits are likely to make you a good life partner, not least because you rate your partner's happiness and well-being on a par, if not more highly, than your own. You are clear-headed and confident in a crisis, loyal and kind. There may be a wee chink in the armour of your perfection, however, a tendency to try and keep too many balls in the air at the same time, which can make you seem unfocused and, sometimes, a bit shallow. If this is the case, learning to focus will pay dividends.

Numerology

No. 2: Shows resilience and power in gentleness, often provides the role of mediator, and linked to psychic abilities.

Tarot

Six of Cups: This is the card of the empath, and that of someone who prefers actions to words when it comes to supporting others. With its depiction of offering a white flower in a pot, this card also suggests the cherishing of memories and an ability to empathise with the sadness of others, which may come from something similar experienced in childhood.

Famous birthdays

Natalie Wood American actress
Carlos Santana Mexican guitarist
Nicola Benedetti Scottish classical violinist

July 21st

Gifted homemaker

Unless something is beautiful and pleases you, when it comes to creating your home, this is likely to be rejected. You probably love beauty wherever it shows up – in nature, in art, in the back garden – and are likely to prioritise this either by making beautiful things yourself or supporting others who do. You are unlikely to be that bothered about excessive material success, but your home takes priority, and you are likely to invest in this. When there are funds to spare, you'll probably spend them at the auction house adding to your vintage porcelain collection or at the garden centre buying a specimen ginkgo tree. You're likely to be a generous, loyal and supportive partner, because you hold yourself (and others) to a pretty strict moral code, unforgiving of those who let you down. Your apparently strong outer shell and confident nature belies great sensitivity, and if someone breaks your heart, it will be a long time before you find the courage to love again. This could make you appear somewhat diffident, so allow those you care for time to get to know you in return.

Numerology

No. 3: Creative with the gift of imagination and an ability to communicate in writing, art or speech.

Tarot

Queen of Pentacles: There's something very earthy, if not a little 'witchy', about the woman depicted in this card. This is someone who loves being outdoors, is very in touch with nature and is never happier than when spending time in the garden. Probably an animal lover, too, and someone who is grounded by having both feet planted firmly on the earth. The lesson here is that you have everything you need for a happy life and it's worth remembering this if the grass sometimes looks greener on the other side of the fence.

Famous birthdays

Robin Williams American comedian and actor
Ernest Hemingway American writer
Josh Hartnett American actor

July 22nd

Flamboyant dramatist

You're unlikely to be someone who needs to be told life is yours for the taking, because if you see something you want, the chances are that you'll go for it without worrying too much if you can pay for it or if it's rightfully yours. Born in the sign of Leo, ruled by the Sun, there's something unshakeable in your belief that you can control your own destiny. This tendency might cause friction in close relationships, possibly because you don't want to hear anything that might contradict your world view and you probably enjoy a bit of drama, too. This may find you wherever the action is, centre stage, right in the thick of it, unlike those spectators you dismiss sitting on the side lines. Some people will find you a touch flamboyant and you may want to channel your obvious artistic flair and need for self-expression into a career where that quality excels, including fashion design or art curation. This penchant for drama may make it difficult to commit to a monogamous relationship, so bear in mind that this may be off-putting for some and may require a little more thoughtfulness in order for you to achieve the close harmony that you also cherish.

Numerology

No. 4: Invested in the physical world, centred earth energy that is practical in application.

Tarot

Knight of Wands: This card is all about flamboyance and drama, with the Knight of Wands racing into the world on his trusty horse, wielding his upright wand with emphasis. Wands are always depicted in leaf, full of life, and this card is about the individual journey that life will take you on. A knight is usually on a quest for some truth, however, as you may be, and this is another clue – it may take you some time to actually find what it is that you most require and desire.

Famous birthdays

Willem Dafoe American actor
Selena Gomez American singer
Don Henley American musician and singer-songwriter

July 23rd

Fiery idealist

You are likely to have such energy in life, it's as if the Lion (Leo) has waited patiently all this time, then been released and pounced. Idealistic and high-minded, you see yourself as starring in the movie of your own life where you are also the writer, director, producer and publicist. You stick to the narrative that you are here to blaze a trail that others will follow. What may not be immediately clear is that this narrative is also about doing the best for others, too. This in part encapsulates all it means to be born a Leo. The shadow side of a sunny nature and generous, leonine courage and strength, however, is likely to be a big ego, a whole lot of vanity and a tendency to self-indulge. You probably have a natural gift for performance and will do well in a career that plays to this strength. For a meaningful, long-term relationship, seek out a partner who will reciprocate your loving loyalty, but who will also understand your need for the space and freedom to go it alone from time to time, not just in body but also in mind. All that powerful energy needs some time out.

Numerology

No. 5: Impulsive and restless by nature, spontaneous and likes to discover the world through the senses.

Tarot

Strength: Not surprisingly, this card speaks of leonine energy but also of the strength, or fortitude, of the woman holding the lion. It's as well to remember that for strength to endure, it sometimes needs to be tempered by gentleness and working with others to achieve outcomes that support everyone. It can take a gentle gesture to realise this, and helps us to understand that working with, rather than against, our best interests sometimes involves pausing to consider the whole picture.

Famous birthdays

Woody Harrelson American actor and playwright
Daniel Radcliffe British actor
Alison Krauss American singer and musician

July 24th

Extrovert rescuer

You probably show up as a larger-than-life personality, ready to rescue those in need, and sometimes those who aren't. Your desire to make things better for people is admirable and will be with you for life. As you mature, it's likely that you will find it easier to work out who genuinely needs you and who doesn't. This is an important distinction and may save you from putting others so insistently ahead of yourself that you can become exhausted in the process. As you are also likely to be a strong character, this may be less of an issue, but it's worth being aware of it. You will do well in life, but you will want to be acknowledged for what you do, either as a leader or a senior team-mate, so you might be happiest self-employed or running your own business. Once you make a love match you will be a generous, loyal and affectionate partner, but this is not always unconditional, as you definitely expect to receive as much as you give. And as you give a lot, this may not always feel equal. Just reflecting on why this may occur immediately makes a difference and developing awareness of this possible tendency will help ensure a smoother ride.

Numerology

No. 6: Empathic and nurturing, can problem-solve in an emotional and physical way, responsible and cares deeply about family and friends.

Tarot

Four of Cups: The Cups represent emotions, and in this card a young man is being offered the chance to grow, to increase his empathy and understanding of the world and of others. Like all teenagers (with apologies, but we've all been one), he thinks he already has all the answers and knows best. Do you sometimes have a tendency to offer help without stopping to learn more about what is really going on or asking what help is actually needed? This card is telling you to turn off the transmission and turn on the receiving antennae just once in a while and listen, which will help you discern more.

Famous birthdays

Jennifer Lopez American singer and actress
Robert Graves British poet
Amelia Earhart American aviation pioneer

July

July 25th

Generous empath

As gregarious as any of the Lions that share your sign, you are likely to be an interesting mix of extrovert and introvert. This can make you hard to fathom because it can come across as two personalities, which is unexpected for the usually straightforward Leo. Your empathy and compassion towards others are genuine and while you share a love of admiration, you can and do put others first. You sometimes come across as an old soul or an old head on young shoulders, and you have such a generous and warm nature that others can see you as a 'soft touch', so make sure people don't take advantage of your kindness and sunny nature. You may choose to work as a counsellor or a campaigner where your empathic nature will be a good fit and where the air of mystery that surrounds you (it's as if you have the answers to some question the rest of us don't even know to ask) will reassure your clients. In matters of love you are passionate and loyal but need your freedom, while sometimes struggling to respect the same need for independence in a partner.

Numerology

No. 7: Very analytical and detail-oriented, likes to observe and investigate things, and has a keen, inventive eye.

Tarot

Nine of Wands: This card serves as something of a warning to those empaths and kind-hearted souls who have a tendency to give, give, give and, eventually, wake up one morning to discover there's nothing left for themselves. The Wands represent our communication not only with others, but also with ourselves, and in this card so many wands have been thrown away that there is only one left for support. This reiterates the warning above, which is not to let people take unfair advantage of your kind and generous nature.

Famous birthdays

Matt LeBlanc American actor
Rita Marley Cuban-Jamaican singer
Rosalind Franklin British chemist

July 26th

Witty charmer

You probably have so much *chutzpah*, you put the capital 'I' in 'individual', and where you lead, others will willingly follow. You were probably Headboy or Headgirl at school (or the equivalent) and with the confidence this early success gave you, you've not looked back since. Your naturally outgoing nature is likely to get you noticed, whether at work or among friends, as someone who doesn't really mind if people rate or ridicule you and your more unusual ideas, just as long as they are taking notice. A natural self-publicist, you may as well take these skills into the world of work and find or more likely create a role in the media, but you probably don't have the time or patience to write a book or build followers on Instagram. Patience, clearly, is unlikely to be one of your virtues but being strategic is, and this applies to your private life, too. However well people may think they know you, you will guard your private life fiercely and only drop your guard to those closest to you. You are a genuinely affectionate lover, and nothing is too much trouble for those whom you love and trust.

Numerology

No. 8: Sees the big picture and aims for it, linked to abundance and material wealth, and uses financial success to give back to others.

Tarot

Death: One of the powerful Major Arcana cards, this does not mean a literal death, rather it is a symbol for the death of something or some relationship that no longer serves your higher purpose. For you, this may be the death of the public persona you have created at the point where you decide it is time to step away from this and develop your inner resources, including your spirituality. And because it will have been your decision, this will not feel like a loss, although there may be a temporary sense of loss when something that has loomed large in life fades away. But this also creates room for new opportunities to become available to you.

Famous birthdays

Jacinda Ardern New Zealand prime minister
Sandra Bullock American actress
Carl Jung Swiss psychiatrist and psychoanalyst

July 27th

Competitive winner

There are some people who seem to be the glue that keeps a group, whether work, family or socially, together. For those born on this date, it's often a key feature of how they operate in the world. With a determined and dynamic character, you probably don't do anything by halves, but throw yourself into all your commitments and responsibilities with the energy of a lion. Self-assured, committed and idealistic, you are here to win, but that's not as selfish as it sounds because whatever the winnings, you will be happy to share and use your resources to make things better for everyone around you. You'll be naturally competitive in nature, even if you keep this hidden, and if you did opt for any sort of sporting career, you're more than likely to have a corporate back-up plan because one of your priorities is to make sure your family and those you love most are taken care of. In intimate relationships you have the characteristic Leo need for constant reassurance and attention, so look for a partner who understands that stroking your ego is likely to be an essential part of the deal between you.

Numerology

No. 9: An old soul that looks to spiritual awareness to solve life's problems and likes to help others to do so in the same way.

Tarot

The Emperor: This is a strong card because while there may be threats to the Emperor's throne, he's not rattled and won't be handing over his power any time soon. His power in this card is depicted by the sceptre and orb, symbols of monarchy, held securely in each hand. As a fire sign, it's the energy of the lion that gives you a strong self-belief, but this card amplifies your strength of purpose and commitment. It doesn't matter what others think, as you are secure in your own judgement.

Famous birthdays

Jo Durie British tennis player
Roxanne Hart American actress
Indiana Evans Australian actress and singer-songwriter

July 28th

Multi-talented strategist

The fact you are ruled by the Number 1 is quite telling in as much as it will be a lifelong challenge for you to learn your needs won't always come first and nor should they. You share a healthy competitive streak with your fellow Leos, but your task will be not to tip it over into something infinitely less attractive. You are likely to be a multi-talented individual, so that when this competitive nature is channelled in a healthy way, everyone wins. You'll soon realise that to get the acclaim you desire, you have to earn it, and your superb strategy skills will come to the fore to be used for the greater good. Keep in mind that admiration is not the same as love, so it may be necessary to reflect on the difference between the two. You may be a little bit combative in relationships, which can be tiresome for someone more laid-back, so be careful you don't alienate the very people you'd like to impress by coming across as selfish and inconsiderate. At work, you can be a force of nature and not least because you have no fear of confrontation or employing tactical game-play to outwit your opponent – all great qualities for a career in the military or in politics, of course.

Numerology

No. 1: A powerful entity and results-oriented force, all about initiating action and getting things done.

Tarot

The Chariot: There's something very single-minded about this card, and possibly about you. Maybe it's the determined glare of the chariot driver who is looking neither right not left but straight ahead, towards his goal. With some signs, the chariot (one of the Major Arcana cards) will be travelling at a genteel pace, but with you it's much more likely to be full throttle and full steam ahead, regardless of whoever and whatever is in the way. Maybe work on opening a space for negotiation to get around those obstacles instead of just riding rough-shod over them to get to what you want.

Famous birthdays

Jacqueline Kennedy Onassis Former First Lady of the United States
Barbara La Marr American actress and screenwriter
Sally Struthers American actress and activist

July

July 29th

Strong-willed leader

You share all the leadership potential of those born under this sun sign, but in your case, you're probably more interested in using those skills to lead a group or an organisation towards a better future that benefits all, rather than for yourself. You may find yourself working in social activism or politics or the law but, whichever field you choose, you are likely to motivate and inspire others with good organisational skills and a commitment to the greater cause. You show generosity towards your own tribe and feel very protective of the members of your own family (the Lion's 'pride'). While you've probably no objection to the idea of having a meaningful, mature relationship with a partner, you may just struggle to put your concern for others aside long enough to focus on one special person. If that's the case, don't be surprised if they don't wait around for you to ever prioritise them. There's a possible danger you could find it emotionally easier to give your all to the common good, so risking the ultimate sacrifice of neglecting your own happiness and emotional welfare.

Numerology

No. 2: Shows resilience and power in gentleness, often provides the role of mediator, and linked to psychic abilities.

Tarot

Nine of Cups: Busted! The trouble – or the great delight, depending on your point of view – of the Tarot is that it can sometimes turn a card where there is no place to hide! The Cups in the Tarot deck represent our emotions, so what is this character guarding and keeping safe? His feelings! Are you guilty of the same? Always putting the needs of everyone else before your own can sometimes be just another way of holding the people who would like to be closer to you at arm's length, while pretending that they don't matter to you. They do, so be sure to let them know it.

Famous birthdays

Benito Mussolini Italian dictator
Alexandra Paul American actress
Fernando Alonso Spanish F1 racing driver

July 30th

Logical thinker

You are unlikely to make any issue or apology about the trajectory you are on. Personal gain is likely to be your goal and since you are probably a clear-headed and logical thinker, you'll have no trouble working your way towards the lifestyle you've set your sights on, especially if you choose a career in finance or the corporate business world. You are likely to be able to accurately assess the situation in a room faster than anyone else, and to have devised a winning strategy, rarely losing a deal because of anything you have said or done. You will be a fantastic life partner for anyone sensible enough to be looking for someone caring and steadfast with whom to make a match and start a family, because you will make them feel they are the reason for working long hours. The paradox with you is that there is a whole other more creative layer just below the surface of this worldly-wise persona. You share your birthday with Emily Brontë, one of the greatest writers the world has ever seen, and it may be that you use creative writing, especially poetry, to decompress at the end of a tough working day.

Numerology

No. 3: Creative with the gift of imagination and an ability to communicate in writing, art or speech.

Tarot

Seven of Pentacles: This is the card that denotes financial success as a result of hard work and dedication, and not as the result of a lottery win or inheriting the family pile. The Pentacle in the Tarot is a talisman and represents our resources and what we might do with these. This card shows a pile of pentacles, signifying prosperity, that have been amassed and is being contemplated by someone considering what to do next with his treasure. Invest or spend, maybe?

Famous birthdays

Arnold Schwarzenegger Austrian actor and businessman
Lisa Kudrow American actress
Henry Ford American industrialist and founder of the Ford Motor Company

July 31st

Ambitious achiever

You may have a tendency to dream of applause, accolades and awards because, for you, success is probably defined by recognition and admiration. Because of this, you are likely to put the work in to achieve the material success and status you feel you deserve. You probably have a public face that is sunny and cheerful (your ruling planet is the Sun), but this may mask a steely determination to succeed at all costs. In matters of the heart, you are quite an old-fashioned traditionalist. Marriage and family are likely to be important to you and when you make a union you will want it to be one that is for life. You'll likely choose a high-profile career where the spotlight naturally falls, so entertainment, the media or even scientific research, as long as there's the hint of acclaim when you publish your brilliant findings. Words like 'razzmatazz' and 'pizazz' sum up your approach to life, although in your quieter times you may admit to a little vulnerability and allow those you trust to see that you are not always as confident as you seem. Part of the lesson for you in this life may be learning to manage, face and explore those insecurities.

Numerology

No. 4: Invested in the physical world, centred earth energy that is practical in application.

Tarot

Three of Pentacles: Unsurprisingly for an ambitious achiever, this is a card that suggests worldly fame and recognition. Here an apprentice is being elevated and may be in receipt of acknowledgement and reward. Translated to modern times, this could be the equivalent of a theatrical award or becoming the public-facing advisor expected to perform well on a televised debate. Fame of some description is literally written in the cards here. The warning is to avoid sacrificing everything for the limelight which can switch off just as quickly as it can be switched on.

Famous birthdays

Wesley Snipes American actor
J.K. Rowling British writer
Geraldine Chaplin American actress

August 1st

Born leader

Your fiery energy and sunny disposition pave the way for a charmed passage through life with you at the helm, and not only in charge of your own destiny, but frequently that of many others as well because your leadership skills are often very good. Like many Leos, you are also a natural performer, so could be drawn to the worlds of entertainment, sport or politics. Or you may choose the written word as your preferred platform, taking up your pen to entertain the masses as a writer of thrillers or historical romances. Talking of romance, there's no stage big enough to accommodate your lofty ideas of what it means to fall in love and woo or be courted. Unfortunately, this is your Achilles heel because no love affair is likely to live up to the grand romance in your head and will suffer because of some of the mundane necessities of everyday life. Remember this, that the security of the double bed has a lot to offer after the hurly-burly of the chaise longue, as the saying goes. When you do find someone willing to pamper, adore and love only you, remember that you can re-ignite earlier passion if it begins to wane rather than rushing off to find someone else.

Numerology

No. 1: A powerful entity and results-oriented force, all about initiating action and getting things done.

Tarot

Temperance: Temperance is always about balance and moderation and the ability to regulate our emotions, instead of feeling overwhelmed and swept away by them. Try and avoid the highs (followed by the lows) of extremes and work towards finding a more supportive and balanced middle path that you can comfortably rely on to see you through life's bigger challenges.

Famous birthdays

Herman Melville American writer
Jean-Baptiste Lamarck French naturalist
Yves Saint Laurent French fashion designer

August 2nd

Fiercely loyal

You are one of those straightforward people who doesn't waste time playing power games; you will steadily make your way to the top of your chosen career through a combination of hard work, diligence, an awareness of team values and good strong leadership skills. You are exceptionally well-organised at work, which means people know they can rely on you, and you may be drawn to a career built around innovation and science which will help satisfy the intellectual curiosity you have had since childhood. Over time, you gain the confidence to stand by your convictions, both at work and in your personal life, and you are never afraid to be the only person in the room standing up for a value you believe in or arguing a different course of action to that being championed by the herd. At home, you are a loving partner and a devoted parent. There is nothing more important to you than protecting the pride (your family) and you will move mountains to help your children find the happiness they seek as they step out into their independent lives.

Numerology

No. 2: Shows resilience and power in gentleness, often provides the role of mediator, and linked to psychic abilities.

Tarot

Two of Wands: This card depicts a wealthy merchant holding a small globe in his right hand, symbolising both his love of adventurous travel and the possibility, in the future, of broadening his horizons still further, based on the success he has already achieved. There is great enthusiasm for life, and in middle age you may well want to step out of your comfort zone into new experiences, which are likely to include travel.

Famous birthdays

Myrna Loy American actress
Peter O'Toole Irish actor
Wes Craven American actor and film-maker

August 3rd

Visionary wordsmith

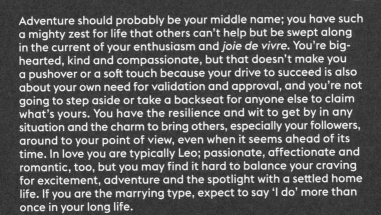

Adventure should probably be your middle name; you have such a mighty zest for life that others can't help but be swept along in the current of your enthusiasm and *joie de vivre*. You're big-hearted, kind and compassionate, but that doesn't make you a pushover or a soft touch because your drive to succeed is also about your own need for validation and approval, and you're not going to step aside or take a backseat for anyone else to claim what's yours. You have the resilience and wit to get by in any situation and the charm to bring others, especially your followers, around to your point of view, even when it seems ahead of its time. In love you are typically Leo; passionate, affectionate and romantic, too, but you may find it hard to balance your craving for excitement, adventure and the spotlight with a settled home life. If you are the marrying type, expect to say 'I do' more than once in your long life.

Numerology

No. 3: Creative with the gift of imagination and an ability to communicate in writing, art or speech.

Tarot

Six of Wands: This is the card of your leonine dreams depicted by a young man crowned with a victory wreath leading a celebratory procession into town. This is a card of triumph and success, praise, acclaim and pride. Like you, he is focused on the next goal. He has put distractions aside and can confidently expect a life well-lived and a successful outcome in all of his endeavours.

Famous birthdays

Martin Sheen American actor
Dolores del Rio Mexican actress
P.D. James British writer

August 4th

Rebellious persuader

You may not share her politics, but you do share the iron will of the UK's first ever female prime minister, Margaret Thatcher, who famously once said: 'The lady's not for turning.' This can mark you out as something of a loner. It's not that you don't care about others; in fact, you care a great deal about things like justice and fairness. So, you may even campaign and work to address these issues in society. But you tend to be very sure of your own opinion and, in childhood at least, this may have marked you out as someone with a rebellious streak and a problem with authority. Actually, it is less about your dislike of being told what to do or how to behave and more about your fear of losing any of your hard-won freedoms. All this is likely to be balanced by a persuasive charm that will enable you to work well with others should you choose. Try not to be suspicious of those who genuinely just want to help you and try not to push people away or you may end up a successful but very lonely Lion, which would be a shame as you are also capable of great love and commitment to those who share your values.

Numerology

No. 4: Invested in the physical world, centred earth energy that is practical in application.

Tarot

The Magician: For most people, the Magician appears in a reading as a reminder to draw on all their talents to reach their goals, including and especially those that are still untapped. He also shows up to remind us that we are all here to learn and, for you, as the saying goes, when the student is ready the teacher will appear, so be aware of this and be open to those who will help you explore and develop your full potential in life.

Famous birthdays

Louis Armstrong American jazz musician
Barack Obama 44th President of the United States
Percy Bysshe Shelley British Romantic poet

August 5th

Volatile individualist

Those born on this day are ruled by the Sun and it's likely that you care greatly about creating the most gorgeous kingdom to call your own, just like Louis XIV of France who was dubbed the Sun King. He took himself and his position very seriously, adopting the view that anything that was good for him was also good for the country, a sentiment you may share because you believe that what's good for you will also be good for your work colleagues, family and friends. You hide strong emotions behind an impressive self-discipline, which will serve you well whatever career you choose. You probably have a powerful need to express yourself, whether that is through the way you furnish your home or how you dress, which can be colourful, flamboyant and certainly stylish. Temperamentally, you may well have a tendency towards volatility, which can be a challenge in close relationships and even scary to quieter souls, but your leonine roar is genuinely worse than your bite. This volatility can mean you're exciting to be around and you are an ardent partner as long as you don't feel your freedom is being curtailed.

Numerology

No. 5: Impulsive and restless by nature, spontaneous and likes to discover the world through the senses.

Tarot

The World: One of the Major Arcana cards, this represents an invitation to step up and engage more fully with the external world in order to pursue and achieve goals and dreams. With you, it is more about stepping back into your internal world to find the courage to drop the mask and let others see who you really are. Whenever this card appears in a reading, it speaks of success, but it is also the very last card of the deck and as such denotes a pause, a breathing space if you like, before gathering all your resources to step out and into the next adventure.

Famous birthdays

Neil Armstrong American astronaut
Marine Le Pen French politician
Guy de Maupassant French writer

August 6th

Moral champion

The Number 6 of your birth date tempers the typically fiery and demanding nature of the Leo sun sign and you really are pretty chilled for most of the time. You are charming and easy-going, and your mild-mannered way of presenting yourself belies a strong will. You have no fear of pushing boundaries to make social, scientific or political progress on a global scale. You are also not afraid to let it be known that you have a strong moral code guiding you through the decisions you make, and it may be that you have and cherish a strong sense of faith and a commitment to a particular religion. Friendship and kinship are both very important to you, and again, you'll make no secret of your morals or the fact you prefer to be surrounded by those who, even if they don't share them, respect them. Love, romance and partnership are also important to you, although as you mature, you'll need to build in the time and space for solitude within the framework of a committed family life because changing the world takes time and energy, and sometimes all your resources.

Numerology

No. 6: Empathic and nurturing, can problem-solve in an emotional and physical way, responsible and cares deeply about family and friends.

Tarot

Five of Swords: Our hero has three of the five swords in his safekeeping but two remain on the ground. This is a card of potential conflict, and of overcoming the odds, but also serves as a warning as to the true cost of such skirmishes. There is no absolute winner, as nobody is walking off with all five swords. When you take on the problems of the world, you take on things many prefer not to see. You have some defences (three swords) but will need to take care to choose your battles wisely.

Famous birthdays

Robert Mitchum American actor
Andy Warhol American artist
Geri Halliwell British singer

August 7th

Sensitive soul

You love the limelight as much as the next Leo, but you may have a fear of anyone seeing quite how vulnerable you sometimes feel or discovering that you have a strong solitary streak and need plenty of downtime. You may have a tendency to be over-sensitive and can sometimes feel misunderstood and unappreciated, which can tempt you to show your Big Cat claws and snarl at those who offend you. Sometimes sentimental and easily moved to tears over the plight of others, if you do well in life, you're likely to want to share your good fortune via philanthropic and charitable giving. You are here, so you say, for the good times, so you may be guilty of a little over-indulgence when it comes to the good things in life. In love, you want to give all of yourself and feel madly loved and hugely appreciated right from the get-go. If this doesn't happen your elation can quickly turn to depression and it may take you a while (or more likely a new love affair) to feel like your bouncy self again. You like to feel good about yourself and those you love, so find a love match that feels the same.

Numerology

No. 7: Very analytical and detail-oriented, likes to observe and investigate things, and has a keen, inventive eye.

Tarot

Knight of Wands: Depicted by a knight riding into town in his full regalia, this is a card of action but sometimes without much forethought. Like you, this knight is not concerned about what dangers may lie ahead but feels on top of the world. The warning in this card is to be mindful, especially when it comes to matters of the heart, and avoid rushing in where angels fear to tread, as the saying goes.

Famous birthdays

Mata Hari Dutch courtesan and dancer
Bruce Dickinson British singer-songwriter
Megan Gale Australian actress

August 8th

Quiet performer

Whatever success comes your way – and there will be plenty of it – you will earn it all. Nothing is being handed to you on a plate, but unlike the cynic who knows the cost of everything and the value of nothing, you, more than most, understand the value of patience, determination, self-belief, resilience and hard work. You also know that once you reach the top of your chosen profession, you're unlikely to be toppled because you're standing on solid ground. You may have chosen a career in or around the limelight because you understand the power of personal narrative, but even those who know you well will sometimes find you reserved, watchful and in control of your emotions. You may also experience feelings of loneliness at times, but this will have nothing to do with whether you're alone or in a partnership, and probably dates from a period in your life when you had to learn to cope on your own. This experience may have made you more careful than most in your life choices, so that when you do choose a life partner you can be confident in that choice and that you will love and be loved for who you are.

Numerology

No. 8: Sees the big picture and aims for it, linked to abundance and material wealth, and uses financial success to give back to others.

Tarot

Five of Cups: This is the card of childhood sorrows, but it is also the card of those sorrows transcended by recognising these as lessons learned. It's tempting to see this solely as a card of grief, but it reminds us we have much to learn through this experience and can emerge stronger, kinder, more compassionate and more determined to help others avoid going through similar pain.

Famous birthdays

Keith Carradine American actor and singer-songwriter
Dustin Hoffman American actor
Roger Federer Swiss tennis player

August 9th

Witchy warrior

Witches and wiccans (the ones working for the greater good) hold the annual Feast of the Fire Spirits on this day, which you probably already know because you are no doubt highly sensitive and possibly even psychic, even if you don't want to be. You may also have had an imaginary friend as a child, who felt as real to you as any of your school mates. In addition to this sensitive side, you are likely to have a classic Leo drive towards, and need for, success and recognition, but combined with a need for privacy and solitude. This could mean that you may spend your twenties and thirties flipping between these competing needs until you find a balance that suits you. People can sometimes mistake your soft heart and kindness for weakness and may get a rude awakening if they do, because being on the receiving end of the roar of the Lion is not to be underrated as you won't be taken for a fool. Creative and idealistic, you may gravitate towards social work, music, art or a particular religious practice. Eventually, you will embrace your deep-rooted spiritual nature and find peace, with one foot in this world and the other in your dreams.

Numerology

No. 9: An old soul that looks to spiritual awareness to solve life's problems and likes to help others to do so in the same way.

Tarot

Queen of Swords: Here the Queen of Swords is depicted gazing fixedly straight ahead because she has the clarity of vision and understanding of a mature woman, and while she can and will (thanks to her sword) offer great protection, she is really about self-reliance and listening to your own truths. She will protect all those who need her help but, like you, she will not be taken advantage of and if you try it, you will feel the edge of her tongue.

Famous birthdays

Whitney Houston American singer
Melanie Griffith American actress
Eric Bana Australian actor and comedian

August 10th

Powerful influencer

The phrase 'larger than life' might have been invented for you and often applies to those born on this day. At any gathering, all eyes tend to focus on you because there's something charismatic about you. You are likely to be creative with an eye for the fantastic, with a strong sense of destiny shared with other Leo sun signs, so unsurprisingly where you go others tend to follow. You thrive on excitement and wilt when confronted by anything ordinary and mundane, and there's a pretty good chance your entrepreneurial spirit has been evident since your early teens. In matters of the heart, your self-assurance and love of the limelight may prove too much for some, so you may need to temper some of that Leo fire. But if you find someone who is a match for you in the confidence stakes, there may be quite a bit of jostling for pole position before you figure out a way you can both enjoy the spotlight while cherishing the private moments together that are yours alone to share.

Numerology

No. I: A powerful entity and results-oriented force, all about initiating action and getting things done.

Tarot

Two of Swords: This card depicts a blindfolded woman with two swords held crossed in front of her and a crescent moon above. This is a card of quiet meditation and suggests there may need to be more of a balance in your life to ensure that you can make best use of all that energy without burning out. Remember to factor in some more contemplative, restorative times for the good of your body and soul.

Famous birthdays

Antonio Banderas Spanish actor
Rosanna Arquette American actress
Leo Fender American inventor and guitar-maker

August 11th

Forensic researcher

What are you after, sitting there hour after hour examining the evidence again and again? The truth, naturally. You were born for detective work, either as a police officer, a scientific researcher, a lawyer, a social justice campaigner or, indeed, anyone else for whom the truth holds such importance. Sometimes, there will be a flash of insight – genius even – thanks to a psychic hunch, so don't ignore these. You have the Leo yen for drama and excitement to banish the mundane from daily life, but the Number 2 of your birthday tempers that and you are less self-mythologising than many who share your sign. You really do want to use your talents to make the world a better place and if a little status, money and admiration come your way in doing so, that's all to the greater good. Your tendency to whittle away until you get to the truth and then to speak it boldly, regardless of the consequences for yourself or others, can make intimate relationships difficult. You are a generous and loyal lover, but may need to lighten up a little if you are serious about a long-term union.

Numerology

No. 2: Shows resilience and power in gentleness, often provides the role of mediator, and linked to psychic abilities.

Tarot

Ten of Wands: This is a card of responsibility, depicting a young man carrying the heavy load of ten large wands towards a home on the horizon. For you, this card is a reminder of the need to take better care of yourself as you dig for the truth, wherever you need to dig and wherever you need to go to do so. Make sure you don't burn out before you get the answers you are seeking, and allow others to help you.

Famous birthdays

Alyson Stoner American actress, singer and dancer
Viola Davis American actress
Chris Hemsworth Australian actor

August

239

August 12th

Logical thinker

When assessing a new situation or looking for the answer to a conundrum you don't just cast your net mid-stream and hope for the best. You have an appreciation that a solution is as likely to lie overlooked in the past as in the future, and so will adopt a forensic approach to working out what's going on, who's involved, what's not being said and why: all great qualities for some kind of investigative career, particularly in the media. Your communication skills are second only to your research skills and powers of observation, and the more you hone these traits, the better you will be able to see off all pretenders to your primetime throne. There's a danger when you're as good as you are at persuading others to your point of view that you'll end up dominating every conversation and stifling all debate. Avoid this unless you don't mind taking off your studio mic and heading home to eat alone. Patience is a virtue and if you are to enjoy harmonious relationships with your lover and family, you might want to work on this elusive part of your otherwise charismatic and attractive character.

Numerology

No. 3: Creative with the gift of imagination and an ability to communicate in writing, art or speech.

Tarot

The Knight of Cups: This Knight is happy to move forwards, always forwards, at a slow but steady pace. He, like you, has his eyes set firmly on the prize and there is nothing in the barren landscape that surrounds him to detract him from his goal. He is depicted as carrying the cup in his right hand, careful not to let his emotions spill. And, like you, he is on a mission to leave behind a better world than the one he rode into.

Famous birthdays

Mark Knopfler British guitarist and singer-songwriter
Helena Blavatsky Russian philosopher and writer
Cara Delevingne British model and actress

August 13th

Ambitious workaholic

With the Number 4 comes a huge sense of responsibility and, as a result, it's not unusual for those of you with this birthday to slip into the habits of an ambitious workaholic. You are super competent and always at least ten steps ahead of the competition, but unless you learn to trust others and delegate, then burnout is a serious risk. You need, even crave, the respect and admiration of others (even if the opposite seems true), but you are more than willing to earn it and so will go the extra mile to achieve both work and personal goals. And when you get the success you have worked so hard for, you can bask in a warm glow of pride in your achievements, knowing you've done all this yourself and so you're not beholden to anyone else. In matters of the heart, you are a warm and passionate lover but can become a little bit clingy and possessive, especially when you feel your partner is preoccupied by something (other than you) and you're not getting the attention that all Leos crave. Try supporting your partner when they have demands on their time and energy and you will be rewarded by a deeper sense of connection and a more mature love that will stand the test of time.

Numerology

No. 4: Invested in the physical world, centred earth energy that is practical in application.

Tarot

King of Wands: This successful man is all about skilled communication, so it may be that you have chosen to take your skills into teaching or science or some other field where the need to convey ideas and explore solutions is critical. He also has the ability to make people from all walks of life feel at ease, which is another useful attribute in life.

Famous birthdays

Alfred Hitchcock British director
Fidel Castro Cuban revolutionary and politician
John Logie Baird Scottish inventor of television

August 14th

Global change-maker

You are likely to have the ability to read the room and assess people's true motivations, regardless of what they are saying or doing. An intuitive ability to apparently read people's minds is a useful skill in journalism, documentary film-making and social justice campaigning. You are nobody's fool and won't think twice about giving someone an honest appraisal of their own character if you think it means they will change their ways for the better. You probably enjoy people-watching and can happily spend time scrutinising the words and actions of everyone you meet. This might be fun, and even invaluable in your profession, but people don't like being judged or scrutinised, and if you're not careful, you'll find it hard to make meaningful personal relationships. Try and work on developing a little more empathy. You'll be a better social commentator or documentarian if you bother to think about why someone is acting the way they are and then those who want to get close to you will be less scared to do so.

Numerology

No. 5: Impulsive and restless by nature, spontaneous and likes to discover the world through the senses.

Tarot

The World: With such exceptional observational and analytical skills, there's a strong probability you will work on a global stage and what this card (one of the Major Arcana in the Tarot deck) tells us is that everything is aligned for the work you have come here to do. Whatever your vision, now is the time to use all the resources and channels at your disposal to disseminate and share it.

Famous birthdays

Halle Berry American actress
Marcia Gay Harden American actress
Steve Martin American actor and comedian

August 15th

Extrovert leader

You were born to lead and so will flourish in any work environment and field where you not only have the freedom to set the strategy but the privilege of leading a team. You are likely to develop extremely logical and practical skills to help formulate and execute a strategy, and you hold yourself to the same high standards, at home and at work, that you set for others. If you've chosen a career in the world of business, you will rapidly work your way up to management or if you work in sales, it won't be long before you are leading the regional team. Take care, though, that you don't unwittingly slide into becoming too bossy and authoritarian; a good leader is also a good listener and has the confidence to be able to accommodate ideas that may come from others but are better than those he or she has proposed. When it comes to love and finding your life partner, you are open, warm and hugely generous, but try not to overwhelm your loved ones with your commanding nature. Work on developing even more empathy towards those you love, and those you work with, and remember you, too, are here to learn and grow.

Numerology

No. 6: Empathic and nurturing, can problem-solve in an emotional and physical way, responsible and cares deeply about family and friends.

Tarot

Six of Pentacles: This card speaks to us of both great generosity and a commitment to social justice. We see a mature and successful merchant holding an old-fashioned balancing scale and distributing alms to the needy. It signifies a person who cares deeply and who will work towards a society that is fair for all.

Famous birthdays

Ben Affleck American actor
Jennifer Lawrence American actress
Walter Scott Scottish writer

August 16th

Innovative visionary

You're a more complex person than it might first appear. An idealist, you may seem a tad crusading when it comes to the causes you support, but there's often a trail of mystery in your wake and not everyone can quite figure you out. On the outside, you're charm personified, but on the inside you probably have more than a passing interest in esoteric and spiritual matters. These two traits make for an attractive combination and you'll never be short of admirers, but beneath the surface, you are focused on achieving your goals, and since you think like a visionary, there are very few that can keep up with you. Those that can't often end up mistrusting you, which means you will probably work best and most happily when you work alone. Likely to be extremely loyal, almost to a fault, you expect this to be returned in a romantic partnership. If not, you're likely to become a little possessive, not wishing to grant your partner the same independence you value so highly for yourself. Address this as a priority, to ensure a loving, long-term relationship.

Numerology

No. 7: Very analytical and detail-oriented, likes to observe and investigate things, and has a keen, inventive eye.

Tarot

Judgement: One of the powerful Major Arcana cards of the Tarot deck, Judgement is a wake-up call. You may not think this applies to you, but ask yourself, is something getting in the way of genuine connections with others? Are you holding someone who wants to love you at arm's length because you are afraid of being truly known? Ponder this and the answer will come. Then you can do something about it, before it is too late.

Famous birthdays

Madonna American singer and actress
Charles Bukowski German writer
Angela Bassett American actress

August 17th

Independent trailblazer

Determined to live life on your own terms, you are 'one of a kind' and likely to be so strong-willed that you will have an equal number of devoted fans and unimpressed detractors. The truth is, you won't much care whether you offend people because if they don't agree with you, then, in your world, they simply don't exist. You are made for public life or a work environment where being in charge or questioning the *status quo* – teacher, campaigning activist, team leader – is seen as a plus. You are unlikely to back down about what you hold dear and so you may find your personal relationships can be volatile, which can be draining for all parties. Protective and generous to those whom you love, you may struggle to feel quite so loving when family members try and go their own way. Try and see that this is no different than when you chose an equally independent path. Make time to listen to and consider their reasoning in a respectful way, especially if it is your children shaking off the shackles, or you will just come across as a bully and someone others may choose to avoid.

Numerology

No. 8: Sees the big picture and aims for it, linked to abundance and material wealth, and uses financial success to give back to others.

Tarot

Three of Pentacles: This card is all about public recognition of some kind. The man depicted is being honoured and perhaps he is being shown the itinerary for a day of celebrations to be held in his honour. Whatever the details, the key message is that public recognition is likely to be a feature of the contribution you've made, possibly campaigning to help create a better society.

Famous birthdays

Robert de Niro American actor and director
Mae West American actress and comedian
Maureen O'Hara Irish actress and singer

August 18th

Selfless crusader

Injustice in any form, to your fellow man or animals, is likely to offend you and you are equally likely to step in without immediate concern for the consequences. While this makes you a selfless crusader, it does not always serve you well, so one of your challenges may be to stop and think before you jump in. You can be a complicated mix of confident and unsure, action and inaction, and while you enjoy the same excitement your fellow Leos seek, you also yearn for a tranquil and quiet home life. You are also likely to have an artistic temperament, which will make you well suited to acting, music, writing, art, design, politics, social work or religion. In fact, the latter may become an important focal point for you since you have a deep interest in spiritual matters and will want your life choices to be underpinned by a deep faith in whatever you believe in. You can be as impulsive in love as you are in your fight for justice, but try not to let your heart completely rule your head when you consider a partner as the potential for a happy and meaningful union might elude you.

Numerology

No. 9: An old soul that looks to spiritual awareness to solve life's problems and likes to help others to do so in the same way.

Tarot

Ace of Swords: The ace cards in the Tarot deck tell us there is a great deal of spiritual support for the path taken, especially when motivated to fight injustice and improve society for all its citizens. The Swords indicate mental agility, quick thinking and an ability to slice through perceived obstacles to our goals.

Famous birthdays

Edward Norton American actor
Patrick Swayze American actor and dancer
Robert Redford American actor, director and activist

August 19th

Shining star

You probably believe you were born to love and be loved, and you probably have the sort of charisma that lights up a room. In fact, you appear to have been born under a lucky star and are likely to have such a lovely zest for life that it would be impossible to ignore you for long. But you also win fans for your willingness to tell it like it is and speak your truth, and often find yourself shaking others out of their complacency or hypocrisy. Enthusiastic, optimistic and industrious, you are happy to throw yourself into every project and seldom shy away from taking your share of responsibility. This means that whatever your talent and whatever path you take, there is a starring aspect in its outcome. Whatever you choose to make your career or role in life is likely to be a success, for you are astute enough to choose what most reflects your abilities. In order to also accomplish another of your goals, a secure and happy relationship with a similarly like-minded soul, the challenge will be not to let the brightness of your own star blind you to that of others. Keep the romance in your life for sure, but temper it with some reality, otherwise you might find yourself slightly out of step with your partner from time to time.

Numerology

No. I: A powerful entity and results-oriented force, all about initiating action and getting things done.

Tarot

Ten of Cups: This is considered to be one of the most joyous cards in the entire Tarot deck. The Cups represent our emotions and ten cupfuls provides us with plenty. The happy family depicted on this card is also framed by a rainbow which sparkles over the entire landscape, reinforcing your sense that you were born into a happy and hopeful world.

Famous birthdays

Matthew Perry American actor
Bill Clinton 42nd President of the United States
Coco Chanel French fashion designer

August 20th

Charming diplomat

You are a highly skilled networker, and sometimes, occasionally to your own detriment, a people-pleaser. This is because you are all about the collective and think in terms of the greater good, which also makes you an excellent and thoughtful life partner. Charming, gracious and competent in whatever you take on, you have the ability to move back and forth with ease between different social circles and so have become the consummate diplomat. You are fun to be around because you are likely to enjoy and be stimulated by the company of others. In the workplace the word 'collaborative' was invented for you, since you are all about joint ventures and activities. You will do very well in any public-facing role such as charity work, public relations, political lobbying or running an NGO which needs more money. Thanks to your good connections, success is likely to be yours, but be careful you don't lose yourself in all this to-ing and fro-ing between such different networks or organisations. You need to stay clear about your own needs and goals, too, so it's important to keep these in mind to avoid over-stretching yourself. Look for a life partner who is your equal in terms of competence but also one who knows the value of intimacy and support, as these are important to you, too.

Numerology

No. 2: Shows resilience and power in gentleness, often provides the role of mediator, and linked to psychic abilities.

Tarot

Seven of Cups: This card is about knowing what is really important in life and making sure it is available, which is highly relevant to you. The Cups represent our emotional life and six out of the seven depicted contain what we might desire or be tempted by. The contents of the seventh cup is an obscured figure, reminding us to pay attention to what we know at heart is important to us.

Famous birthdays

Robert Plant English singer-songwriter
Joan Allen American actress
Demi Lovato American singer-songwriter

August 21st

High-minded idealist

Your inner narrative is one of you as a hero blazing a trail for others to follow in order to make the world a better place. In your quieter moments you might recognise this sense of destiny, but how to achieve it might not be clear for some time. You might also find the mundane necessity of graft tricky to reconcile with your blue-sky concepts, but what's clear is that you are probably happiest doing things your own way and only dipping into the collective when needs must. Happily, there are many career paths that will not only afford you this personal freedom but celebrate your ideas and ability to plan: project management, publishing, media, advertising or some aspect of higher education. You can often cut a somewhat solitary, even lonely, figure in your professional life, but there's a whiff of romance about being seen this way so, again, this may suit you. In matters of actual romance, you like the idea of love, partnership and undying loyalty, but the reality may prove a tad confining for you. Try and push through this barrier because a foundation of loving support given and received can really ground and replenish you.

Numerology

No. 3: Creative with the gift of imagination and an ability to communicate in writing, art or speech.

Tarot

Eight of Cups: Often, a hero's journey is a tale of emotional pain overcome and a transition from ignorance to understanding. For example, we may travel the world only to arrive back at the same place, but this time with a greater understanding of ourselves and our goals in life. What we also learn, and which this card reminds us of, is that it's often through trial and error that important lessons are mastered.

Famous birthdays

Carrie-Anne Moss Canadian actress
Usain Bolt Jamaican athlete
Kenny Rogers American singer and musician

August 22nd

Secretly sensitive

Like all those born close to the cusp between two different sun signs, you could be something of a mix of what has gone before (Leo) and what is being heralded (Virgo). Like all Leos, you will probably tend towards an artistic temperament with a possible flair for the dramatic, but sometimes, like Virgo, you can be painstaking and analytical, which could make you an intriguing if sometimes contradictory blend. You may also have big-picture ideas married to a scrupulous attention to detail, which is a great combination and your secret weapon for success at work, whatever career you choose. With a tendency to be gregarious and fun-loving, you can occasionally come across as picky and judgemental, and the difficulty for you can sometimes be working out whether to listen to your heart or your head. You might struggle with this but, eventually, since you are a Leo, you're more likely to follow your heart. In your relationships you probably express more balance than the more overtly romantic Leos, but your heart is genuinely big and warm, and unless you are disappointed once too often or your partner doesn't quite live up to your high ideals, you probably won't have much reason to be otherwise.

Numerology

No. 4: Invested in the physical world, centred earth energy that is practical in application.

Tarot

Temperance: Could there be a better representation of what you sometimes feel? Temperance is about harmonising and balancing two things, and this card is a depiction of the eternal struggles of duality. Life/death, good/evil, light/dark and, in your case, flamboyant/retiring. This card speaks of the challenge in learning to regulate between head and heart which, for you, is likely to be lifelong.

Famous birthdays

John Lee Hooker American musician and blues legend
Tori Amos American singer-songwriter
Pope Leo XII Former Italian pope

August 23rd

Analytical achiever

Your birthday brings us to the first day of a new sun sign, Virgo, whose key characteristics, which will show up in some form in everyone born under this sign, include cleverness, quick thinking, orderliness and sometimes a mercurial streak. Sound familiar? You can sometimes give the appearance of being somewhat aloof, but that can be a defence mechanism to shield you from your own feelings, rather than a lack of caring. You'd rather be thinking about intellectual or physical challenges and if you are honest, it might be your emotions that make you feel uncomfortable. You may choose a caring profession that combines practicality with hands-on organisation, merging your strengths in a career that is related to people but possibly at arm's length. Whatever path you choose, your work life is often prioritised, sometimes to the detriment of your personal relationships. In romantic unions you can be nurturing and caring, but then flip suddenly into pickiness which is not nice to be around. So, take care to choose someone who understands your critical streak, won't take offence, won't try to cramp your style and, just as importantly, afford them the same courtesies.

Numerology

No. 5: Impulsive and restless by nature, spontaneous and likes to discover the world through the senses.

Tarot

Two of Wands: This is a card about success and possibly on a world stage, but this may come at a price, so it presents you with a positive prediction but also a question. Yes, the success you wish for can be yours as you are willing to work hard for it, but do love and personal happiness have to be sacrificed to achieve those goals? There is no right or wrong answer, just what is right for you.

Famous birthdays

River Phoenix American actor
Gene Kelly American dancer and actor
Louis XVI Last King of France after 1789 French Revolution

August 24th

Psychological explorer

Those born on this date are likely to be life's observers. Highly engaged with learning about others and what makes them tick, you may have an almost clinical interest in human behaviour. You could make a gifted therapist, counsellor or psychoanalyst, or you may just be drawn into a field where you can comment on human behaviours as a writer, artist or songwriter. The realms of human relationships and of social systems will be a lifelong fascination for you, however you choose to use the knowledge you gain from studying them. You may have a tendency to focus on the smallest detail in your quest for knowledge, which will make you a formidable researcher, so perhaps your path will take you down a more academic route. In your own personal relationships, you are affectionate but realistic and all too aware of the ebb and flow of loving relationships. You may sometimes be a touch too objective about those you love, which could appear as criticism, so be mindful of the power of the words you use as, once spoken, they may be difficult to take back. Tempering your clear-eyed vision with love should help, and remember that discretion is often the better part of valour.

Numerology

No. 6: Empathic and nurturing, can problem-solve in an emotional and physical way, responsible and cares deeply about family and friends.

Tarot

King of Cups: Grounded and calm, the king depicted in this card is blessed with great insight, represented by the Cups. His real strength lies in the fact that he actively likes people and is fascinated by them. So, he is truly motivated to do his best by them. The ability to take an unprejudiced view of people is helpful in all relationships, and this is something that probably comes quite easily to you.

Famous birthdays

Anne Archer American actress
Jean-Michel Jarre French composer and musician
Stephen Fry British actor and comedian

August 25th

Original thinker

Editors and publishers often use a phrase that they all intuitively understand but struggle to explain when asked to put into words; they talk about a writer's 'voice'. This is something you too understand intuitively because, whether or not you write, you have developed a 'voice'. Some may share your vision, others may question it, and there will be others still who just tell you that you've got it all wrong, but no one will deny that it's uniquely yours. You will probably use this voice to campaign for what you believe in and you are likely to retain an altruistic streak, in one form or another, throughout your life. It is as if your voice is your anchor, your guide and your moral compass. You were probably born kind-hearted and caring, and these qualities are natural to you and those that are likely to be remembered about you, whatever path you choose. The only place where your voice might let you down is in your intimate relationships, where you may feel shy about expressing your own needs. Your partner will quickly learn that you tend to show love through actions more than words, and that your devotion is sincere.

Numerology

No. 7: Very analytical and detail-oriented, likes to observe and investigate things, and has a keen, inventive eye.

Tarot

The High Priestess: Like you, our bookish and intuitive High Priestess is a student of human life and behaviours. She, like you, may sometimes appear somewhat detached from the hurly-burly of everyday life with its transitory gains and eternal losses. And she is both teacher and eternal student, loving to learn and sharing her values and ideas.

Famous birthdays

Sean Connery Scottish actor
Tim Burton American director
Claudia Schiffer German model and actress

August

August 26th

True romantic

You may occasionally have the tell-tale rather aloof exterior of a typical Virgo, but at heart your greatest expression is through romance. You have a passion for relationships and while you can still be a bit moody and tricky to live with at the start of a new relationship, once you have conquered your insecurities, you are loving, loyal and absolutely dependable. Ambitious in work and life, you probably have the patience to wait, keeping your cards close to your chest until the time is right, holding out for the best possible opportunity before making your 'Big Move' in both love and your career. Fools may rush in where angels fear to tread, but you won't be among them and this sets you apart from the crowd, which is often inclined to jump on the first thing that comes their way so as not to get left behind. With such a good Virgoan analytical mind combined with the passion that is your trump card, you would probably do well in business or industry, education, government or science. While you tend to proceed with caution and will closely scrutinise all aspects of a situation before deciding on the best course of action, this is a good route to success that you trust and which will instil trust in others, too.

Numerology

No. 8: Sees the big picture and aims for it, linked to abundance and material wealth, and uses financial success to give back to others.

Tarot

The Lovers: You have no intention of passing through this life without the joy of a great love and if you have to wait until middle age to find it, so be it. You just know, deep down in your gut, that your soulmate is out there, and your paths will cross. The Lovers card is elusive in readings and rarely shows up. Why? Because most people settle for something less than the soulmate relationship you're holding out for.

Famous birthdays

Macaulay Culkin American actor
Mother Mary Teresa Albanian-Indian Roman Catholic nun and saint
Shirley Manson Scottish singer-songwriter and actress

August 27th

Natural healer

You may not have chosen healing as your formal career path, but if not, you may end up involved in the healing arts in some way because you have both a natural gift and a strong desire to be of service to your fellow humans (and probably to animals, too). Insightful, observant and mentally sharp, you have the ability to listen carefully to what someone has to say before giving counsel and you have an uncanny ability to cut right to the heart of things. With a strong moral compass, you may come across as a little judgemental at times, but you are actually lighter in spirit than most initially realise. This is because Virgo's ruling planet, Mercury, has probably given you the gift of witty repartee and this you use to your advantage both at work and at play. Just be careful that your wit doesn't turn to sarcasm, which could wound more sensitive souls. You won't be short of admirers because there's usually a genuine warmth and positive interest in others in your interactions that makes you a good listener and which is part of your healing capacity. In love, you are warm, funny and romantic, and expect the same in return.

Numerology
No. 9: An old soul that looks to spiritual awareness to solve life's problems and likes to help others to do so in the same way.

Tarot
Ace of Wands: This is a very powerful, positive card and all about being an ace in communication, a skill that already lies at the heart of your potential healing capacity. It is up to you to decide whether you accept this gift or use it in some profession that benefits both you and those around you.

Famous birthdays
Lyndon B. Johnson 36th President of the United States
Tom Ford American fashion designer
Jamala Ukrainian singer-songwriter and actress

August 28th

Fiercely independent

There's probably no following the crowd or going along with the herd for you. Being independent is a natural state of affairs and you probably can't understand why anyone wouldn't relish it. You can tend towards perfectionism (which can be a source of irritation to others), so when you commit to something this can lead to spectacular success because this is usually combined with a highly rational mind and the ability to communicate new ideas to diverse audiences. All of which makes you perfect for scientific research and business leadership, but also the literary arts. Like many Virgos, that Mercury influence also ensures a quick sense of humour, which helps balance some of that analytical intensity. You enjoy the romantic side of relationships but ultimately you are probably more interested in forming a partnership based on a meeting of minds, which underpins everything for you, than on grand romantic gestures and teenage butterflies. Emotionally, you can sometimes struggle with strong feelings, with a tendency to blow hot and cold, which could leave a partner feeling confused. This is often just a sign of less-obvious insecurities, so be aware of this and understand your own need to feel secure.

Numerology

No. 1: A powerful entity and results-oriented force, all about initiating action and getting things done.

Tarot

Seven of Wands: The Wands in the Tarot deck signify our communication skills and not surprisingly (since communication is likely to be one of your key skill sets) we see plenty of them in this card. But this card also brings a gentle warning, which is that learning to bend a little and knowing when to yield can also be a fruitful communication strategy.

Famous birthdays

Jason Priestley Canadian actor
Jack Black American actor and comedian
John Betjemen British poet

August 29th

Team player

You're a great believer in the work hard, play hard maxim and as a result, whatever success comes your way will probably have been earned through diligence and attention to detail. You hate being alone, have zero interest in being independent and won't be happy until you've met and bonded for life with your chosen mate. The only word of caution is to avoid falling in love with the idea of being in love, so make sure you choose someone who is equally able to return your commitment. You tend to hate discord of any kind and will work hard to keep the peace at home and at work. Happily, you have buckets of tact and even a smidge of psychic foresight, which makes you a skilled diplomat, probably more than able to both build and repair bridges. Because you set such high standards of behaviour for yourself, you are frequently disappointed by others falling short of perfection. Try and curb this because nobody likes being judged and found wanting, and for all you know they may be doing the very best they can under circumstances you know nothing about.

Numerology

No. 2: Shows resilience and power in gentleness, often provides the role of mediator, and linked to psychic abilities.

Tarot

Strength: This is a great card for you because your real strength is actually hidden from the world and only revealed to those closest to you. This strength has nothing to do with physical prowess or any show of force but arises directly from your self-restraint. It takes fortitude (strength) to hold back, make a calm assessment and only act when you have all the information you need to make an important decision.

Famous birthdays

Rebecca de Mornay American actress
Richard Attenborough British director
Ingrid Bergman Swedish actress

August 30th

Shrewd investigator

With your clever mind and deeply rooted interest in people and what makes them tick, you're not about to take anything you see or hear at face value. You probably need constant mental stimulation and, growing up, may have driven your parents nuts with your questions. You share your fellow Virgoans love of orderliness and need for perfection, but you are a little more adaptable and pragmatic than many and are even prepared to compromise if it makes the difference between reaching a goal or not. You like nothing better than working out someone's hidden agenda or strategy and then implementing one of your own. It may sound obvious, but you would relish police work or a career in academic research or work related to documentary film-making or investigative journalism. Both the written and spoken word come easily to you and with your unusual adaptability you may even strike out on your own as an entrepreneur. In matters of love you may feel the need to take all the responsibility for a relationship, but you need to remember that love works best when it's a two-way thing. Being aware that this tendency may arise from your own insecurities can help you accept another's equal need to contribute to what makes it work between you.

Numerology

No. 3: Creative with the gift of imagination and an ability to communicate in writing, art or speech.

Tarot

The Chariot: Sometimes this card signifies a steady direction of travel from A to B, but in your case the direction is probably not the issue because you know exactly where you are going and how to get there. Independence is a fine thing, but great joy can be found in learning to trust another, so you can probably ease up on the reins a little and share responsibility for this ride.

Famous birthdays

Cameron Diaz American actress
Anne-Marie of Greece Former Queen of Greece, born in Denmark
Joan Blondell American actress

August 31st

Hardworking pragmatist

Efficiency could be your middle name since you probably have little time for time-wasting or procrastination. You want to see practical results in return for investing your time and energy, so when a process needs streamlining, or someone needs to create order out of chaos, you are highly likely to be considered for the job. One of your key strengths is your ability to stay focused, avoiding would-be distractions until you've got the task done. You are well suited to a career in finance or business where the bottom line counts, but you are also likely to have a strong social conscience and may actually prefer to give your talents to a shared project that improves things for your local community. As a partner you are reliable and make a virtue of being so, and this often compensates for a Virgo inclination to criticise others if they fall short of your high personal standards. When you first fall in love you can be as sentimental, romantic and idealistic as the most passionate of lovers, but you may struggle when you have to accept the gap between your dreams and everyday reality. Most of all, you like to be admired for your hard work and good sense, and you may choose a path that makes this likely rather than one where your efforts go unnoticed and unpraised.

Numerology

No. 4: Invested in the physical world, centred earth energy that is practical in application.

Tarot

Three of Cups: Good friendships are very important to you and this happy card symbolises the importance of the efforts of a group sharing a common goal and the role of community in our lives. These are values you are likely to cherish, too, and the appearance of this card for your birth date tells you something you hopefully already know: you have much to celebrate and be thankful for.

Famous birthdays

James Coburn American actor
Van Morrison Irish singer-songwriter
Richard Gere American actor

September 1st

Silver-tongued persuader

You have such great self-knowledge and confidence in who you are, what you want and where you are heading in life that you're unlikely to have problems persuading others to come on board and help fight the good fight to improve the world for all. You're not averse to simultaneously bettering yourself and your own status as a result of your sterling efforts and will probably take the view that what matters most is not anyone's true motivation but getting the outcome you want. You are definitely more of a charmer than a fighter and use your eloquence to convert others to your way of thinking. One of the most admirable things about you is your ability to remain steadfast in the face of adversity, which also makes you one of the best people to have around in a crisis. You may take to performing or writing, or a career in sales and retail; anything where you can use your considerable powers of persuasion. Be careful you don't become so goal-orientated that you neglect your personal life and those trying to love and support you. You value that support but need to give something back in order to keep a healthy balance.

Numerology

No. 1: A powerful entity and results-oriented force, all about initiating action and getting things done.

Tarot

The Hermit: One of the important Major Arcana cards, the Hermit may be lighting the way for others, trying to reach the same elevated position or trying to find his way back from reflective solitude. The message is that it's fine, necessary sometimes, to retreat but also important not to stay away for too long.

Famous birthdays

Barry Gibb British singer-songwriter
Gloria Estefan Cuban-American singer-songwriter
Lily Tomlin American actress

September 2nd

Courteous diplomat

If anyone is going to get what they want without offending others, it's likely to be those born on this day, because they have such impeccably good manners that they can easily sidestep objections without anyone noticing they've been outclassed. You may appear to be more chilled than many who share your sun sign, but only because you're better at hiding your true feelings and somehow know intuitively there are lots of ways to get what you want without causing confrontation. This doesn't, however, make you a pushover, because when you need to stand your ground, you will, but it does make you one hell of a negotiator and/or mediator. Is the fact you appear to be more cooperative than you actually are a case of smoke and mirrors and something of a magic trick? Maybe. You will likely be drawn to those careers where this skill can be used to its full potential, including and especially the law and business, where you can build your reputation on your charm and exceptional negotiating skills. You have a deep desire to love and be loved but value intellectual rapport and mutual respect far more than flakier notions of romantic love and passion.

Numerology

No. 2: Shows resilience and power in gentleness, often provides the role of mediator, and linked to psychic abilities.

Tarot

The Emperor: He has everything we look for when we want to trust someone, particularly a steady and attentive gaze. Anyone would feel safe putting their welfare into the hands of the Emperor, who represents wisdom and responsibility and all matters relating to the law and mediation, and this card suggests it's a gift you share.

Famous birthdays

Keanu Reeves Canadian actor
Jimmy Conners American tennis player
Christa McAuliffe American astronaut

September 3rd

Quiet change-maker

Your quiet, often thoughtful, manner belies a steely determination to work in a meaningful way that will help improve the lives of those who most need a helping hand. You really are someone who prefers 'the walk' to 'the talk' and will likely train in some practical skill such as engineering or scientific research that you can take back out into the world to make an actual difference to those communities who need extra support. You aspire to a world which runs smoothly for all its participants and feel passionately about using your skills to help bring about the changes that need to happen to make this a reality. If you have to resort to confrontation, you are probably capable of doing so, but you'd rather use the persuasive powers of the spoken word to get your point across. You may often feel misjudged by others who can sometimes fail to see past your quiet demeanour to your steely core, but you are forgiving, too, and won't bear a grudge. In matters of the heart, you are usually quite a realist, but can sometimes be guilty of holding potential partners to impossible ideals of romantic love and passion.

Numerology

No. 3: Creative with the gift of imagination and an ability to communicate in writing, art or speech.

Tarot

Death: Not what it might seem or what we might fear, this card shows up to speak of the end of something old, which is always the start of something new. The horse on which Death is depicted riding picks its way between bodies strewn on the ground, representing the ideas, beliefs or things that no longer serve us. The old must give way to the new.

Famous birthdays

Charlie Sheen American actor
Ferdinand Porsche Austrian-German car engineer and founder of Porsche
Alan Ladd American actor

September 4th

Independent idealist

There are those who only start to look for meaningful work once they approach middle age but, for you, it's likely embracing hard work that embodies your core values has been your priority from the start. But you are an independent thinker and have learned to trust your own judgement more than anyone else's, which can, in turn, make you something of an outlier. You have a keen intellect that others can sometimes find a bit intimidating and you may be drawn to academic research or non-fiction writing where you will relish the autonomy to work at your own pace (fast) to explore new ideas. You are actually very good-natured and can function as part of a team, as long as you don't feel your autonomy is being curtailed. Yours is not an ambition for personal glory, rather an ambition to bring your idealistic visions to reality and leave a legacy you can feel proud of. You bring the same independence to your personal relationships, which means that while you may have some meaningful intimate relationships, you may choose to live alone and not least because, unusually among earth sign Virgos, you may have little interest in the mundane business of running a home.

Numerology

No. 4: Invested in the physical world, centred earth energy that is practical in application.

Tarot

Six of Cups: This card is full of emotion, and often comes up when there has been sadness in someone's childhood, but it can also indicate someone who has great compassion for others and will do whatever they can to make things better for anyone who is suffering from or had trauma in their past.

Famous birthdays

Liz Greene American astrologer and psychologist
Beyoncé American singer and actress
François-René de Chateaubriand French politician and writer

September 5th

Unconventional visionary

You tend to be unusual among those Virgos that crave order and work to create and maintain it, because it's likely that you have the happy capacity to tolerate change. You thrive whenever the established order has been rocked and usurped, and you will be more than happy to play your part in causing that temporary chaos. Some might call you *avant-garde,* others might mutter the word 'crazy'. True, some of your ideas can appear to be lacking in reason and rationale, but this kind of innovative creativity can also take everyone by surprise and change accepted wisdoms overnight. You may choose a career in the arts or entertainment where such unconventional thinking will be welcomed, or you could take your ability to think outside the box into politics, medicine or sport. Whichever field you choose, you will likely quickly make a name for yourself, even if not everyone approves of your unconventional methods. In your intimate relationships, you may tend to favour freedom over commitment, and if your view of romantic love is somewhat idealised, this can make it tricky for a partner to live up to your expectations.

Numerology

No. 5: Impulsive and restless by nature, spontaneous and likes to discover the world through the senses.

Tarot

The Fool: Like the image on this card, you have little fear of stepping into the unknown. In fact, you thrive on the thrill of taking a risk and not knowing where your next step could lead you. The Fool also has his little white dog (representing his instinct) to protect him and stop him leaping into a complete abyss. Be reassured that you can trust your instincts about the choices you make, too.

Famous birthdays

Michael Keaton American actor
Freddie Mercury British singer-songwriter
Rose McGowan American actress and activist

September 6th

Dedicated humanitarian

Those born on this day often feel compelled to find work that allows them to combine their concern for others with a need to challenge and fully exercise their intellectual abilities. What this translates to in practice is that they are well suited to those careers like law and medicine that reflect their deep-seated desire to effect change for the better, while perhaps allowing them to do so in a slightly remote way. You can come across as a complicated, even highly strung, character to those trying to get to know you, and at times you're probably aware of being something of a prickly pear. There may also be an aspect of you that comes across as solitary or preferring to be alone but, again, you could say that this is simply a pragmatic ability useful when advocating on someone else's behalf. This same somewhat reserved quality, which is characteristic of many Virgos, may make you take your time before committing to a loving relationship. But, when you do, you will also want a loving and supportive relationship with someone that you consider your equal in character and attitude.

Numerology

No. 6: Empathic and nurturing, can problem-solve in an emotional and physical way, responsible and cares deeply about family and friends.

Tarot

Two of Pentacles: The Pentacles represent our resources, including, but not restricted to, money. In your case, it probably refers to those intellectual abilities and your compassionate qualities. You will probably need to find a way to give equal weight and balance to both these drives, which can be something of a delicate juggling act for you.

Famous birthdays

Dolores O'Riordan Irish singer-songwriter
Macy Gray American singer-songwriter
Idris Elba British actor

September 7th

Enigmatic seeker

You're unlikely to be someone that takes anything much at face value or accept something as being true just because everyone says it must be so. Discovering the truth for yourself is more important than the opinions of others, and only then will you trust something as being a fact. You can come across as quite secretive, mysterious even, because like many Virgos you tend to be quite self-contained and happy with your own company, often needing solitude and time to think. Number 7 is your ruling number, which also suggests a spiritual dimension to your character that you may want to explore and requires solitude to do so. When this happens, don't hold back, because with your unique outlook you have much to contribute. Solitude allows you to manage your emotions, too, which can be quite a focus. You are happy being single, but you won't spend your life alone as a loving relationship is important to you. You seek the tenderness and intimacy that a deep connection with another brings. Like many Virgos, however, you may have a critical streak, but you are capable of applying this equally to yourself as to others.

Numerology

No. 7: Very analytical and detail-oriented, likes to observe and investigate things, and has a keen, inventive eye.

Tarot

Knight of Wands: Wands are about life, and the journey ahead for the Knight of Wands depicted here may be across a spiritual or emotional landscape rather than an earthly one. But whatever lies within his gaze, but out of ours, there's a slight nervousness. Like you, he needs to trust that the process of this life's emotional journey will take him where he needs to be.

Famous birthdays

Chrissie Hynde American singer-songwriter
Buddy Holly American singer-songwriter
Gloria Gaynor American singer

September 8th

Dynamic leader

You already know you cannot please all of the people all of the time and that being a leader means you may end up more respected than liked by other people. Happily, this doesn't bother you. Your determination to help others on the right path for them is admirable and your conviction and ability to support someone without actually interfering is probably key to some admirable leadership qualities, whether that's reffing the local football team or heading up a company. You can, however, come across as rather a force of nature, but fortunately you're also likely to have the communication skills it takes to persuade others to go along with your usually very well thought-out ideas. Organised and often analytical, you tend to take a pragmatic approach to work, and possible career paths might include politics in some form or investing time and effort in more creative, entrepreneurial ideas. The same approach probably goes for your personal life where, although it may take a patient partner to open up the more loving and demonstrative side of you, that can get buried.

Numerology

No. 8: Sees the big picture and aims for it, linked to abundance and material wealth and uses financial success to give back to others.

Tarot

Ten of Pentacles: This is a card of self-made success and also one that depicts a happy family, complete with two dogs, a comfortable home and much to be grateful for. All these blessings lie in wait for you if you can just take a step or two towards compromise when you meet your soulmate.

Famous birthdays

Peter Sellers British actor and comedian
Pink American singer
Patsy Cline American singer

September 9th

Independent observer

Even when you're in the thick of it and pulling your weight as a 'team' member you will come across as a somewhat solitary soul at work and at play. This is because, although you will take part in shared activities, you can't help but take up the position of an independent observer, which will quickly set you apart. The truth is, this is often due to shyness and insecurity which you can successfully transcend as you mature, particularly if you find a loving partner who offers you the unconditional love and support that will make you feel brave enough to pile into the fray. You have a strong social conscience and if you don't choose a specifically humanitarian career path, you will choose work that benefits as many people as possible, including perhaps education or scientific research. You are an original thinker but hugely sensitive, which means if you cannot convince others of the innate value of a solution you are sure of, you will battle on alone to prove you were right and worth listening to. You will likely have a strong spiritual streak or a deep faith underpinning this desire to make the world a better place.

Numerology

No. 9: An old soul that looks to spiritual awareness to solve life's problems and likes to help others to do so in the same way.

Tarot

The Magician: The Magician knows what needs to be done and holds the connection, earthly and spiritual, between all four Tarot suits: Cups, Wands, Pentacles and Swords. He has all these resources at his disposal and when it feels just too hard to keep going it alone, his power is available to you.

Famous birthdays

Hugh Grant British actor
Leo Tolstoy Russian writer
Michelle Williams American actress

September 10th

Natural leader

This is leadership with the lightest of touches. The way you motivate others to give their best is by making them feel they are the most important person in the room, which makes them want to give more. You probably hold yourself to the same high and exacting standards. The difference between you and those around you is that you are likely to have your eye very clearly on a position of power and prestige and be more than prepared for the necessary graft required to get there. You have a warmth towards other people, finding it easy to make and nurture those networks that will help you get where you are going and keep you there. You know what you want, and this clarity is very helpful in your dealings; you are not afraid to go after it and others will respect you for your ambition. You are also happy to be the power behind the throne, especially if this can facilitate your aims, so may choose an advisory career. In matters of the heart, you fall easily in and out of love, but the recipient of your affections may have to tolerate a sense that you blow hot and then cold, as your incisive brain switches gear, often overriding your heart.

Numerology

No. I: A powerful entity and results-oriented force, all about initiating action and getting things done.

Tarot

Three of Wands: Depicted here is a successful merchant, a self-made man smart enough to know that while he has done well in the world, he still needs to keep a close eye on his resources, which in this case happens to be the merchant ships sailing away in the distance to trade with other lands. Figuratively, these ships also represent all the rewards our canny merchant has earned finally coming home to his estate and safekeeping. This card suggests you keep a close eye on your own resources in order to manage them successfully.

Famous birthdays

Colin Firth British actor
Guy Ritchie British director
Karl Lagerfeld German fashion designer

September 11th

Gifted communicator

You won't want to waste your communication skills which, coupled with the organisational talents common to many Virgos, means that you are likely to soldier on even when others have given up on a task. You have the courage of your convictions even when the going gets tough and will feel compelled to continue to champion what you believe in, whether this is a work project or a love interest. With a strong empathic streak, you are probably easily moved (even to tears) by the plight of those who struggle with inequity and if you're not taking centre stage as a speaker to highlight and raise awareness, you'll be pushing for social change through social media or taking radical steps as an activist to make people sit up and listen. Oddly, while you are prepared to be unconventional – radical even – to fight for change, deep down you are likely to be highly traditional, believing strongly in family values and stable family relationships. Friendships and more intimate family relations can be tested by the fact that you are not shy about sharing your strong opinions and there's a good chance that learning to listen may be the single biggest challenge of your life.

Numerology

No. 2: Shows resilience and power in gentleness, often provides the role of mediator, and linked to psychic abilities.

Tarot

Death: As with so many of the powerful Major Arcana cards, Death calls for a deeper interpretation because it brings a single question to the table, asking: What needs to die for something better to flourish? You may think you already have the answer, but the fact that this card has shown up suggests you need to think again. Are you only thinking of the obvious? Is there something you are not seeing that needs to go for good?

Famous birthdays

Moby American singer-songwriter
D.H. Lawrence British writer
Harry Connick Jr American singer and composer

September 12th

Honest communicator

There are likely to be times when it might be better for you to stop and think about the consequences of what you are about to say and filter your response accordingly. However, you may have neither the time nor inclination to tone down what you want to say. Luckily, you are highly personable and great fun to be around, which more than helps pave the way for you to say what is on your mind and get away with it. You are likely to be very good with words, spoken or written, and probably well able to judge what to say for best effect and when to say it, because you're not going to risk the success of a project or your own reputation by blurting something out at the wrong time. But when the time is right, your reputation is for being forthright. You may be drawn to a career in education, science or the law and have no problem standing up in a room full of strangers, or even detractors, to get your point across. Your reputation for honesty helps people trust you, and you make friends readily. There's also an adventurous streak in you, unusual in many Virgos, that may be either physically or mentally adventurous, but probably means you enjoy travel and new experiences. You are a good partner and value intimacy, unlikely to be unreliable but prone to boredom, so pick someone who likes adventure, too.

Numerology

No. 3: Creative with the gift of imagination and an ability to communicate in writing, art or speech.

Tarot

The High Priestess: This is the card of the eternal student who will always want to study, learn and share with a wider collective. She also represents the secret place where your imagination fires up before bursting into the world to demand truth and change. Don't underestimate the gifts you've been given, which may take time to mature and flourish.

Famous birthdays

Ian Holm British actor
Barry White American singer-songwriter
Jennifer Hudson American actress

September 13th

Gifted problem-solver

You are likely to have quite the analytical take on life and are never happier than when you're facing a real tangle of a problem that demands tenacity and resolve. This total absorption with the task in hand makes you an excellent problem-solver but may also mean you are less engaged with the more mundane side of life, which can be frustrating for partners and co-workers. Actually, there probably aren't any co-workers unless they are members of the team you lead, because you may well be inclined to choose a career where you can work independently and without interruption from others. You may be drawn to scientific research, design and innovation or the business of business. Whatever you choose, you will probably thrive as long as the right circumstances allow you to apply your highly original and innovative approach. Generally, you come across as a positive and good-humoured person, but it's a different story when you feel blocked from getting on with what you see as a priority. That's when we might see a slightly short-tempered Virgoan whom others may describe as a workaholic. In matters of love, you are just as dedicated and goal-orientated and happy to lead by example, but you'll need to learn to make space for your partner's wishes, too.

Numerology

No. 4: Invested in the physical world, centred earth energy that is practical in application.

Tarot

The Tower: This can be a difficult card and one that can serve as an advance warning more than a prediction and deserves a closer look. A flaming tower with its occupants trying to escape before it collapses – are you capable of overlooking things in your life that could fall apart unless you give them your full attention? Your relationship? Your work? Your health?

Famous birthdays

Bill Monroe American singer-songwriter
Claudette Colbert American actress
Goran Ivanišević Croatian tennis player

September 14th

Eternal student

There's an element of the student in many Virgos because an enquiring mind is a feature of this sign. You are so busy asking how and why, it's astonishing that those standing close by can't hear the constant whirring of your brain as you shift between gears looking for answers that often raise more questions. You are charming and articulate and like nothing more than exploring your ideas with like-minded individuals, but you can become easily bored and so the truth is, you don't tend to hang around for long with one person or one group. This can make you seem aloof or intriguing or, once it is obvious you have no intention of giving away any more of yourself, a tad selfish. The truth, as ever, is more complicated, and it can't just be said that you're selfish. Because you're not, but you sometimes find it difficult to engage with feelings – both those of others and your own. The fact that you are independent, assertive, intelligent and ambitious means you will do well in your chosen career, but this reserve of yours can be misinterpreted and cause problems in your personal relationships, meaning that you might struggle with the gap between your romantic ideals and the everyday reality of love.

Numerology

No. 5: Impulsive and restless by nature, spontaneous and likes to discover the world through the senses.

Tarot

The Moon: If we had to choose one word to sum up the message of this card that word would be 'obfuscation', which is the act of making something obscure or unclear. We know you have no problem communicating your ideas, so this card is talking about your emotions. What are you obscuring and why? How would it be if you came out of hiding and revealed your true self to someone? Risk this – it might be the best thing you ever do.

Famous birthdays

Amy Winehouse British singer-songwriter
Mary Crosby American actress
Sam Neil Irish actor and director

September 15th

Compassionate idealist

You are probably someone who feels that they need to take care of others, especially those who cannot take care of themselves. This nurturing side may find you drawn to a career in public service, social care, politics, education, catering, charity, the law or the area of well-being. Whether you are feeding people, rehoming people, advising people or championing people, helping other people is likely to lie at the heart of what is important to you and is probably what gets you out of bed in the mornings. Often, people will be grateful to you, but there will also be those who may resent your input and so you will probably need to learn to find the balance between offering help where it is genuinely needed and keeping your nose out where it has been made clear it is not welcome. Sometimes, taking care of others becomes an effective strategy for avoiding taking care of ourselves and for ignoring our own issues. Helping others makes us feel good about ourselves, but you will be more effective and your support more sustainable when you, too, are in a good place and those you love and who love you will recognise this and encourage it.

Numerology

No. 6: Empathic and nurturing, can problem-solve in an emotional and physical way, responsible and cares deeply about family and friends.

Tarot

Five of Pentacles: This card depicts a couple battling through a snowstorm, passing by the stained-glass window of a church. Burdened and bowed down, neither notices the Pentacles (resources that could be theirs) in the window. What might this tell us about labouring so independently that we miss out on help that's available?

Famous birthdays

Tommy Lee-Jones American actor
Oliver Stone American director
Agatha Christie British writer

September 16th

Exuberant live wire

Unusually for a Virgo, your feet don't touch the ground for long as you probably race from one thing to the next, bringing the full force of your passions to so many different interests that it can be difficult for others to keep up. Likely to have a lightning-quick, somewhat mercurial mind, you have a tendency to want to blaze a trail, leaving less energetic souls in your wake. Far from being a dilettante, however, you bring enormous tenacity to anything you undertake and probably won't be persuaded to pause until the job is complete. Getting results is important to you, as is being recognised and praised for your efforts, which means you may choose a field of work like manufacturing or the arts, where your personal contribution is clear for all to see. You are also likely to be drawn towards a mentoring role quite naturally as you mature and the same applies to your friendships and family relationships, because while you relish your intellectual independence, you are not a loner but have a deep desire to share both your life and your discoveries with those who cherish you.

Numerology

No. 7: Very analytical and detail-oriented, likes to observe and investigate things, and has a keen, inventive eye.

Tarot

Six of Wands: This card absolutely represents those qualities of natural leadership that you probably have in spades, even if you've not realised that yet. We know, whatever their recent exertions, that the young man on his horse has triumphed because the wand the leader carries is decorated with a celebratory laurel wreath – a symbol of success in the Tarot deck. Once you have acknowledged and begun to focus your key skills, you are likely to be very successful in life.

Famous birthdays

Mickey Rourke American actor and screenwriter
Lauren Bacall American actress
David Copperfield American magician and illusionist

September 17th

Lateral thinker

The positive outlook on life, focus and drive that are linked to this birth date mean you have all you need to make things happen. With a tendency towards single-mindedness, when you set your mind to a task or project nothing much will get in the way. This quality, combined with a Virgoan attention to detail, can make you a force to be reckoned with. However, you are also likely to be quite sensitive and empathic towards the needs of others, giving you good opportunities to come up with solutions that help others with their problems. These qualities can make you a gifted and generous team leader, so whatever career path you choose you will enjoy working with and inspiring others towards a common goal. In all your relationships, including your more intimate connections, you feel a tremendous responsibility for the welfare and well-being of those you care about and will think nothing of topping up someone's bank account to help them through a sticky patch or of supporting them in some other practical way. You probably have a great sense of humour, which you bring into all your relationships, and once past your initial shyness, you are a lively and engaging lover and friend.

Numerology

No. 8: Sees the big picture and aims for it, linked to abundance and material wealth and uses financial success to give back to others.

Tarot

King of Cups: The Cups in the Tarot deck represent our emotional natures, and here the king is a caring and empathic person whose calm and steady exterior hides a highly sensitive nature. He is immensely protective, especially of those he can see are in some sort of need. The indication is that you may sometimes come across as too emotional and, as a result, a little indecisive, but that's a small price to pay for being so thoughtful about the needs of others.

Famous birthdays

Anne Bancroft American actress
Hank Williams American guitarist and singer-songwriter
Roddy McDowall British actor and director

September 18th

Strong-minded worker

You are probably interested in and want to learn about many diverse things, but far from being flighty or flippant, you have the classic Virgoan steadfastness that encourages others to look to your opinion. You probably appreciate company and beauty in many different ways, and you have an earthy sense of humour. You are unlikely to have trouble attracting lovers or friends; what might confuse people is that you also need your downtime and will retreat, like a hermit, when you need to. This need can come across as being at odds with your otherwise sociable and fun-loving nature, and can sometimes be misinterpreted, so it's as well to be aware that this element of reserve may inadvertently offend. At work, the chances are it will be in a field that allows you to express some aspect of your refinement and good taste, even if this is only in how you dress or the attention you give to your uniform, should you need to wear one. There's also likely to be a strong humanitarian streak running through you and in whichever field you work, you will have an eye out to protect the underdog. Those privileged enough to be allowed into your inner circle can expect an easy and relaxed relationship, in which you are happy to devote special attention to them and their needs.

Numerology

No. 9: An old soul that looks to spiritual awareness to solve life's problems and likes to help others to do so in the same way.

Tarot

The Magician: There may be more than a hint of psychic ability, which you probably think of as strong intuition, in your make-up and this is something the Magician card tells us you can develop further as you travel through life. He forms a bridge between this world and 'the Other' and is the custodian of all the suits in the Tarot deck. Call on him when you have difficult decisions to make and remember him during times of solitude.

Famous birthdays

Tara Fitzgerald British actress
Greta Garbo Swedish actress
James Gandolfini American actor and producer

September 19th

Competitive risk-taker

You probably make no apology for the fact that you like to come first, and with a naturally competitive streak, it's probably never just about taking part for you but also about winning. This may lead you to look for work and life opportunities where winning is part of the game, from sports to business, and in other areas where being competitive can pay dividends. Ambition for recognition and personal success is also likely to be on your agenda, and you may often give the impression that you have no insecurities at all. But you are only human and sometimes that self-confident mask is there to project your feelings. You are more in touch with your emotions and more romantic than many other Virgos, which can sometimes result in you being more easily hurt when it comes to matters of the heart. When you do find a soulmate, you are a loving and loyal partner who will expect your devotion and generosity to be returned in equal measure. You're also likely to be calm in a crisis where fast decision-making is necessary, making you a good person to have around when a quick brain and precise actions help ensure a positive outcome.

Numerology

No. I: A powerful entity and results-oriented force, all about initiating action and getting things done.

Tarot

The Lovers: Being more in touch with your feelings than many Virgos means that love is one of your top priorities, and even though you seem to be so independent, the truth is you want to share your life with someone who really is your equal. Choose a mate wisely so that your loving relationship not only remains blessed but also allows you the independence you need to function at your best.

Famous birthdays

Jeremy Irons British actor
Cass Elliot American singer
Twiggy British model and actress

September 20th

Aspiring peacemaker

There's likely to be an aspect of your nature that makes you shy, which might mean that trusting relationships and sharing your feelings is difficult for you in your early years. But don't give up on this dream because there is someone out there for you; it may just take a little longer for you to find them. When you do, this partnership is likely to be a priority and the place where you share similar ideals, even a working partnership as well as a love relationship. It's possible that you will seek out a career, even if not immediately, where you will be of service to others, which is where you might expect to find your fulfilment. Because of a likely commitment to a common cause, you may be quite a skilled peacemaker, able to understand all sides of an argument and, just as importantly, able to navigate a resolution that all parties can live with. Dispute resolution in some form is probably a skill that you will develop, bringing together your intellect and compassion. Most people you meet will find you agreeable, but woe betide those that mistake your kindness for weakness, because you are no pushover, and your bite is more than equal to that quiet bark.

Numerology

No. 2: Shows resilience and power in gentleness, often provides the role of mediator and linked to psychic abilities.

Tarot

Justice: This is a powerful card that reflects those traits outlined above. It depicts an adjudicator sitting with a sword of the intellect in one hand and the balancing scales of a more emotional mindset in the other, weighing up the arguments presented to find in favour of peaceful resolution and fairness.

Famous birthdays

Sophia Loren Italian actress
Kenneth Moore British actor
Nuno Bettencourt Portuguese guitarist and singer-songwriter

September 21st

Stylish optimist

You are likely to be highly interested in new ideas, new trends, new ways of thinking about old problems and even new fashions. Sociable and probably with a quick wit and sense of humour, you will have no difficulty building impressive influencer networks to help disseminate your ideas, designs or political ideas across the globe. It may appear that the good things in life come more easily to you than to others, but that's more likely because of the hard work, dedication and self-belief behind the scenes, usually kept hidden away. You probably have that deceptive ability to make it all look not only effortless but also great fun. And you are also likely to be blessed with the great old-fashioned value of common sense, which means you aren't fickle but grounded, like many other earth signs. You're stylish but not flashy, and it's possible that you'll gain a name for setting trends in popular culture even if you work in apparently unrelated fields. You probably have a perfectionist streak like many Virgos, which can cause problems in love as reality may never quite live up to your romantic ideals.

Numerology

No. 3: Creative with the gift of imagination and an ability to communicate in writing, art or speech.

Tarot

Nine of Pentacles: The Pentacles represent what resources are available to us, including money, but also other qualities such as happiness, resilience, optimism and health. The card depicts a very stylish woman of leisure taking a wander through a vineyard at harvest time, petting her favourite bird of prey sitting on her gloved left hand. She has everything she needs and more and, like you, knows how to make the best of all she has.

Famous birthdays

Bill Murray American actor and comedian
Stephen King American writer
Leonard Cohen Canadian singer-songwriter

September 22nd

Forthright communicator

If you're not already blogging or using some form of social media to flag up your concerns or strategic solutions, then it probably won't be long before you find some outlet for your desire to work towards the common good. And you may have been the child running a lemonade stall for charity because you wanted to make a difference. You may find yourself working in public service as a consequence of this desire. But this might not be enough for you and finding a way to communicate your concerns to a wider audience via social media might well fit in with your ethos. As a forthright communicator (you may not know how to tone it down even if you wanted to), it's as well to be aware that you could alienate those who have more to gain by maintaining the *status quo* that you might be working so hard to shatter. This means that confrontation could be a feature of your working life. Make sure this doesn't detract from what your nearest and dearest need, and allow them to give you the unconditional support you may sometimes require in order to keep going.

Numerology

No. 4: Invested in the physical world, centred earth energy that is practical in application.

Tarot

Page of Pentacles: This card reflects the humanitarian who puts the needs of others before their own, depicting a young man holding up those resources – the pentacle – he has and will use to support others. There's a youthful energy and selflessness in the way this is being offered, which is evident in the qualities associated with this birth date, too.

Famous birthdays

Nick Cave Australian singer-songwriter
Michael Faraday British scientist
Billie Piper British singer and actress

September 23rd

People-pleaser

In astrology, what the Libran scale demands is that often tricky balancing of opposing principles or desires and, in your case, it's possible that there's a balance to be struck between selflessly helping others and doing so purely in order to please them. The fact is, you probably have a deep empathy for the plight of others and may want to find meaningful work where you can help highlight injustice and inequality, and work to correct it. These are good reasons, but it's important not to do things purely to please others, which can lead to resentment. Balance is fundamental to everyone's well-being, including yours, so any tendency towards the more negative connotations of people-pleasing may be worth addressing. The upside of this willingness to try to please is an empathy, consideration, generosity and loyalty that attracts great affection and often equal commitment, providing the balance that is necessary to ensure happiness in a reciprocal relationship. This is also important to you, providing you with the balance you seek to live harmoniously in the world.

Numerology

No. 5: Impulsive and restless by nature, spontaneous and likes to discover the world through the senses.

Tarot

Ten of Cups: An emotional and joyful card which hints at a life well-lived and fulfilled. You already know that love matters greatly. You are generous with your care, compassion and love for others, and this card signifies that good things really do come to those who work towards them. It might not be quite apparent to you yet, but balance those scales and you will be more than able to achieve this happiness.

Famous birthdays

Mickey Rooney American actor and comedian
Bruce Springsteen American singer-songwriter
Cherie Blair British lawyer

September 24th

Compassionate campaigner

It's likely that, for you, loving and being loved must be in balance. Not for you the passion of unrequited love, as love is too important a feature in your life not to expect to have it returned in equal measure. You are considerate towards others and probably have the Libran knack of being able to sense someone's unhappiness. You will want to step in to help make things better and a little more hopeful for them. You expect the same in return but may need to bear in mind that not everyone is as empathic and compassionate as you. You are likely to find distress in other people and animals something you feel compelled to do something about, so you may find yourself campaigning for those organisations that tackle these issues. You probably also have a love for the written word and will always have something to say and share about injustice where you see it. Unexpectedly for someone seemingly so sociable, you also have a deep need for solitude during which you can reflect on more spiritual and esoteric matters and indulge in your own interests. Again, you will seek a partner that is able to recognise and balance these needs, expecting to return the same courtesy.

Numerology

No. 6: Empathic and nurturing, can problem-solve in an emotional and physical way, responsible and cares deeply about family and friends.

Tarot

The World: This is your stage, if you want it to be, and not least because many of the issues you want to tackle, and redress, take place on a global stage. This card captures the deep sense of engagement you have with life and your compassion for all who share the planet and who are distressed. You have the vision and the skills to redress the balance and make a difference, even if this comes to you later in life.

Famous birthdays

F. Scott Fitzgerald American writer
Jim Henson American animator and puppeteer
Nanda Costa Brazilian actress

September 25th

Spontaneous traveller

Because you relish the excitement of meeting new people and exploring new places, you may be something of a traveller who takes any opportunity to flit off. Spontaneity helps ward off boredom, but if you are doing this to avoid making any real connections, this may cause loneliness. Equally, if it's also a way of avoiding responsibility, this too may create problems, especially in later life. When you take the time out to reflect on why this constant need to be on the move occurs, it may help resolve the issues you may have about making a commitment to people or places. You have a strong psychic streak and may eventually end up settling down somewhere long enough to work in the healing arts and share the wisdom you have gained from all your travels and exposure to alternative ideas. Love, however, presents a real dilemma for you. The romantic part of you craves an intimate and loving connection, but you could be nervous about what you see as the prospect of being tied down. Seek a partner to whom you can open up about this and you may find that the person who attracts you actually feels the same way as you.

Numerology

No. 7: Very analytical and detail-oriented, likes to observe and investigate things and has a keen, inventive eye.

Tarot

Knight of Cups: The Knight of Cups suggests someone who is tentative about settling down in one place. The knight depicted in this card isn't giving his horse full rein but seems to be pausing in contemplation, considering the pros and cons of moving on. You may find it useful to reflect on why the urge to leave people or places is so strong.

Famous birthdays

Will Smith American actor
Christopher Reeve American actor
Catherine Zeta-Jones Welsh actress

September 26th

Studious perfectionist

This may not be how you would choose to describe yourself on a dating app, but it may be typical of a logical way you have of thinking and your Libra preference to have things just so. In any event, whether you are drawn to the sciences or the arts, study in one form or another is likely to be important to you throughout your life. You constantly want to improve at what you do, and also to use your skills to help others, either by mentoring or teaching or just swapping ideas during social activities like debating or playing basketball. You have a strong imagination coupled with the self-discipline to bring new ideas to fruition, and others may admire your drive. Your route to success may not always be obvious to outsiders, but you are likely to intrigue and leave them wanting to know more about your thinking and methods. In matters of the heart, you will probably need a nudge or two to get started, and a few more to keep you on track, because you may have a tendency to put work above all else. You can also be prone to neglecting your own emotional needs, as well as those you love and care about.

Numerology

No. 8: Sees the big picture and aims for it, linked to abundance and material wealth, and uses financial success to give back to others.

Tarot

The Chariot: This card is all about the direction of travel you choose (forwards) and the skills you need to stay on a middle path, veering neither to the left nor the right. It is particularly apposite for you when you struggle to balance the opposing pulls of your emotional and work life. For you, this is a card that urges moderation; you can work hard, yes, but ensure you stay grounded by making the time and space for love.

Famous birthdays

Serena Williams American tennis player
T.S. Eliot American poet
Olivia Newton-John Australian singer and actress

September 27th

Stealthy observer

You are someone who is likely to be enthralled by the diversity of human nature and really enjoy the challenge of working out what makes someone tick and why they make the choices they do. As a consequence, you probably have highly developed observational skills. You are also likely to have the chameleon's knack of blending in with whichever group you choose, partly because you prefer to be the observer than the observed, often hiding behind an easy-going façade. There's a good chance you've chosen a career that legitimises your almost psychic ability to read people's minds, work out their motivations and predict their reactions. Psychology attracts you, as do other areas of work that involve people's motivations and behaviours. You are also a peace-loving Libran soul and will do almost anything to avoid confrontation. In your own relationships you're a generous and loving partner who likes to anticipate a partner's needs, but remember to allow someone to cherish you, too, otherwise you could end up feeling a little resentful. With all the insight gained through observing others, it can also be useful to reflect on our own motivations.

Numerology

No. 9: An old soul that looks to spiritual awareness to solve life's problems and likes to help others to do so in the same way.

Tarot

Ten of Cups: With this card we see a self-satisfied merchant sitting in front of ten cups, so we know that there's plenty of emotion here, but nobody is getting access. Our merchant is sitting with his arms folded defensively and nothing is getting past this barricade unless he chooses to let down his guard. Remember that it's equally important to be able to receive, as well as to give, love.

Famous birthdays

Gwyneth Paltrow American actress
Meat Loaf American singer
Barbara Dickson Scottish singer

September 28th

Independent thinker

You probably have very little interest in learning by rote or being told what to think, as you want to discover the world for yourself before drawing your own conclusions. A constantly questioning attitude could make you something of an outlier, which may be difficult when you are young but will become a badge of honour as you mature. It allows you to explore ideas that others may shy away from and as you delve deeper into more artistic and spiritual concerns, you find yourself moving further and further away from those who put their emphasis and build their value systems on money and status. This air of detachment lends you a mysterious aura, but others are likely to be drawn to it. You demonstrate a clear concern for the happiness and well-being of others, and you may well choose to work in or around the healing arts, either conventionally in a medical field or in some more esoteric way. However, this emphasis on healing others may impact on your own personal relationships, as showing any emotional vulnerability may not come easily. You probably won't want to give up your freedom to think or live as you wish and may find the compromises that close relationships demand difficult to manage, especially when you're young.

Numerology

No. 1: A powerful entity and results-oriented force, all about initiating action and getting things done.

Tarot

The High Priestess: Often referred to as the Eternal Student, this card frequently shows up in the tarot readings of those who have deliberately taken an alternative path to delve deeper into the esoteric mysteries and healing arts. This is a card for someone who understands the power of gentle action and the need for a life of meaning.

Famous birthdays

Brigitte Bardot French actress and animal rights campaigner
Helen Shapiro British singer and actress
Jennifer Rush American singer

September 29th

Tenacious champion

You may well struggle to understand why putting the needs of others before your own is not always the best option. The best way to explain this is to think about the safety drill on an airline where we are told to put our own oxygen masks on before attempting to help anyone else. This is because we can't attend to the needs of others if we haven't attended to our own. How might this apply to you? Championing the needs of others comes naturally to you and as a Libra you are ever the diplomat, but that doesn't mean always putting others first in order to avoid confrontation. Your compassion for others is admirable, but there are times when it's essential to show the same compassion to yourself and allow yourself the time and space to recharge your own batteries. It's likely that you derive real pleasure from seeing others prosper and thrive, and your friends and family alike know that you are the best person to turn to in a crisis. But you must also remember to champion your own desires, in order to maintain a balance between giving and receiving. Otherwise, lovers in particular may find it frustrating that you won't allow them to share some of the load.

Numerology

No. 2: Shows resilience and power in gentleness, often provides the role of mediator and linked to psychic abilities.

Tarot

The Lovers: This card is here to remind you that one thing that will sustain and support you in all your endeavours is a grounded and stable home life with a partner who, even if they don't share all your ideals and dreams, actively supports you and them, and vice versa. Remember to allow for this possibility, as it will enrich your life.

Famous birthdays

Silvio Berlusconi Italian media tycoon and politician
Jerry Lee Lewis American singer and pianist
Anita Ekberg Swedish actress

September 30th

Gifted storyteller

You probably have something of a reputation for being a networker with the names of lots of influential people on speed-dial. This comes from being highly social in person and online, and something of a raconteur. You're also likely to have a breezy cheerfulness that's a plus at any gathering. Your love of storytelling often finds you centre stage, but your Libran discretion means you stop just short of gossip, making it unlikely that you'll offend. A public-facing role will likely come naturally as you probably enjoy performing, which may find you attracted to the performing arts or even doing some amateur stand-up comedy. Or you might just sell your skills as the best party planner in town and combine all your favourite things into one role. As much as you say you'd like a committed relationship, this may not happen until later in life. The truth is, you are having too much fun for a domestic life and can be a bit fickle in your attachments. Happily, as you mature, you value friendship and companionship over and above romantic love, and so when you do settle down you can expect a very happy union, which will allow you to show the more tender and considerate side of your nature.

Numerology

No. 3: Creative with the gift of imagination and an ability to communicate in writing, art or speech.

Tarot

Ace of Wands: Lots of people tell good stories and make others feel good about themselves, but with you it's a gift that has been elevated to an art form, and with this card we see why. The Wands represent our animation and the Ace of Wands, which shows a hand passing you this incredible gift, tells us that this really is likely to be your birth right.

Famous birthdays

Deborah Kerr Scottish actress
Marc Bolan British singer-songwriter
Buddy Rich American jazz drummer

October 1st

Strong-willed idealist

Tucked away out of sight and hidden beneath your air of lovely Libran charm, there's an unexpected will of steel. You hide an ambitious nature and a burning desire to succeed in life, but you may struggle with the head versus heart decision-making that can keep your scales tipped too far one way or the other. This can make you seem indecisive or, when you do suddenly make a decision, rash and impetuous. You are likely to have a deep-rooted Libran idealism and a strong sense of justice, so will happily focus on and campaign for the things you believe in. That said, your energy ebbs and flows, and so while some days you'll put in an 18-hour work shift and leave no obstacle unconquered, other times you'll have an inclination to switch off the alarm clock and while away the whole day apparently getting nothing done at all, but the cogs will be whirring away while you appear to idle in first gear. These seeming extremes of behaviour can catch those trying to get close to you off-guard, never entirely sure which side of you will show up. This style of maverick creativity makes you comfortable working in the media, the arts or the world of entertainment. In love, you are an affectionate and loving partner and value the support of a long and lasting union.

Numerology

No. 1: A powerful entity and results-oriented force, all about initiating action and getting things done.

Tarot

Eight of Cups: This card depicts the journey we must all make from being at the mercy of our emotions (childhood) to being able to regulate them (maturity). We see a traveller walking away from the eight cups (emotions) to traverse a new and uncertain landscape. Are past sorrows being left behind? Or have some very difficult feelings been conquered by learning that you don't have to act on them every time?

Famous birthdays

Richard Harris Irish actor
Julie Andrews British singer and actress
Theresa May British politician and former prime minister

October 2nd

Lovable live wire

Your *joie de vivre* is infectious and put simply, you are likely to be an absolute pleasure to have around, whether that is at work, at home or in a friendship group. Unlike many of your fellow Librans, you don't tend to suffer from indecisiveness but may be a bit too prone to making instant decisions, some of which you might look back on with a tinge of regret because you didn't really think things through. You love the idea of helping others but can be so gung-ho in your analysis of the situation that you neglect to consider the shades of grey that may harbour the better solution, so your advice could sometimes be better considered before its shared. People like your straight-talking and tendency to call a spade a spade, but some who have gone along with your emphatic decision-making in the past may now tend to be less persuaded. If you can develop a more nuanced decision-making process, then you have all the other qualities that make for a good leader. In matters of the heart, you like honest communication and won't have any trouble attracting a mate who believes in you almost as much as you believe in yourself.

Numerology

No. 2: Shows resilience and power in gentleness, often provides the role of mediator, and linked to psychic abilities.

Tarot

Two of Pentacles: The Pentacles in the Tarot deck represent the resources at our disposal (including money). This card shows a young man juggling the two pentacles at his disposal. This constant considering of two options can be time-consuming and make you indecisive. Sometimes it's better just to pause and wait and see what the better outcome might be.

Famous birthdays

Mahatma Gandhi Indian political activist and spiritual leader
Don McClean American singer
Sting British singer-songwriter

October 3rd

Focused perfectionist

You have a strong streak of perfectionism, which is a quality you share with many other Librans, although it is particularly pronounced in those of you that were born on this day. This can lead to you being perceived as somewhat critical in both your work and your personal relationships. This can result in some people tending to steer clear, and you may wonder why. Remember that your goal is to do your very best and encourage others to do the same, so perhaps temper your perfectionism with a little compassion for those who may see things differently to you. You have a good mind and a knack of seeing immediately how systems can be enhanced and improved, so you may well be drawn to a career in science or research, or even as a motivational speaker. You are extremely resourceful, which people admire. You actually like people and want to be involved in ways that benefit the collective, so it's likely you'll seek a wider stage, although you'll be just as effective in your local community. In matters of love, you are a reliable and practical partner, but you have a tendency to put work first, which can cause problems at home.

Numerology
No. 3: Creative with the gift of imagination and an ability to communicate in writing, art or speech.

Tarot
Five of Cups: Five is the number of change and with this card we see that while three cups are now lying on the ground, two remain standing upright. Are you focusing too much on what has been spilled or lost, rather than the possibilities of what the upright cups might hold? Focus on what you've learned from the past and look to the future with more confidence at this point of change.

Famous birthdays
Clive Owen British actor
Neve Campbell Canadian actress
Eddie Cochran American singer

October 4th

Relaxed realist

Reality may sometimes be something of a brutal departure from a more romanticised view of the world we'd all like to believe in, but being such a realist means you have the valuable gift of knowing what will work and what won't. This means you can save us all time (and possible disappointment) by identifying those goals that can actually be achieved. I'm not suggesting that you don't dream big alongside your fellow Librans, because you can and you do, but you like to see results and will shape your dreams according to what you believe is realistic. This means you are likely to be drawn towards those professions where you can see real results based on a combination of your vision and efforts. You have a genuine interest in helping others and such a good nature that most people are happy to be in your company. And where some Librans can be hypercritical, you have a very relaxed attitude towards the fact that most of us are fallible and many of us have feet of clay. Which is all part of your realistic approach to life. In affairs of the heart, you are a loving and uplifting partner because you have a tendency to be optimistic, which your family and friends love about you.

Numerology

No. 4: Invested in the physical world, centred earth energy that is practical in application.

Tarot

Seven of Pentacles: This card reminds us that the only place where the word 'success' comes before the word 'work' is in the dictionary. You are likely to take stock of your resources (Pentacles) and build on these, through hard work. This dedicated but realistic determination to get results and succeed comes from the investment you make in your own personal resources.

Famous birthdays

Susan Sarandon American actress
Charlton Heston American actor
Buster Keaton American actor

October 5th

Naturally attractive

You are several moves away from the classic Libran charmer who would avoid causing offence to another at all costs. You are much more comfortable looking for compromise and team effort and working to benefit the group, as long as things are done your way (and you benefit, too). You have plenty of Libran charm and can communicate easily with everyone, but you may have a wilful and wayward streak. This means that when push comes to shove, you'll prioritise 'me' not 'we', which may be exactly what's necessary at the time. What is going on here is the Number 5 (which is all about freedom) is pushing everything else aside because the one thing that probably matters most to you, even if this is subconsciously, is your freedom. This doesn't mean you can't be part of a committed relationship because you can, as long as it is one that protects and allows you to cherish your free spirit. You are naturally funny, clever and stylish, and will always have plenty of people interested in sharing your life. Fortunately, you rate equality and intellectual companionship above romantic love, which bodes well for a happy union when you do meet your love match.

Numerology

No. 5: Impulsive and restless by nature, spontaneous and likes to discover the world through the senses.

Tarot

Four of Wands: The Wands represent communication and with this card we see that a happy union is possible for you, provided it is built on a meeting of minds as much as physical attraction. The happy couple celebrating their love are depicted outside a wall, neither restricted nor hemmed in. This card reminds us happy unions are possible.

Famous birthdays

Kate Winslet British actress
Karen Allen American actress
Clive Barker British writer and director

October 6th

Highly persuasive

It'll be a huge waste of one of your biggest talents if you are not working in some kind of sales-related field, either retail or well-being, where you may be promoting a new kind of treatment. You have a gift for networking and bringing people together and work in such a collaborative way that nobody will quite know there is still a hierarchy with you at the top. You thrive in beautiful surroundings and may be drawn to the arts, working in a gallery or an auction house. You are a fantastic host, love to party and generally enjoy entertaining, like many Librans. Your persuasive skills, strong moral code and sense of fair play would make you an excellent charity fundraiser and you probably already support a number of charities in one way or another. A loving relationship with another is likely to be top of your priorities as you have no intention of living alone, but until you let go of the idea of 'being in love with love', there may be a few false starts and more than a few broken hearts trailing in your wake. When you do finally find your soulmate and settle down you will feel more in balance.

Numerology

No. 6: Empathic and nurturing, can problem-solve in an emotional and physical way, responsible and cares deeply about family and friends.

Tarot

The Star: This card is all about beauty: beauty in nature, the beauty of the naked human form, and the beauty of everything working together harmoniously and in balance. It is also the card that suggests someone involved in the healing arts, either as a practitioner or someone who understands the body/mind/spirit link and is happy to explore it. It also suggests that the stars are aligned for you to do whatever makes you happy.

Famous birthdays

Carole Lombard American actress
Ioan Gruffudd Welsh actor
Britt Ekland Swedish actress and singer

October 7th

Radical idealist

You believe, deep down, that you are only here to make a positive difference to the lives of others and if this means making a few enemies along the way, then that's a price you probably consider worth paying. It's not that you don't care when people dislike you, it's more that you probably don't want to engage with what you see as petty nonsense, saving your energy to get what you see needs doing, done. You have your share of Libran charm, wit and imagination and will use all those qualities to win others over to your point of view. But you know progress can only be made when someone rocks the boat and you're probably more than prepared to do this. You may work as an activist of some sort, an environmental or social campaigner perhaps, and even if you have a more conventional job, you'll be promoting good causes in your spare time. Your courage and compassion for others will inspire followers, so perhaps you've found your voice on social media. In your intimate relationships you reveal a less combative side and more of those innate and loving Libran qualities.

Numerology
No. 7: Very analytical and detail-oriented, likes to observe and investigate things, and has a keen, inventive eye.

Tarot
Death: Don't panic, this card doesn't foretell a personal death, but it may be banging a death knell for the old order so that a new and more equitable one can replace it. However, people hate change, even when it's for the greater good, so this is where you can make good use of your Libran ability to persuasively balance attention to detail with charm to promote your cause.

Famous birthdays
Simon Cowell British TV presenter and entrepreneur
Thom Yorke British singer
John Mellencamp American singer-songwriter

October 8th

Original visionary

Anyone choosing to live outside the accepted 'norm' could be called eccentric (at best) and outright crazy (at worst), but you're not bothered. Being an outlier probably isn't a choice for you, but just how it is and how you are. You don't much care if others find your dreams and ideas unrealistic because nobody ever broke the mould by following the herd. The truth is that, however fantastical your goals might appear to be, you have a sharp mind and the drive to power through the strongest of objections. If you're not an entrepreneur, you could find yourself pushing the boundaries of areas of research or financial investment. And so, what if the best idea you ever had came through in a dream? The German chemist Friedrich Kekulé discovered the structure of benzene as the result of a dream and three of his students went on to win Nobel Prizes! You're immune to the mockery of the ideas you believe in, which is likely to gain you admiration from those working alongside you, whatever your field. But in matters of the heart, it's a different story. You can come across as remote and sometimes critical when potential partners fall short of your ideals; temper this so that when you do find a good partner you are more able to commit.

Numerology

No. 8: Sees the big picture and aims for it, linked to abundance and material wealth and uses financial success to give back to others.

Tarot

Two of Wands: Nobody would call the successful merchant depicted on this card an oddball. He is standing, symbolically, on higher ground looking into the far distance. A combination of hard work and the courage of his convictions have brought him to this place. Like you, he didn't concern himself with the opinions of the crowd but pushed through their mockery to realise his vision.

Famous birthdays

Sigourney Weaver American actress
Matt Damon American actor
Chevy Chase American actor and comedian

October 9th

Talented artist

There's probably a personal magnetism about you that you're largely unaware of, but it means that whatever career choice you make, many will recognise and be happy to applaud you and your talents. And if you did embark on a career in the arts, especially as a writer, singer or musician, you're likely to have a loyal fan base for life. You are probably a keen student of human behaviour and everything you observe or experience for yourself is likely to turn up in some form in your work. Your creativity is balanced with a compassionate streak, so there's a good chance your personal quest in life will take you on something of a spiritual journey at some point, and if it does, don't be surprised by the feeling that you've been this way before. You are likely to be considered something of an 'old soul', such is your wise take on many things. In your relationships you can be very giving, but sometimes rather reserved and passive, so be aware of this and don't let this put you off getting involved when you meet someone new, as it can take time for lovers to get to know you.

Numerology

No. 9: An old soul that looks to spiritual awareness to solve life's problems and likes to help others to do so in the same way.

Tarot

Page of Wands: A card in the suit of communications (Wands) depicting a young man dressed in his finery, including a feather in his cap, standing tall and looking ahead. This suggests a link to great change, heralding something new, something good and something better coming. This is a good-news card: something positive will occur and you will have been a significant part of it through your talent and endeavours.

Famous birthdays

John Lennon British member of The Beatles
P.J. Harvey British singer-songwriter
David Cameron British politician and former prime minister

October 10th

Reliable organiser

This may sound a bit dull, but it's a huge gift: you may find that you're drawn to chaos like a moth to a flame because you love to bring order. You don't much like chaos in any form and believe a smooth road to progress requires an organised and tidy workspace, as well as an organised and tidy mind. You're probably happily methodical in all you do and think, able to see precisely what needs to be done to prevent wasting time or the worst happening. Not surprisingly, whatever career you choose, you can expect rapid advancement to management level via a variety of team leadership and supervisory roles. You are a safe pair of hands and the calm support all organisations need. You are unlikely to be a fan of drama, either at work or at home, and will probably bring the same steadfastness to your domestic life, too. You're more than happy to support those you love emotionally and financially, and as soon as you make a commitment to a partner, they will have the joy of discovering you are far more sensual and loving than anyone might guess from that highly efficient-looking exterior. In typical Libran style, you also relish the finer things in life and someone to share them with.

Numerology

No. I: A powerful entity and results-oriented force, all about initiating action and getting things done.

Tarot

King of Swords: Here he comes, confident, decisive and in no mood to suffer fools, depicting someone that is all about cutting through chaos and the restoration of law and order. Although this can sometimes come across as a little bit cold and ruthless that's only because it's a big responsibility cutting through other people's muddles to bring order to bear. This is the person everyone wants around when chaos threatens, and that person is likely to be you.

Famous birthdays

Charles Dance British actor
James Clavell Australian writer
Chris Penn American actor

October 11th

Calming mediator

You probably have something of a reputation for peace-making. And you already know that you catch more flies with honey than vinegar, which makes you a gifted mediator. You have an amiable and calming presence that can take the temperature down several degrees just by being in the same room where there's a disagreement going on. This comes from being a Libra, able to see both sides of an argument. Fairness is important to you but you're no pushover, so when you do finally deliver an opinion and communicate how reparation might be made, others are likely to listen. To you, being able to do this is easily accomplished. You've been mediating since you were at school and may even have built a career on this. You probably approach problem-solving with analytical detachment and that's how you are able to resolve complex disputes and disagreement. And put simply, people trust you. In intimate relationships, however, you lean towards an overly romantic view of potential partners and it may take you time to balance this with your more rational side, to achieve a lasting union.

Numerology

No. 2: Shows resilience and power in gentleness, often provides the role of mediator and linked to psychic abilities.

Tarot

Justice: This is one of the most empowering cards in the whole Tarot deck, depicting both the scales and sword of justice. It speaks of truth and of balance, of course, but also of the necessity to use these tools with care, weighing up each situation in its own context. This takes experience and maturity, so bear this in mind and know that some gifts evolve over time.

Famous birthdays

Joan Cusack American actress
Eleanor Roosevelt American diplomat, activist and former First Lady
Luke Perry American actor

October 12th

Optimistic achiever

You have the charm, wit, eloquence and insightfulness to make a success of whatever career path you choose, but you are particularly good at working and communicating with other people. For this reason, you may well gravitate towards a career in teaching, the law or even local government. With an enthusiasm that others find attractive, you probably have such a wide range of interests and are so determined to get the best from life that this carries you a long way. Just like everyone else, you'll have your share of ups and downs, but you have such a strong self-belief that you are never down for long. You are naturally resilient, funny and honourable, and people enjoy being around you. It's really only in your more intimate relationships that this may not work quite so well for you. You will need to find the balance between your need for love and companionship, and the independence and freedom you also value. Take care to choose a life partner who balances your interests with theirs and shares similar enthusiasms.

Numerology

No. 3: Creative with the gift of imagination and an ability to communicate in writing, art or speech.

Tarot

Three of Cups: This is a card of friendship, celebration and fun. The Cups in the Tarot deck represent our emotions, and in this scene we see three friends toasting to the good things in life and their friendship. This joyful card reminds us that while material things may come and go, it doesn't really matter because what human beings really crave is connection.

Famous birthdays

Hugh Jackman Australian actor
Luciano Pavarotti Italian opera singer
Teresa Benedicta Polish philosopher, saint and martyr

October 13th

Intellectual progressive

When it comes to problem-solving, particularly in conflict resolution, whether this is between unhappy toddlers, work colleagues or global governments, the same strategic principles apply. There's probably something in your balanced, methodical approach to life that makes you more than happy to roll up your sleeves and get stuck in. You may occasionally be more combative when you feel the need to shock people out of their complacency and into the kind of action that will benefit society at large. But the thing you probably love most is the opportunity to debate a problem, because this is where you excel, objectively communicating the facts. You will probably want to use your skills in some public-facing capacity, perhaps even in politics in some way, but somewhere where communication is a factor. Strip away a little of your communications polish and it becomes evident that sometimes your more worthy humanitarian projects work better in the abstract than in reality, and the same could be said of your intimate relationships. Remember that the detachment needed to help resolve arguments needs to be tempered with warmth when it comes to friends and family. This is also the place where you can balance those needs for your personal happiness.

Numerology

No. 4: Invested in the physical world, centred earth energy that is practical in application.

Tarot

Strength: The strength of this card suggests your resourcefulness and refusal to give up on anything or anyone. If it doesn't work one way, then you'll try another, convinced you can think your way through a problem. To some, this can appear implacable, but your moral conviction is also part of your strength and you will want to do your best by everyone.

Famous birthdays

Margaret Thatcher British former prime minister
Sacha Baron Cohen British comedian and actor
Paul Simon American singer-songwriter

October 14th

Pragmatic humanist

Mastering the trick of balancing a desire for loving companionship without losing freedom is one that needs to be struck by many, but none more so than you. In some ways you live in your head, but you can sometimes feel overwhelmed by your feelings, and this may make you appear rather restless at times. You are genuinely predisposed to being kind-hearted and considerate, and fundamentally believe that the world is a good place. But you may sometimes struggle to communicate this. On an objective level, the way people behave genuinely interests you and your observations often make you a shrewd judge of character, so you may choose a career where you can utilise this, perhaps in teaching or counselling, finding that level of involvement with others rewarding. When it comes to finding your partner, you probably have a romantic streak but are astute enough to know that true love doesn't conquer all and you still need to pay the rent. Maintaining your freedom will always be important to you, and you may find that it is through an initial friendship based on similar interests that your more intimate relationships flourish rather than a *coup de foudre*, however attractive that might initially appear.

Numerology

No. 5: Impulsive and restless by nature, spontaneous and likes to discover the world through the senses.

Tarot

Ace of Swords: The Swords represent our intellect, and the Ace of Swords suggests an ability to cut through limitations and obstructions on an intellectual level. This card frequently shows up for someone who is more cerebral than emotional and whose head is likely to overrule their heart. Bear this in mind and remember that our feelings are important, too.

Famous birthdays

Lillian Gish American actress
Roger Moore British actor
Cliff Richard British singer and actor

October 15th

Highly individualistic

No one likes to feel restricted or tied down, but you may be someone who takes this to a whole new level if there's a threat to your freedom and independence, of mind as much as body. This will make your closest relationships a challenge unless you find a partner who can tolerate your need to freely express and debate every thought and idea. Happily, although you are likely to prize your independence, you are also highly sociable with a strongly empathic streak. You may genuinely enjoy being around other people from a diversity of backgrounds and probably have a strong sense of social justice and concern. Nothing will make you happier than knowing you might be able to pioneer positive change, and so you may find yourself choosing a role in life where you can accomplish this. Your take on life probably means that you relish the challenge of finding more progressive ways to solve problems and may even end up being publicly recognised for your contribution to this. Ironically, for someone for whom their own freedom feels so important, you sometimes struggle to allow others the same.

Numerology

No. 6: Empathic and nurturing, can problem-solve in an emotional and physical way, responsible and cares deeply about family and friends.

Tarot

Six of Cups: This card suggests some lingering sorrow (sometimes actual trauma) from earlier times, but also tells us that it is never too late to find happiness. The cup filled with white flowers signifies hope, but this may take time to flourish into something beautiful in your life. Make sure that you allow space for this possibility.

Famous birthdays

Friedrich Nietzsche German philosopher
P.G. Wodehouse British writer
Keyshia Cole American singer-songwriter

October 16th

Straight talker

With your charisma and charm, it's no surprise people are drawn to you. What may be more of an issue is that in contrast to this, you may sometimes be rather undiplomatic and even abrupt. You find people and their behaviours utterly fascinating, but don't feel any need to suffer fools and may prefer working with animals rather than people as a consequence. You have a gentle demeanour and don't like confrontation, but you're no pushover, and if needs be, you'll retaliate, which may surprise some who don't know you. You like to think for yourself and will explore both spiritual and political beliefs that fall outside the mainstream. Although you're naturally inclined to be sociable, you need time alone to recharge. If you are someone who needs to retreat into solitude occasionally, it might leave others feeling you're a bit elusive and difficult to get to know. You can be an exciting and generous lover with the right partner, and while intimacy is important to you, you're unlikely to commit until you feel sure of their feelings first.

Numerology

No. 7: Very analytical and detail-oriented, likes to observe and investigate things and has a keen, inventive eye.

Tarot

The Moon: The Moon's cycle moves through shades of reflected light and dark as it waxes and wanes, much like our intuition, which is stronger at certain times than others. Sometimes what's around us is easily perceived; at other times, not, and being aware of this can be helpful in our dealings with others. Plus, what we show or hide changes the way others perceive us, too, which is worth remembering.

Famous birthdays

Tim Robbins American actor and director
Angela Lansbury British actress
Oscar Wilde Irish poet and playwright

October 17th

Philosophical educator

You were probably known as something of a 'why?' child growing up and continue to ask questions of yourself and others even now. When it comes to what you believe, your inclination to research and base your opinions on information you've checked out for yourself enables you to carry an argument with conviction. And this comes partly from an enthusiasm to share what you're personally curious about, but also from a passion to educate others. While you are mostly pretty philosophical about life and present a calm and controlled persona to the outside world, underneath you can also be a bit of an adventurer and curious about exploring new things. This could extend to sometimes being a bit physically reckless in your excitement to dive in. The balance you seek may come through a committed relationship, but you don't always make it easy on your partner because that slightly detached, philosophical stance can occasionally come across as a bit critical. Bear in mind that we don't always need to be educated or hear the unvarnished truth, and it's often better to pause and consider other people's feelings before commenting, even if we know we're right.

Numerology

No. 8: Sees the big picture and aims for it, linked to abundance and material wealth and uses financial success to give back to others.

Tarot

King of Swords: This card represents an incisive thinker and often shows up when there are important decisions to be made which require some careful thinking and planning. This is very much your approach to life anyway, so this card should reassure you that your instinctive approach to check and educate yourself with facts is a good one.

Famous birthdays

Rita Hayworth American actress
Eminem American rapper-songwriter
Montgomery Clift American actor

October 18th

Responsible protector

The welfare of others, particularly those you perceive as the underdog, are often a priority for you. This empathy, balanced with objective skills, may find you working in social justice in some way, in a legal field, as a campaigner or even as a social media activist in your spare time. Your clever brain also needs opportunities to explore and express new ideas, and this may mean that you thrive when working alone rather than within the restrictions of an established team. But your conviction is sincere, and this will be clear to those around you. Your weak spot might be your inclination towards the more luxurious side of life, because you probably believe it's better to have one high-quality garment than three cheaper ones. You're as generous with others as yourself, though, easy-going and often with a strong sense of humour that occasionally borders on the absurd. You may have to check that the scales are balanced when it comes to personal relationships, however, so you don't end up being the one doing all of the giving. It's as important to know how to receive as it is to give.

Numerology

No. 9: An old soul that looks to spiritual awareness to solve life's problems and likes to help others to do so in the same way.

Tarot

Wheel of Fortune: This is always an important card, predicting good fortune as long as the wheel is spun in the right direction. It takes a certain amount of time and experience to work out the right direction, so it may not be until later in life that success and love come to you, but rest assured they will.

Famous birthdays

Chuck Berry American singer-songwriter
George C. Scott American actor
Jean-Claude van Damme Belgian actor

October 19th

Talented innovator

Not everyone has the originality or creative talent to innovate, but when it comes to problem-solving or finding new ways to do things better, those born on this birthday usually have a head start. Not only that, but you will want to develop and use your ability in this area to work for the greater good of your family, friends or society as a whole. This may be on a small or large scale but is no less important for that – whether it's your ability to fix a tap or invent a clean-water system for a developing country, your talent is for finding new ways to do old things. You are also likely to be something of a free spirit and may sometimes come across as a rather solitary soul, but this is primarily because you approach your more intimate relationships with care. When you do find the right life partner for you, you'll know because then you will feel confident enough to share your softer and more loving side. This may occur later in life, but then you are an affectionate and generous mate, very much able to adjust to the different demands on your relationship over the years.

Numerology

No. I: A powerful entity and results-oriented force, all about initiating action and getting things done.

Tarot

Three of Wands: The Wands represent communication, and this card depicts a man surveying ships either sailing into or away from the harbour, which suggests that travel and hard work were involved in his success. You, too, may travel through life successfully inspiring others to join you on a journey of innovation.

Famous birthdays

Trey Parker American actor
Michael Gambon Irish actor
Rebecca Ferguson Swedish actress

October 20th

Extrovert introvert

For those born on this date, your challenge in life can be learning how to balance your confident, outgoing side with your quieter, more contemplative one. How this appears to others can also complicate things: to some, you are probably the leader of the pack; to others, the quiet confidante. This is also enhanced by the numerology, so it may not be until adulthood that things fall into place and you can easily move between the two, depending on what is being asked of you. This duality might also show up when you have to study, for example, which comes surprisingly easy to someone who appears to be a party animal at times. It will probably take time for others to get to know you as you come to know yourself, but when they do, this will be an easy friendship that can also tip over into romantic love. Often Librans find their most intimate relationships start through friendship, as this is a balance they need, preferring that their lover is also a friend. There's no shortage of romantic inclination, but for you, this probably needs to be rooted in something solid for it to work. Although there's nothing wrong in playing the field first!

Numerology

No. 2: Shows resilience and power in gentleness, often provides the role of mediator and linked to psychic abilities.

Tarot

Temperance: This suggests something of a thermostat that influences how we balance our lives, ensuring there is a manageable mix between the highs and lows, the rough and the smooth, the ups and downs, all of which can be tempered by the decisions we make. In life, we have more control than we sometimes think, if we just take the time to think things through.

Famous birthdays

Danny Boyle British director
Tom Petty American singer-songwriter
Snoop Dogg American rapper

October 21st

Skilled negotiator

One of your most useful talents is your ability to perceive how things really are, rather than how you might wish them to be. This is what probably lies at the heart of being able to improve these skills and then use them to your best advantage.It's more than being a good researcher and keeping your ear on the ground; it's a sort of intuition about what's around the corner, which helps you in the judgements you make. This is likely to be balanced with a knack for reading people accurately, born from observation and understanding, because you are interested in what makes people tick. This is a great skill for a politician, lawyer or journalist and most definitely a diplomat, whether on a domestic or world stage, especially when it comes to negotiating. This also extends into matters of the heart, which are equally important to you. It will be through your intimate relationships that you also open yourself up to what makes you tick, particularly when you find a soulmate in whom to place your trust. On this basis you will be happy to build your domestic life.

Numerology

No. 3: Creative with the gift of imagination and an ability to communicate in writing, art or speech.

Tarot

Two of Swords: Swords represent our ability to cut through to what's important, but in this card, the woman is depicted as blindfolded. This suggests that our ability to 'see' doesn't just rest with our eyes, but that we can also trust our ability to assess how things really are by using our perception. Challenge your intuition but know you can often trust it.

Famous birthdays

Carrie Fisher American actress and writer
Jade Jagger British jewellery designer and former model
Alfred Nobel Swedish chemist and engineer

October 22nd

Devoted partner

Some born on this date are Libra and others are Scorpio, so you will need to know your birth time and place to know for sure. But there's a streak of devotion towards those people you care about that runs very deep. There's also a thoughtfulness about the way this devotion is expressed, and it is often extended to those outside your immediate circle, especially if they are struggling in difficult circumstances. It's possible that you'll look for work that allows you a way to defend or champion the rights of others, or you may work within the arts to try and accomplish this. There's an independent streak that can make you confront any restrictions on your personal freedom head on, which may make you tricky to live with. This is also complicated by the fact that because you set such high standards for yourself, you find it difficult to lower them for others. It's possible that your sense of purpose in life might set you apart from those who don't share the same commitment, and this may need to be tempered in order to allow others to get close, because devotion needs to work both ways in a balanced relationship.

Numerology

No. 4: Invested in the physical world, centred earth energy that is practical in application.

Tarot

Seven of Pentacles: This is the card of hard work and dogged determination, where success isn't handed on a plate but available to those who earn it. The Pentacles symbolise an abundance of internal resources, as well as our finances, and this card represents a treasure chest of talents and positive qualities to be used.

Famous birthdays

Jeff Goldblum American actor
Catherine Deneuve French actress
Joan Fontaine American actress

October 23rd

Ambitious strategist

To an outsider, a strategy isn't always obvious until it's accomplished its goals, and those born on this date often have the ability to develop and deliver strategies that are more ambitious than most. To an outsider, it sometimes looks as if you make life more difficult than it needs be, and sometimes this might be true. What you are probably doing is taking the long view, which may not yield results immediately but is generally successful in the end. This is partly because, like a chess player, you are able to look ahead and anticipate countermoves, all of which you love, as otherwise there is a lot about the routine of daily life that tends to bore you. Your ideas sometimes come across as rather radical, but your enthusiasm generally gets others on-side, whether at home, work or play, because your creative imagination is much admired. As a lover, you are generally passionate but occasionally demanding of partners, possibly pushing them away by inadvertently being rather controlling. That said, once you find the right life partner you are a protective, caring and fair-minded soulmate, but with a possible jealous streak.

Numerology

No. 5: Impulsive and restless by nature, spontaneous and likes to discover the world through the senses.

Tarot

King of Pentacles: This is the card of the self-made person, someone who does it their own way and uses all their talents to get to the top. The Pentacles represent all the resources at our disposal, and the King of Pentacles is a statement of potential success, so it is likely that you will work hard with what you have to get to where you want to be.

Famous birthdays

Ryan Reynolds Canadian actor
Briana Evigan American actress and singer
Pelé Brazilian footballer

October 24th

Level-headed organiser

You're probably one of those rare people that relishes the detail, the one who reads the small print and then methodically tackles any problem. This is a great approach that pays off well, especially in careers like finance and engineering, although it's equally successful in more creative areas like event management. You probably like to lead by example as well and prefer to take a hands-on approach to problem-solving. In fact, you are a very safe pair of hands, whether dealing with matters at work or at home, making you both a valued team player and the family member others turn to. You won't take any unnecessary risks and you will delegate or recruit additional support to get the job done when you need to. You don't suffer fools gladly, but equally you don't let your own pride get in the way, so, if someone else has more expertise than you, you're happy to hand over the reins. Home, however, is where a more critical and perfectionist stance can kick into play and you may attempt to try to improve not only the space in which you live, but also those you share it with. Curb this if you want a more harmonious domestic life, as your partner may see your attempts as undermining, even if they are lovingly meant.

Numerology

No. 6: Empathic and nurturing, can problem-solve in an emotional and physical way, responsible and cares deeply about family and friends.

Tarot

Nine of Cups: The Cups represent our deepest emotions and with nine depicted here it's not the case that you don't feel strongly about things because you clearly do. But here, the suggestion is that you might be withholding your feelings from those you care about, which could make relationships unnecessarily complicated.

Famous birthdays

Kevin Kline American actor
Adrienne Bailon American singer and actress
Monica Denise Arnold American singer-songwriter

October 25th

Stubbornly opinionated

If there are three little words that are unlikely to pass your lips, they might well be: 'I don't mind', because the truth is, you probably do even if you don't let on. You know what you want and once you've made up your mind about something, you're unlikely to it. This combination of stubbornness and Scorpio's more secretive side could make life rather difficult for you. A benefit of this strong will is likely to be a resilience to life's knocks, but you may need to temper this so that you receive fewer of them, otherwise you may experience more than your fair share of disappointments. Tempering your opinions, or keeping them to yourself, may be a useful strategy both at work and at home. At work, this strength of character will help you in careers where you need to be able to take the knocks without feeling undermined, perhaps in a public-facing capacity, from sales to performance, to political campaigning or social media activism. In love, you will probably have to learn the art of compromise in order to share a home harmoniously.

Numerology

No. 7: Very analytical and detail-oriented, likes to observe and investigate things and has a keen, inventive eye.

Tarot

Knight of Cups: Cups represent the emotions, and this card depicts a youthful person fiercely protecting a drinking cup. Water also represents our emotions, so he is being doubly challenged to express his feelings in order to move forward. This card often shows up for someone who is wary of emotional involvement for whatever reason, and this may be something you need to look at.

Famous birthdays

Katy Perry American singer
Ciara American singer-songwriter and dancer
Adam Goldberg American actor and musician

October 26th

Formidable ally

An ally is always a good thing, but a formidable one can also be an opposing force to someone else, so for those born on this date, it's worth considering the pluses and minuses of this position. While you're likely to be a force to be reckoned with at work, finding a career path that makes best use of this aspect of your character may take you some time, because you are probably also interested in succeeding financially, too. This may not be so obvious, thanks to a secretive side to your Scorpio nature, but a desire for financial success may also drive you. To this end, you're probably prepared to work twice as hard as anyone else, and whatever your chosen field, you're likely to aim for the top. There's also a strong sense of duty to your family, who you want to protect because of your love for them, which also influences your commitment to success. Don't fear showing your more vulnerable side, however, to those you love, so they can be your allies, when you need them.

Numerology

No. 8: Sees the big picture and aims for it, linked to abundance and material wealth and uses financial success to give back to others.

Tarot

Five of Swords: Well-armed, this is the card that shows just what a formidable ally (or opponent) you can be. The battle over, the hero has vanquished his opponent and retained three of the five swords to fight another day. Always be mindful that you need to keep something in hand to continue a successful endeavour.

Famous birthdays

Hilary Clinton American politician and former First Lady of the United States
Rita Wilson American actress and singer-songwriter
Bob Hoskins British actor

October 27th

Artistic idealist

You're probably quite used to being the centre of attention, not because you deliberately set out to grab the limelight but because you are such a lively communicator, you can't hold back from taking the floor to share your enthusiasms and views. There's no question that you'll thrive where communication is important, from journalism to teaching, or through the art of music, writing or acting. Whether you pursue the latter as an amateur or a professional, your idealism helps elevate and ensure the realisation of these talents. You are also likely to be comfortable with your emotions, which can be an important part of an artistic nature, and you may often react with your heart before your head. At some point in your life, you may also find you have a serious interest in spirituality and moral issues and wish to explore this in some way. As a partner, you're likely to expect at least as much back as you give emotionally, but you are also less intense and much more fun to be around than might first appear. You'll want to share all your passions with your partner, but they may need to accept sharing you with a wider audience as well if you've developed a public persona.

Numerology

No. 9: An old soul that looks to spiritual awareness to solve life's problems and likes to help others to do so in the same way.

Tarot

Three of Pentacles: This is the card that denotes some kind of public recognition for the work you do, either in the future or even perhaps on social media in some way. Along with this recognition also come rewards, which may be part of the incentive for you as you seek to communicate your idealism through your work or art.

Famous birthdays

John Cleese British comedian and actor
Vanessa-Mae British classical violinist
Kelly Osborne British actress and singer

October 28th

Emotional powerhouse

Your emotions probably don't alarm or overwhelm you and, in fact, these are available for you to use very much to your advantage, as you often feel your way toward success. You have the combined stealth and strategic planning skills of those who share your sun sign but you're much more forthright about your approach than some, which helps makes communicating with others so much easier. Along with your emotional side, there's an objectivity that helps power through other people's more subjective objections, which will gain you respect as long as you don't bludgeon people with it. Fortunately, you are also likely to have the charm to temper your more direct approach, encouraging others and making you something of a leader. Working in business, industry or science in some way all hold an attraction for you, especially if you can use your emotional strength to support your goals. You are capable of huge loyalty, too, which potential life partners also value, and once committed to another, this is likely to be for life.

Numerology

No. I: A powerful entity and results-oriented force, all about initiating action and getting things done.

Tarot

Queen of Swords: If this card represents anything it's the ability to be decisive. Swords in the Tarot deck represent our intellectual capacity and wielding a blade to cut through obfuscation and get to the truth is often the goal. An ability to weigh up a situation and to be decisive is yours to utilise and will help you throughout life.

Famous birthdays

Bill Gates American business magnate and philanthropist
Julia Roberts American actress
Joaquin Phoenix Puerto Rican actor and environmentalist

October 29th

Accomplished tactician

If anyone is going to be guarding the element of surprise and only using it where and when it will have maximum impact, it is likely to be you because you probably don't make a move until you have planned all that will follow. To you, perhaps, life isn't so much like a game of chess, it *is* a game of chess, and you've no intention of losing. An independent thinker with a tactician's mind, you're likely to work towards any outcome quite secretively until you're sure of your next move. If this is starting to sound a bit like military-style manoeuvres, then that could be a clue to your perfect career, but you'd also thrive in police work, investigative reporting or that most Scorpio of careers, the secret service or its equivalent in domestic life. You are tenacious and loyal, and your colleagues admire this quality as much as your ability to problem-solve. You're likely to be adamant that your work and home lives remain separate, and at home there is a softer version of you available to those you love and care for. You are likely to be very protective of loved ones, but also playful and very committed to the idea of family life.

Numerology

No. 2: Shows resilience and power in gentleness, often provides the role of mediator and linked to psychic abilities.

Tarot

The Chariot: Driving purposefully into the future, this vehicle is depicted rather mysteriously as being drawn by two sphinxes, those enigmatic and inscrutable mythological creatures. So, be guided on your life's journey by something other than facts; learn to trust your intuition as well.

Famous birthdays

Winona Ryder American actress
Rufus Sewell British actor
Richard Dreyfuss American actor

October 30th

Accomplished communicator

There's probably a natural kindness towards your fellow man that influences your approach to others and, because you have zero interest in going it alone at home or at work, this works well for you. This makes you likely to engage with your personal community at quite a deep level, wanting to get involved and improve things for everyone. You also have an inclination to get things done rather than just talk about them, which makes you a valued contributor to any group. To this end, once you've harnessed all you need to know to get on with the job, you're so accomplished in communicating your ideas that others are only too happy to go along with them. That kindness and caring you show when communicating may find you choosing to work in social services, teaching or healthcare because of the great satisfaction it brings you to make a positive difference to the lives of others. This same caring aspect is more than evident in your more intimate relationships, where you easily prioritise their needs, making you a valued partner with whom to share the ups and downs of life.

Numerology

No. 3: Creative with the gift of imagination and an ability to communicate in writing, art or speech.

Tarot

Six of Swords: Here the Swords are indicative of action, specifically the action of taking care of others, using what resources we have to help them move towards an easier existence. This card suggests that this action is taken in response to another person's sorrow, where our kindness can help counteract life's hardships.

Famous birthdays

Ruth Gordon Jones American actress and screenwriter
Ivanka Trump American businesswoman
Diego Maradona Argentinian footballer

October 31st

Analytical thinker

When the cool intellect of a scientist is combined with the emotional temperament of an artist there can sometimes be some tension, but it can also fuel a lot of exciting ideas. For those born on this date it usually works to their advantage where a more entrepreneurial approach to work shows up, often in a new take on an old idea, about which you are likely to be very shrewd and well focused. You also realise that getting others on board will help your plans for success whatever your career choice, and this comes more easily to you than some because you have a genuine interest in people. In addition, you are more likely to be driven by a desire for recognition rather than more obvious financial rewards, and this is probably what fuels the energy you need to succeed. That energy buzz may find you burning the candle at both ends, so it's also as well to apply an analytical take on your own well-being. You also want and need love and affection to flourish, but it may take you time to realise that you have to make time for this, too.

Numerology

No. 4: Invested in the physical world, centred earth energy that is practical in application.

Tarot

Queen of Cups: Cups in the Tarot deck represent emotions and here the Queen of Cups is holding fast to her emotions, which is a reminder not just to hold on to but also to express how we feel. Remember that it is as important to receive as it is to give, and if we don't share how we feel, it can make it difficult for others to support us.

Famous birthdays

Vanilla Ice American rapper and actor
Rob Schneider American actor and director
John Keats British poet

November 1st

Enthusiastic explorer

Those born on this date are likely to roll up their sleeves and get stuck in rather than sit around thinking about a problem for more than a minute or two. You're also likely to be fearless in the face of obstacles and opposition, and because of this, others tend to look up to you. You may come across as a little impulsive and restless because you find it difficult to slow down long enough to take stock. But your enthusiasm and energetic drive more than compensate for the odd mistake you make in your rush to get things moving in the right direction. You will do very well in business, especially when you're able to work on your own initiative, and you may even step into the world of entrepreneurship. What you are unlikely to enjoy is the routine of a nine-to-five desk job, where it feels as if one day merges into the next. But once you find yourself in the right job, you probably give 100 per cent and may even be at risk of pushing yourself too far, so take care to avoid burning out. This commitment may also impinge on your personal relationships, so be sure to take time out for these and don't neglect those you love.

Numerology

No. 1: A powerful entity and results-oriented force, all about initiating action and getting things done.

Tarot

Six of Pentacles: This card shows us your desired outcome and why you give your work everything you've got and more. It is symbolic of someone who has worked hard in order to give back to society, but it also carries a warning: a set of scales. The warning is to make sure you have a good work/life balance and not to give so much you risk burning out.

Famous birthdays

Jenny McCarthy American actress
Anthony Kiedis American singer-songwriter
Toni Collette-Galafassi Australian actress and singer-songwriter

November 2nd

Protective idealist

You are someone whose intentions are benevolent, but sometimes the way you go about offering help and advice may seem a bit overbearing, especially when your input has not been asked for. You probably have plenty of opinions and ideas on how to go about things and all that's being suggested here is that sometimes you need to allow others to do things their own way, however much you want to step in and protect them. You are probably as opinionated about what you believe to be right and fair in life, with a humanitarian concern about which you are deeply authentic. You have a tendency to say what you mean and have probably had to learn to pause sometimes before you share your convictions. And while you won't go looking for confrontation your idealistic nature won't shy away from it if you think it necessary. This strength of character might find you making a commitment to political, humanitarian or environmental causes, out of which you may forge a career. You are generally full of goodwill towards others and also very committed to your partner, because you're also likely to believe that charity begins at home.

Numerology

No. 2: Shows resilience and power in gentleness, often provides the role of mediator and linked to psychic abilities.

Tarot

Ten of Pentacles: A very positive card that depicts great happiness and material success gained through hard work and commitment to the wider world. Contentment in this outcome is also a shared pleasure as there are two people depicted enjoying the fruits of their labours.

Famous birthdays

David Schwimmer American actor
Marie Antoinette Last Queen of France before 1789 French Revolution
k.d. lang Canadian singer-songwriter

November 3rd

Insightful flirt

When it comes to the heart versus head dilemma, for those born on this date there's always a tendency to follow your heart, which in turn can lead to emotional dramas. Learning to manage this may be a lifetime's work because there's no denying that the way you approach life creates an excitement that you probably enjoy. It's not that you crave the limelight, it's just that you often seem to end up standing in its glare. Like a lot of Scorpios who can often see beyond the obvious, you're also likely to have been blessed with the gift of insight, which should help you avoid the worst of the potential dramas. All this may mean that it takes some time for you to find a career that is interesting enough to stick at. Anything that requires a creative edge may suit you, so if you have a flair for PR, for example, you may find more interest in the world of movies than in finance. When it comes to personal relationships, you may be accused of being flirtatious, but this does seem to come naturally to you. You're likely to take some time making a commitment to just one person and may not settle down until later in life. When you do, you'll be committed for life.

Numerology

No. 3: Creative with the gift of imagination and an ability to communicate in writing, art or speech.

Tarot

The Magician: This Magus has all the resources of the Tarot available to him, making him a gifted operator. You are gifted a similar range of possibilities, so once you choose a path there'll be no stopping you from working your way towards the spotlight in whichever career you choose.

Famous birthdays

Lulu Scottish singer and actress
Roseanne Barr American actress and comedian
Anna Wintour British-American journalist

November 4th

Enterprising realist

There's a sensual streak in your make-up common to many Scorpios, but this isn't obvious at first glance because you are also something of a realist. Combined, these traits show up in an enterprising way that often looks towards humanitarian concerns, so you may well seek work that is financially rewarding but will also help others and leave the world a better place. You have a good head for figures and are smart about business. For this reason, if you are successful in areas of finance or commerce, you're likely to turn your attention to philanthropy in some way so that others can benefit from your hard work and good fortune. You bring the same commitment and dedication into the workplace that you show your partner and family at home, and it is admirable how, despite your considerable skills and intellect, you never think a task is beneath you. That's a great asset and will make the necessary grafting more palatable. Watch out for something of an insecure streak, however, when it comes to your partner, as this could make you a little possessive and controlling.

Numerology

No. 4: Invested in the physical world, centred earth energy that is practical in application.

Tarot

Death: This card indicates big change is afoot, the death of the old to make space for the new, and this may well feel uncomfortable while you are in transition between the two. But when you look back, you will see the reasons for it. There may be times in life when you are resistant to change, but trust the process as it will work in your favour.

Famous birthdays

Matthew McConaughey American actor and producer
Loretta Swit American actress
Puff Daddy American rapper and songwriter

November 5th

Intellectually curious

That curiosity may well find you intrigued about what can be improved in established systems and puzzling out how to identify improvements and advances. Looking beneath the surface comes naturally to you and you are likely to be an excellent researcher, enjoying the thrill of one discovery opening the door to the next. This may see you drawn to careers where research is important, from academic or scientific research to journalism or police work. You may even be someone who relishes working alone to find answers, before returning to your team-mates. You probably have Scorpio's telltale confidence in yourself and your abilities, too, and people may admire your analytical skills and creative solutions. This also makes you a much-valued friend, colleague, parent and partner, and you in turn value a happy domestic life to support your endeavours. A stable relationship is important to you, as is your home, which is where you relax and refuel.

Numerology

No. 5: Impulsive and restless by nature, spontaneous and likes to discover the world through the senses.

Tarot

Queen of Pentacles: The Queen of Pentacles is someone you can count on through thick and thin. She has a clear love of nature and it may be that nature is the place you go, or need to go, to recharge your batteries, so that, like her, you can continue to nurture and encourage those around you. This card also denotes prosperity and success for you.

Famous birthdays

Vivien Leigh British actress
Bryan Adams Canadian singer and record producer
Tilda Swinton British actress

November 6th

Generous giver

Your concern for your fellow humans is genuine. Some give in order to receive, but for you the pleasure is purely in the giving, so it's also important to ensure your generous attitude isn't exploited. But like a lot of Scorpios, you're probably insightful enough about people to avoid this. Still waters also tend to run deep and while you may show up in both public and private with an optimistic attitude, behind the scenes you're a little more circumspect. That's a strong combination and it will work in your favour across a spectrum of careers in people-centred industries, from retail to medicine. While you want the best for others, you may occasionally need to remind yourself that they too have free will because a deep-rooted perfectionist streak common to many Scorpios can sometimes try to assert itself. You are generous with your time, money, intellect, effort and heart because you tend to want to make good things happen, not just for yourself but probably for others, too. In love, you have much to give but must learn to expect enough in return.

Numerology

No. 6: Empathic and nurturing, can problem-solve in an emotional and physical way, responsible and cares deeply about family and friends.

Tarot

Five of Cups: This card probably represents the shadow side of you, an emotional part of your character that occasionally spills over, as represented by the toppled cups. Fortunately, the others are standing firm, so it's perfectly possible to accept this aspect of yourself while knowing that it won't completely overwhelm you.

Famous birthdays

Sally Field American actress and director
Ethan Hawke American actor
Emma Stone American actress

November 7th

Natural peacemaker

There's a diplomatic way in which you deal with others and this seems to come naturally to those born on this date. If you need a way to resolve a dispute or disagreement without confrontation, you'll find it. This imparts a sort of stillness and calm about you that others respond to. It may be a skill that develops over time and you may find that it's at work rather than in the schoolyard that this comes into its own. You probably also have more than a passing interest in esoteric ideas and more than your share of seemingly psychic ability. It is as if you use your Scorpio insight to see through the different arguments to break the deadlock, instinctively recognising when people start refusing to compromise that there is often some irrational fear that you can allay, and all will be well again. If you don't get a job with the United Nations, you may think about working in the healing arts. At home and with those you love, this approach helps ensure a balanced relationship and happy domestic life, because for all that peacefulness you are not a doormat.

Numerology

No. 7: Very analytical and detail-oriented, likes to observe and investigate things and has a keen, inventive eye.

Tarot

The High Priestess: Often referred to as the Eternal Student, the High Priestess knows that studying the esoteric world gives us a wider window onto human relationships. Learning to access and utilise this wisdom may be a life's work, but it can help you succeed in both work and love.

Famous birthdays

Marie Curie Polish scientist and Nobel Prize winner
Albert Camus French writer and philosopher
Joni Mitchell Canadian singer-songwriter

November 8th

Original thinker

Your ideas may be considered too original and radical for some, but can someone really be *too* original? You have a remarkable imagination that can sometimes alarm those around you, and as a child you may have enjoyed scaring your classmates with inventive stories. Harnessing this ability may need maturity to work for you, and whether you choose a career in research, science, public broadcasting or investigative reporting, the fact that you can think for yourself is what will make you and your body of work stand out. You know that good research requires paying attention to detail, but this comes easily to you and actually shapes your ideas. Optimistic and resourceful, you have such vitality in your approach to life that you are probably one of the few people that can burn the candle at both ends well into middle age and still appear at breakfast looking fresh and alert. A stable and grounding home life is crucial in supporting you, though, and this may take some time to get right, but this is important to you and so when you do, you will really flourish.

Numerology

No. 8: Sees the big picture and aims for it, linked to abundance and material wealth and uses financial success to give back to others.

Tarot

King of Pentacles: Often interpreted as depicting someone self-made and successful. In your case it is self-determined, as in thinking for yourself and then acting on that original thinking. This card bodes well for your personal success and suggests that you are able to access all the internal and external resources you need to succeed.

Famous birthdays

Tara Reid American actress
Gordon Ramsay British chef, restauranteur and TV presenter
Mary Hart American TV personality and actress

November 9th

Pragmatic psychic

You're probably already aware that you're intuitive and sometimes almost psychic, which is something you could probably develop, should you so choose. In your head, there's not much difference between the past, present or future, and you are probably quite comfortable about the possibilities of alternate universes. In fact, this is not uncommon among Scorpios, but it is often pronounced in those born on this date. This slightly mystical aspect to your character can be deceptive as you are no fool and still have that proverbial sting in your tail when necessary. You will bring these qualities to whichever career you choose, which may also involve some sort of healing, whether in conventional or alternative medicine. For those who wish to get close, there's no point playing games or hard to get, as you can read people well and are seldom fooled, preferring a straightforward approach in relationships. It's not that you can't be romantic, you can, but when it comes to a lifelong relationship, you're likely to take quite a pragmatic approach to any commitment.

Numerology

No. 9: An old soul that looks to spiritual awareness to solve life's problems and likes to help others to do so in the same way.

Tarot

Eight of Swords: This is a card for someone who isn't reliant on what they can physically see in order to wield their power and the figure with access to eight swords is actually blindfolded in order to prove this point. For you, this message suggests you learn to trust and develop what comes naturally.

Famous birthdays

Ivan Turgenev Russian writer
Carl Sagan American astronomer and astrophysicist
Hedy Lamarr American actress and inventor

November 10th

Cerebral creative

What's going on in your head is often so interesting that you may sometimes appear introspective, isolated and depressed to others, particularly if they suggest that you 'cheer up' when you're actually perfectly happy. Your creativity is very much part of how you think, and you probably have little interest in fame or status, but you do want to explore all avenues open to you – spiritual, intellectual and material – to campaign for a better world to share with your fellow man. It might take you some time to work out the best field of work for you, but what's also likely is that you probably have no idea that you leave such a memorable impression on those you meet. You may find a niche in teaching or scientific research that will engage your intellectual creativity, or work in something more arts-related like creative writing in some form. You won't want to compete with your soulmate in terms of creativity, but there's a balance to be struck, and you will probably need someone who understands how much this is a part of who you are.

Numerology

No. 1: A powerful entity and results-oriented force, all about initiating action and getting things done.

Tarot

The Star: This is a very positive card, and it often appears for those with healing talents. It may also affirm your feelings of spiritual connection, and as a guiding light, this star will help you navigate your way through life, balancing your creativity with a role that brings you great satisfaction.

Famous birthdays

Richard Burton Welsh actor
Brittany Murphy American actress and singer
Roy Scheider American actor

November 11th

Emotional powerhouse

You're probably unaware that some people can find you hard to get to know, but if you're honest, that's OK with you. When it comes to your career, you enjoy working in a team of like-minded individuals but are equally capable of working alone. You may choose a hands-on career in construction or build a different kind of business based on research or IT. You're much admired for your values, including your integrity and clear-sighted determination, but even those closest to you often feel they don't know what you're really thinking or who you are privately. It's not that you're secretive exactly, just that you don't like everyone knowing about your business, and what makes this so powerful is your ability to manage and use your emotions effectively. You're not a particularly sombre character, and many find you very attractive, but you may have an unnerving tendency to turn your attention on and off at will, which can be confusing. It's as well to be aware of this because your closest personal relationships are very important to you and they need their home to be a secure haven.

Numerology

No. 2: Shows resilience and power in gentleness, often provides the role of mediator and linked to psychic abilities.

Tarot

The Hermit: Don't underestimate or dismiss the Hermit, who's not anti-social, just discriminating about those with whom he engages. The light depicted in his hand shows an ability to help others see a situation clearly, something you probably share. Being able to communicate clearly to others is important to you in both your personal and work life.

Famous birthdays

Leonardo DiCaprio American actor
Demi Moore American actress
Calista Flockhart American actress

November 12th

Stubborn achiever

When you set goals as ambitious as those that you're likely to set yourself you are going to need to be stubborn to achieve them, making this description of those born on this date a compliment. You're rather like an athlete in your commitment to the training that may be necessary to succeed and are probably able to dig just that little bit deeper to keep going. If you're not involved in sports professionally, they may well be a big part of your social and leisure life, giving you an outlet for this impressive focus. You may also need a similar capacity to steer you through some of life's non-work challenges, because sometimes these can feel a little overwhelming and may take some time to learn to manage. Self-confidence is something you can develop, so remember to trust and believe in yourself, because you do have what it takes to be happy, and this resilience comes from a commitment to what you value. You take your meaningful relationships seriously and are happy to invest time and effort, but only up to a point. Even so, there will probably still be times when you need to retreat to find the emotional balance that's sometimes needed.

Numerology

No. 3: Creative with the gift of imagination and an ability to communicate in writing, art or speech.

Tarot

Five of Cups: The Cups represent our emotions, and this card suggests a complex person who tends to respond with feeling and may have to learn to manage this, balancing what is felt and what is known. From learned experience comes resilience, on which you can draw throughout life, so it's important to remember this.

Famous birthdays

Grace Kelly American actress and Princess of Monaco
Anne Hathaway American actress
Neil Young Canadian singer-songwriter

November 13th

Prudent strategist

With their thoughtful and secretive natures, many Scorpios are born strategists, but those born on this date are likely to take this skill to new levels with their ability to investigate and then plan a strategy. There's probably nothing you enjoy more than diligently looking to find the truth of what's really going on, having qualities of patience, endurance and perseverance to help keep you focused. This prudent approach means your strategies tend to be well-grounded and likely to work, whether you are managing a sales force or argumentative friends. Smart *and* creative, you may take an artistic career path, or you may gravitate towards the sciences, but either way, once you are sure of your facts you are happy to bring your instincts into play, too. This is also often the case for you in affairs of the heart, because you like to know the facts of the person you're interested in before you allow your emotions full rein. Once you trust yourself on this, you'll trust them; otherwise, you may come across as a little detached and aloof, which is probably a way of hiding your own insecurities.

Numerology

No. 4: Invested in the physical world, centred earth energy that is practical in application.

Tarot

The Fool: Don't be misled by the name of this card because there is nothing foolish about the young man depicted. Alongside him is a little white dog that represents the instincts we can develop to guide us. You act on instinct, but only once you have all the information you need, which is something you'll come to trust.

Famous birthdays

Whoopi Goldberg American actress and comedian
Robert Louis Stevenson Scottish writer
Monique Coleman American actress

November 14th

Empathic stoic

Empathy is a lovely quality as long as other people's feelings don't become overwhelming. For those born on this date, this quality is tempered by an ability to create boundaries, which means you can be caring while also able to stand back a little. This is a valuable asset in the caring professions where you sometimes need to make difficult clinical decisions, while still feeling for those in need of your care. Working as a medic in some way may attract you for a career, and that small edge of detachment or stoicism is what makes you a more effective carer than some. But you may also find that you are drawn to other forms of alternative or psychological healing, which create or complement your work life in some way. There's no doubt that your family and friends are important, and it's where you will look to find yourself supported, especially if you work in a profession that demands a lot of empathy. In your more intimate relationships, you can be a passionate lover, but you also need your mate to be a friend who you can talk to and confide in.

Numerology

No. 5: Impulsive and restless by nature, spontaneous and likes to discover the world through the senses.

Tarot

Queen of Cups: In this card the Queen of Cups holds a sacred vessel full of precious oil. You can't access the oil without unlocking the vessel's secret compartments, in the same way that you can't access yourself without unlocking your feelings, too. You may already be aware of this fact, although it may take time to mature into a full acceptance of it.

Famous birthdays

Charles, Prince of Wales Member of the British royal family
Claude Monet French Impressionist painter
Condoleezza Rice American diplomat and academic

November 15th

Underdog champion

When it comes to the underdog, you are likely to want to stick up for them and try and make a difference. This is a feature of those born on this date, not least because they also recognise how easy it is in the society in which we live to become the underdog ourselves. Online bullying might mean we are all only a tweet away from falling foul of the crowd, and this sort of realisation probably makes you want to chip away at some of those structures in society that others aren't even aware of. This sort of insight is also typical of the thoughtfulness of many Scorpios, but it doesn't always make life easy for you, as you're not a natural rebel. For this reason, taking a stance and making a difference may take some courage. This inclination may find you working in the charity sector in some way or some sort of social service, whether professionally or informally. You know what's important in life and you're also smart enough to put together and cherish a close network of family and friends who will be there to support you when you find it hard to keep going.

Numerology

No. 6: Empathic and nurturing, can problem-solve in an emotional and physical way, responsible and cares deeply about family and friends.

Tarot

Justice: This card very much represents your values and what you will work towards generally in life. You may find yourself fighting for vulnerable communities, endangered wildlife or the planet itself, either through work or social media activism. But you will do so happily, whatever causes you've picked up your sword to defend.

Famous birthdays

Jonny Lee Miller British actor
Petula Clark British singer
Beverly D'Angelo American actress and singer

November 16th

Charismatic coach

Many people choose to work as life coaches, but it is those who have the charisma to inspire others who are most successful. This may be an aspect of your professional or leisure life that you may want to develop, whether in business, sport or well-being, and those born on this date definitely have a flair for it. Your natural charisma means people feel drawn to you, and the highly original way you often look at the world will appeal to those becoming tired of the *status quo*. If you're not working as a life coach or a counsellor, you may be heading into community politics or some other form of activism, and you may well have your eye on a global stage. This is not so much about your ego, though; it's about genuinely wanting to encourage others to realise their potential. Watch that you don't become so busy helping others and sharing your hard-won pearls of wisdom with your followers (often complete strangers) that you're neglecting those with whom you share your life and home. It's as important to support those who support you as it is to coach the world.

Numerology

No. 7: Very analytical and detail-oriented, likes to observe and investigate things and has a keen, inventive eye.

Tarot

Page of Pentacles: Pentacles represent our resources, including money, and when the Page of Pentacles shows up it is to tell you that you already have absolutely everything you need to make the next move. Whether you choose to utilise the resources available to you is up to you, but they are there to develop through training and application.

Famous birthdays

Lisa Bonet American actress
Burgess Meredith American actor and director
Marg Helgenberger American actress

November 17th

Persuasive idealist

It's one thing to be an idealist, but tricky if you can't persuade others of the value of your idealism. This isn't likely to be a problem for you as this unique combination makes you communicative in the most persuasive of ways. If you haven't begun to utilise this gift, you soon will because you know you've been incarnated to do something big with your life. You speak eloquently and will aim to use your skills to highlight those things that matter to you. Your dream may be to make a difference in some way, perhaps using some issue of social injustice about which you have personal experience. What you won't be doing is sitting in the corner like a wallflower at a party. You probably have a progressive approach to communications, and so if you want to promote your work, you're likely to do so through online resources and apps. Happier in some ways on an open stage than in private, you may sometimes struggle to open up in an intimate relationship and reveal who you really are. Take the time to do so, because cherishing someone and being cherished will support you in your aims and ideals.

Numerology

No. 8: Sees the big picture and aims for it, linked to abundance and material wealth and uses financial success to give back to others.

Tarot

The High Priestess: This card represents the need for lifelong learning and so often shows up for someone who has the humility to know and accept that life is a learning journey. It's a stimulating path for those who take it and being open to both formal and informal styles of learning is one that greatly enhances how we experience life.

Famous birthdays

Martin Scorsese American director
Danny DeVito American actor
Sophie Marceau French actress and screenwriter

November 18th

Courageous crusader

If you feel you are on a crusade in life, then courage is a useful ally, because this is seldom an easy path for anyone (although one that comes more naturally to those born on this date than others). It's not all heavy-going, either. Some crusades create lifelong relationships that enable us to accomplish more together than alone, which is rewarding. And it doesn't really matter what channels you use to progress your ideas – TV, movies, business, politics, the arts, writing, motivational speaking, music or science – it can be stimulating and fun, enabling you to leave your mark, whichever path you choose. You can probably read a room and the people in it faster than others, and may have an almost psychic-like ability to perceive what's not being said, which also strengthens your position. There's a strong possibility you'll be guiding other crusaders on a similar path, and you'll know that this is an enormous privilege. In matters of love, you have a tendency to give away more than you ask in return, which can create an imbalance in your relationships. If this occurs, be sure to address it; otherwise it may lead to resentment on your part.

Numerology

No. 9: An old soul that looks to spiritual awareness to solve life's problems and likes to help others to do so in the same way.

Tarot

The Hermit: Don't interpret this card too literally. Yes, the Hermit is lighting the way ahead, but we don't know exactly for whom. All that matters is that this energy, which represents hard-won wisdom and esoteric understanding, lies at the heart of your work and is available to you when needed for your own development.

Famous birthdays

Owen Wilson American actor
Kim Wilde British singer and TV presenter
Ant McPartlin British TV presenter

November 19th

Purposeful leader

Despite having an excellent intellect, what probably excites you most is action. You only really value leadership if there's some tangible purpose to it, and if you see something that needs doing, changing or improving, you'll probably be the one to instigate the action required. This makes you a valued member of your community and a safe pair of hands at work, where you seldom put off until tomorrow what really needs doing today. You may well choose hands-on work to help shape how future generations tackle social issues, because you care about your legacy on this Earth. Whichever path you choose, people are likely to trust your word and follow your lead. This is probably because you're also an outgoing and likeable person who attracts a diverse circle of friends and has a happy social life. And if you have a family of your own, you'll work hard to create a loving and stable home. There may be times when you slide from being helpful to being a tad controlling, wanting to do things your own way, but hopefully those who love you will gently let you know.

Numerology

No. 1: A powerful entity and results-oriented force, all about initiating action and getting things done.

Tarot

Ten of Wands: Wands represent the power we have at our disposal and this card provides you with a lot, but it comes with a warning. Struggling to use it all at once can be counter-productive, so it's better to use it purposefully a little at a time without exhausting yourself in the process.

Famous birthdays

Meg Ryan American actress
Jodie Foster American actress
Jack Dorsey American technology entrepreneur and co-founder of Twitter

November 20th

Charming persuader

You have oodles of charm, so it's probably not difficult for you to persuade others to your way of thinking. Because of this, you're likely to find it easy to influence others and generally use this talent for the greater good, rather than your own personal gain. To outsiders, you may come across as quite self-controlled, but the truth may be that you have little patience with either those who don't grasp your suggestions quickly or those who do, but then object. You will always prefer to use charm, but if necessary, there is a sharper alternative. You probably have a good business brain, or may develop one later in life, because you have Scorpio's gift for strategic thinking. These elements may all combine to open up ways to make business more sustainable, in order to stop damaging the environment, for example. You are also more than capable of charming a potential lover but expect the same effort in return because you know your own worth. In the absence of reciprocal emotional investment, you're likely to move swiftly on to find your soulmate.

Numerology

No. 2: Shows resilience and power in gentleness, often provides the role of mediator and linked to psychic abilities.

Tarot

The Lovers: This couple are depicted as well-matched in every way, but far from stepping on each other's toes there's a huge and healthy gap between them. By maintaining their own identities, they keep their love alive. Bear in mind that this may also mean revealing a little vulnerability and feeling safe enough to do so.

Famous birthdays

Sean Young American actress
Joe Biden 46th President of the United States
Kimberley Walsh British singer and actress

November 21st

Cheerful empath

You present a sunny and cheerful face to the world, but for those born on this date, this can provide a useful mask protecting hidden depths that many won't suspect. This is to your advantage, because being empathic to the extent you are can sometimes be exhausting. That you care goes without saying, but one of the ways to demonstrate your empathic concern is to try and lighten the emotional load of others through your natural cheer. You'll likely be drawn to the creative arts, whether professionally or in your spare time, which will allow you to work through these complex responses to the world and the people around you. Expressing this side of yourself provides respite and you may paint, sculpt or write, but whatever you do, it will give you a way to explore those hidden depths. Family and friends are important to you, but top of your list of priorities is your intimate relationship with your partner and lover. As far as you're concerned, success means absolutely nothing without someone special to share it with, plus your partner can hopefully provide that safe space you need to unwind, relax and let go of some of your feelings and fears.

Numerology

No. 3: Creative with the gift of imagination and an ability to communicate in writing, art or speech.

Tarot

The Hierophant: This is the card of the teacher, which might represent you or the necessity for you to find someone you trust from whom to learn. Even experienced teachers find new ways of seeing and engaging with life, so it also means staying open to learning from other people, places and ideas. For the empath, this may also mean learning ways to balance caring with not being overwhelmed.

Famous birthdays

Goldie Hawn American actress
Björk Icelandic singer-songwriter
René Magritte Belgian surrealist artist

November 22nd

Feisty organiser

As we move into Sagittarius, we immediately see the effects of this fire sign, with a sparky energy and a look towards the horizon. You probably feel a natural restlessness and a sense that moving forwards is always important. This restlessness can sometimes make you appear a little dissatisfied with your lot, but this is really just an aspect of your ambitious approach to life. With an eye to the future and a creative knack, you may go into a career in events organisation, from weddings to political conferences, where you're likely to lead from the front. Equally, organising a group holiday holds similar appeal as it combines planning and anticipation, at which you excel. Strong-willed, competitive and energetic, you probably also excel at sports of some sort, or are a very engaged referee. You can be a very caring person but sometimes your enthusiasm for getting stuck in and driving change can get the better of you, making you a little bossy with your colleagues. What's essential is to press pause occasionally, to chill and recharge, especially at home and with those you love; otherwise, they may find it hard to keep up and come to resent it.

Numerology

No. 4: Invested in the physical world, centred earth energy that is practical in application.

Tarot

Nine of Pentacles: These represent our physical and material resources, and this card gifts you a good number, suggesting that you're prepared to put in the graft but that you will want your reward here on Earth rather than in the hereafter. That's fine, but you must also remember to take the time to enjoy it and share it with those you love, otherwise all that effort may be wasted.

Famous birthdays

Jamie Lee Curtis American actress
Terry Gilliam American director and screenwriter
George Elliot British writer

November 23rd

Freewheeling adventurer

You probably have little interest in stability or swapping adventure for security, especially at the moment. You are stimulated by new places and likely to find everyday mundane practicalities like paying the bills a little tedious. Work is very often a means to an end, and you may seek a training that can take you anywhere, from masseuse to software consultant, if that's what's called for. This is because every day brings new possibilities, whether this is securing your next contract or embarking on a three-month hike in the foothills of the Himalayas; you are more interested in the next adventure, whatever its shape or form. This constant need for stimulation may need to be balanced, because such an adventurous attitude to life may also make it difficult for you to commit to someone who wants a more stable existence, or at all. Certainly, you won't lack for potential partners, but not everyone will be able or want to keep up. Human contact is important to you, so there may come a time when compromises need to be made. When you realise that you may have to compromise a little, you may find your adventures become more enduring and the one you most seek lies at home.

Numerology

No. 5: Impulsive and restless by nature, spontaneous and likes to discover the world through the senses.

Tarot

Two of Cups: The Cups represent our emotions, and we see here what looks like the union of a happy couple toasting their love. But there seems to be a lack of mutual commitment and this may be an indication that if you also want to have that adventure, you may have to think about going it alone.

Famous birthdays

Miley Cyrus American singer-songwriter
Boris Karloff British actor
Kelly Brook British actress and model

November 24th

Caring conformer

You've probably no intention of rocking the boat, either at work or at home, but when you sense there are things that need to change, you're more likely to tackle this within the established system rather than from without. Conforming to a system means learning its rules and working out how to change them, which you're prepared to do. You also have the confidence to take the long view, knowing that bringing others on board can secure change, and you're prepared to work at this. For you, rebellion is too insecure a tool, although if you need to ally with activists, you will. Studying the law or working in teaching are two ways that your training and knowledge can work, and you may be drawn to either of these careers in some way. Whatever your professional role, at home the same caring attitude is obvious through the way you give time to your family, and you won't be the first caring conformist that suggests family summit meetings to resolve problems. Demonstrably affectionate and protective of those who you love, you never go to sleep on an argument, either.

Numerology

No. 6: Empathic and nurturing, can problem-solve in an emotional and physical way, responsible and cares deeply about family and friends.

Tarot

Queen of Wands: The Queen of Wands is grounded and wise, and her role is to offer support when it's needed. The sunflower is a symbol of life and there's an energy and strength here that you can call on when you're flagging and your spirits need a little extra push, especially if you are unconfident about moving onto a bigger stage.

Famous birthdays

Henri de Toulouse-Lautrec French artist
Billy Connolly Scottish comedian and actor
Dale Carnegie American writer and lecturer

November 25th

Wisdom seeker

Although you're probably as outgoing as other Sagittarians, there's also a streak of self-reliance that comes from being comfortable in your own company, which is typical of those born on this date. Truth is, you're likely to be on something of an internal journey, trying to work out the ways of the world and forging your own wisdom to live by. This makes you something of an observer, too, happy to people-watch and choosing to interact on your own terms. It's this aspect of your personality that could find you drawn to formalising your thoughts through a training in psychology, whether as the basis for work in human resources or in a therapeutic role, somewhere you can make best use of your wisdom. This is also likely to be a lifelong journey and one that you may not even recognise, because there's unlikely to be any intensity about how you approach your search. You may find that you attract a similar soul as a partner, one who is happy to journey alongside you on your quest. This is likely to be important to you, as you probably love to share your insights and ideas with a like-minded soulmate.

Numerology

No. 7: Very analytical and detail-oriented, likes to observe and investigate things and has a keen, inventive eye.

Tarot

The Tower: This is a powerful card and not always easy to interpret, but its appearance here suggests that, for you, there will be a moment of insight and transformation at some point in your life that is related to your 'search', which could mean a complete career change or even a different location in which you play out your life's journey.

Famous birthdays

Carl Benz German car engineer
Andrew Carnegie Scottish-American industrialist and philanthropist
Joe DiMaggio American baseball player

November 26th

Gifted researcher

Anyone can go through the motions of research, but for those born on this date there's an added extra. For you, you have a gift to make interesting connections with what you find out, which can take you down some innovative pathways. Again, as for many Sagittarians, there's often a journey to be taken and with research one thing can easily lead to another. Because this can also include the thrill of the chase, it's probably something you relish and may well form the basis of your career, either in academic research, journalism or other forms of creative enquiry. What's for sure is that it's something that comes naturally to you, and as a child you probably asked endless questions and took to Google like a fish to water. This talent for research won't be limited to your professional life, either. When it comes to dating and love, you will want to know all about the object of your affections. Try not to get too obsessive – checking someone out is fine, but stalking them on social media isn't, and you may have to remember that in affairs of the heart there's also a role for serendipity and chance.

Numerology

No. 8: Sees the big picture and aims for it, linked to abundance and material wealth and uses financial success to give back to others.

Tarot

Ten of Swords: This card looks rather ominous with a body pinned down by ten swords, but it's really a reminder that when you feel very stuck, you do have the resources to cut loose and find another path. It takes reaching this point before a breakthrough can be made, so it's not to be feared but recognised as part of the process.

Famous birthdays

Tina Turner American singer
Rita Ora British actress and singer-songwriter
agnès b. French fashion designer

November 27th

Rebellious creative

That you are creative in your approach to life is probably obvious to everyone that meets you, but what might be stopping your progress is a rebellious streak which sometimes alienates others. Being in a state of constant rebellion can be exhausting but used occasionally can really energise a situation. You may have to learn to use this power to your advantage, so that the originality of your ideas can actually find expression without being lost in confrontation. Sometimes compromise makes other aspects of creativity possible, so the knack is to work out when this works in your favour. This may be especially important if your professional life relies on teamwork or being told what to do, and it may take you some time to find a role where your style of creativity is well harnessed, so practise a little patience. This may also be a requirement in your personal life, especially with less robust family members who may find your tendency to rebel intimidating. And when it comes to forging intimate relationships, compromise is always going to be part of the picture.

Numerology

No. 9: An old soul that looks to spiritual awareness to solve life's problems and likes to help others to do so in the same way.

Tarot

Eight of Pentacles: Pentacles represent our resources, and this is a card that raises questions about the way we utilise ours. Although this number suggests you are well-equipped, have you worked out the best way to use the resources or talent that you have? Sometimes it takes a while to get this right and there's no harm in pausing to take stock of where you are with this.

Famous birthdays

Bruce Lee Chinese-American martial arts expert and actor
James Avery American actor and poet
Caroline Kennedy American author and diplomat

November 28th

Savvy pioneer

Like many a Sagittarian, there's a touch of the pioneer that's likely to attract you to exploring very different routes, either around the world or to personal success. What's equally true is that you're probably very smart about the choices along the way, so to others there seems to be a logical progression in how you approach things. What makes you a pioneer is an ability to see possibilities where others don't, but it's being savvy about these that actually makes everything seem so feasible. It may take some trial and error on the road to maturity to learn how to communicate this, but when and if you do, it will greatly enhance any leadership skills you want to employ, particularly at work. Others are also likely to gain confidence from the assurance with which you deploy your innovative ideas, in such a way that they seem obvious. This sort of life journey requires an accommodating partner, and you may recognise the possibilities of a lasting relationship before the other party does. If this is the case, be smart enough to allow them the chance to catch up and you'll be in with a chance.

Numerology

No. 1: A powerful entity and results-oriented force, all about initiating action and getting things done.

Tarot

Seven of Wands: You are very well supported by this card, which suggests you can hold your own against all comers, but this defensive position may not always be necessary, and you could exhaust your energy for no good reason. There may be an alternative way to make better use of your power and this is what you need to discover for yourself.

Famous birthdays

Randy Newman American singer-songwriter
Ed Harris American actor
Barbara Morgan American astronaut

November 29th

Robust aesthete

This may sound a contradiction in terms, but while you're more refined than many of your fellow Sagittarians, you probably have the same fire in your belly when it comes to knowing what you want. There's a love and appreciation of art and beauty, and you're likely to be drawn to creating your own art or work with those who do. If you want to take your interest beyond an amateur level, you're also robust enough to take risks to get what you want, which may find you attracted to the business side of art in some way. This aspect of the art world can require a hard nose for negotiation, which may come naturally to you. You're also someone who can probably sense the public's changing mood and read the zeitgeist long before the mainstream, so it may be that you find your way to some sort of social commentary role, even if only on social media. But once established, that following may turn into an income stream. In relationships you enjoy the romance but can be torn between domestic security and being able to come and go as you please.

Numerology

No. 2: Shows resilience and power in gentleness, often provides the role of mediator and linked to psychic abilities.

Tarot

The Magician: Some people fear their sixth sense and never bother to explore it, but it's very often the result of careful observation, and if used wisely can help you when it comes to backing hunches. It can also help you to read other people's motivations, making you an interesting ally or foe.

Famous birthdays

Diane Ladd American actress
C.S. Lewis British writer
Joel Coen American director and screenwriter

November 30th

Focused analyst

You probably hide an incisive and analytical mind behind an unassuming demeanour, which means you can sometimes be overlooked in a crowd. Of course, this allows you to focus without the distraction of interaction or interruption, which sits quite comfortably with the way you like to operate. You can also come across as laidback, but in truth this is more a case of still waters running deep, because your goals are likely to be ambitious, with a methodical plan for realising them that few would even guess at. That focus could make you a natural leader, but you can be so subtle in some of your manoeuvres that it takes a while for others to discover you're actually the boss. There's probably a genuine concern for others that runs parallel to any leadership role you take on, which others will come to recognise and appreciate. Your ability to focus so well may be something you've learned, but it's also an asset in your personal life, because being able to switch off from your work life (which may be a demanding one) when you get back to your family will foster a harmonious domestic life.

Numerology

No. 3: Creative with the gift of imagination and an ability to communicate in writing, art or speech.

Tarot

The World: This may reflect your more worldly ambitions, but they also incorporate your wishes for your world, and you may find you need to wait until the time is right to realise them. Once you're sure of your place in the world, then your aims and objectives will tend to fall into place. There's a pattern to this that you'll soon start to see and be able to work with.

Famous birthdays

Ben Stiller American actor
Mark Twain American writer
Ridley Scott British director

December 1st

Eccentric free spirit

Of course, you're unlikely to see yourself as eccentric, because isn't everyone as free-spirited in the way they live as you? Probably not, but that doesn't matter because you also have a great deal of charm and people find your open-hearted nature easy to engage with. When it comes to work, finding the right profession to suit you may take some time, but remember that no experience is ever wasted, and all can be built upon. It's often the case that you approach things in a less than obvious way, but in creative careers innovative solutions can be a big plus. You may enjoy the companionship of working in a team as long as you're allowed enough leeway to progress at your own speed. People are likely to admire the drive and optimism you bring to the table, but there are times when you will make decisions that may seem reckless to everyone else. In your personal life it may take you a while to settle with one person and you could tend to prioritise friendship before more intimate relationships, but this can form the basis of the beginnings of a very happy one.

Numerology

No. I: A powerful entity and results-oriented force, all about initiating action and getting things done.

Tarot

Six of Cups: Here's a card that reveals how much you like to make other people happy. The offering of one cup (representing emotions) to another contains the message that it is never too late to have a happy life, whatever has gone before. When this card shows up, it's often to remind us that the future begins now.

Famous birthdays

Bette Midler American singer and actress
Richard Pryor American actor and comedian
Woody Allen American director

December 2nd

Easy-going people-pleaser

Easy-going and generally cooperative, you may sometimes be accused of being a people-pleaser, but is that a wholly bad thing? Actually, your priority is for a harmonious life, especially at work where you don't like to waste time, but as people will come to learn, this is probably only on your own terms. You also enjoy doing things for other people that pleases them, in a way that doesn't come across as obsequious. You are something of a diplomat and with the ability to maintain a neutral position and consider both sides, this will make you an asset both at work and at home, and you may have found yourself the peacemaker of the family. You may find that you also have a natural talent for sales, which it would be a shame not to explore, plus you can sniff out a new trend and spot the demise of an old one faster than anyone. Although you're a little less emotional than some Sagittarians, your friendship group is wide and important to you. In your more private life, you can be romantic and affectionate, but your priority is to find a companion with whom you can share life's ups and downs. Once you find this person, you won't hesitate to make a commitment.

Numerology

No. 2: Shows resilience and power in gentleness, often provides the role of mediator and linked to psychic abilities.

Tarot

King of Swords: The Swords represent our intellectual capabilities and decisiveness. Being able to mediate conflict calls for an ability to think clearly and make rational decisions that all parties can respect and accept. The King of Swords is the master of this, able to adjudicate in a calm and neutral way.

Famous birthdays

Britney Spears American singer
Nelly Furtado Canadian singer-songwriter
Gianni Versace Italian fashion designer

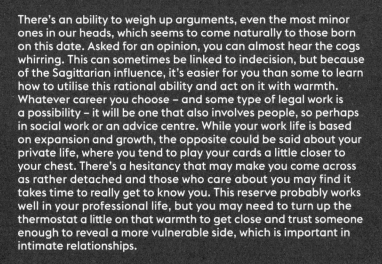

December 3rd

Rational adjudicator

There's an ability to weigh up arguments, even the most minor ones in our heads, which seems to come naturally to those born on this date. Asked for an opinion, you can almost hear the cogs whirring. This can sometimes be linked to indecision, but because of the Sagittarian influence, it's easier for you than some to learn how to utilise this rational ability and act on it with warmth. Whatever career you choose – and some type of legal work is a possibility – it will be one that also involves people, so perhaps in social work or an advice centre. While your work life is based on expansion and growth, the opposite could be said about your private life, where you tend to play your cards a little closer to your chest. There's a hesitancy that may make you come across as rather detached and those who care about you may find it takes time to really get to know you. This reserve probably works well in your professional life, but you may need to turn up the thermostat a little on that warmth to get close and trust someone enough to reveal a more vulnerable side, which is important in intimate relationships.

Numerology

No. 3: Creative with the gift of imagination and an ability to communicate in writing, art or speech.

Tarot

Eight of Wands: This is the card that signifies the beginning of something. This may be a new job or a new way of thinking. Throughout life it's important to be open to the possibilities of this to avoid becoming stuck, especially emotionally. For more rational types, this can take some reflection about what might be holding you back.

Famous birthdays

Julianne Moore American actress
Daryl Hannah American actress
Ozzy Osborne British singer-songwriter

December 4th

Dynamic entrepreneur

If you're not already involved in an entrepreneurial project (or three), that's probably because the right one hasn't come along yet. You probably come across as pretty chilled, but there's an undercurrent of ambition that might surprise some who know you and that dynamism often shows up in someone who finds adapting to change easy. In fact, this is probably what fuels your capacity to see opportunities for development. Communicating your ideas probably comes easily to you, too, which is a useful asset for encouraging others on board, whether you are launching a start-up or angling for a management buy-out. Your energy and enthusiasm are inspiring, and while you have the typical Sagittarian restless streak, this is tempered by the Number 4 in your chart which will keep you on the straight and narrow, so you can realise your goals. When you do take a break, you'll want to travel and explore new places and cultures with the same interest you bring to other areas of your life. In love, you are steadfast, reliable and committed, but you'll need a partner who knows that independence is important to you.

Numerology

No. 4: Invested in the physical world, centred earth energy that is practical in application.

Tarot

Seven of Wands: This is often considered the card of the entrepreneur, because Wands represent our creativity, and this card depicts one in the hand and another six to consider. There may be an element of risk involved, but the strong, upright posture suggests that this is part of the process and a recognised aspect.

Famous birthdays

Jeff Bridges American actor
Jay-Z American rapper and songwriter
Deanna Durbin Canadian singer

December 5th

Resourceful adventurer

Many Sagittarians are adventurers – it goes with the territory – but those who are also resourceful often get more out of it. You're probably as far removed from being a couch potato as it's possible to get and being busy, accomplishing tasks and ticking things off all please you. This makes you a highly valued work mate, whatever your profession, and although you may have a tendency to go off-piste occasionally, in time, as you become more senior, you will come to manage your need for freedom and the expectations of others better. Your adventurousness probably makes you keen to explore places and ideas that more conservative folk might avoid, but those around you feel in safe hands because of your resourcefulness. You have the Archer's clarity of purpose, so while you may want to use that creative streak you're blessed with, you're likely to use it in a way that benefits your longer-term goals, on which you are quite focused. In affairs of the heart, you are generous and passionate, but you won't agree to anything until you're sure it will fit into the bigger picture of how you want to live your life.

Numerology

No. 5: Impulsive and restless by nature, spontaneous and likes to discover the world through the senses.

Tarot

Three of Pentacles: The Pentacles represent our resources, including those qualities we may not always show to the whole world, and this card suggests some public recognition for your work. So, if you are a writer, musician or painter, even if only an amateur, expect to be fêted for this at some point.

Famous birthdays

Walt Disney American animator and movie pioneer
José Carreras Spanish opera singer
Little Richard American singer-songwriter

December 6th

People person

Those born on this date often approach tasks in a rational and organised way, and you're likely to believe that if there's a right way to do things, it's probably the way you do them, making you a safe pair of hands and a joy to work with. All of which is likely to make you a popular team member, whatever your profession, although events organising, project managing and even systems management are among the most obvious options. Your confidence at work partly comes down to a good attention to detail, which comes naturally to some. Although this is something you may have learned to develop, it's likely to inspire confidence in others. What you also bring to the table, both at work and at home, is light-heartedness, which encourages others to take a look at the world through your eyes. This optimism is a real asset in life, helping you feel happy and, secretly, you may even believe that you have been born with a lucky streak. You're always interested in others and never more so than when in love. You may have many partners before you settle down, but even your exes remember you with affection.

Numerology

No. 6: Empathic and nurturing, can problem-solve in an emotional and physical way, responsible and cares deeply about family and friends.

Tarot

Knight of Wands: Wands depict our energy and this card's message is one of readiness for action. Challenges are just another adventure and the recommendation here is that you pause for a moment to consider the implications before accepting them, as it doesn't always pay to be impulsive.

Famous birthdays

Alberto Contador Spanish cyclist
Sarah Rafferty American actress
Dave Brubeck American jazz pianist and composer

December

December 7th

Unconventional observer

If you were ever tempted to have a motivational statement tattooed somewhere on your body, it's likely to say something like: '*Dare to be different*'. With you, this attitude isn't really even a choice, as you've probably always felt that your take on life was different to that of your peers. You're interested in what the majority thinks, but it seldom makes sense to you to just follow the herd when there are more interesting avenues to be explored. You probably can't stand being intellectually or emotionally stifled, so the chances are you'll need meaningful work that allows for creative time spent alone. You're not a loner, as you actually care a lot about others and even feel responsible for their welfare and happiness, but loneliness isn't an issue and you probably relish times spent on your own projects, whatever your profession. In your personal relationships you're a devoted partner and friend, but with the important caveat that people accept you for your unconventional self and don't set about trying to change you. Chances are, you'll find someone as unconventional as yourself with whom to share a happy life.

Numerology

No. 7: Very analytical and detail-oriented, likes to observe and investigate things and has a keen, inventive eye.

Tarot

The High Priestess: The original Eternal Student, the High Priestess is her own person and would have it no other way. Her opinions and values are formed according to her own research into human nature, the Universe and the esoteric influences we can only guess at. As a role model, she has a lot to offer.

Famous birthdays

Tom Waits American singer-songwriter
Noam Chomsky American linguist and philosopher
Jennifer Carpenter American actress

December 8th

Romantic adventurer

You're determined to live life to the full and when you aim and shoot your archer's arrow at someone or something you are interested in, you do so wholeheartedly. Your take on life veers towards the romantic and one of the biggest challenges you may face is learning to accept the limitations that sometimes arise here. You're likely to have to pace yourself when the next great idea strikes, so you don't burn out. You have a strong desire to make others happy, so all this action is not about being selfish or trying to fulfil your own needs, which are actually pretty modest, but often to realise the romantic dreams of others. You want to be happy, but you want those whom you love and care about to be happy, too. Financial success alone is unlikely to motivate you, and you're not particularly ambitious for power or status, either. Although your grand ideas can sometimes prove extremely fruitful, there's often an element of risk involved in your endeavours. When it comes to your intimate relationships you may need to be a little more realistic and give those you care about something solid to rely on.

Numerology

No. 8: Sees the big picture and aims for it, linked to abundance and material wealth and uses financial success to give back to others.

Tarot

Ace of Pentacles: The Pentacles represent our resources, including money, and the Ace of Pentacles always tells us that you are on the right path, doing the right thing and being guided by an unseen hand making sure you have everything you need to leave the world a better place than you found it.

Famous birthdays

Kim Basinger American actress
Sammy Davis Jr American singer and dancer
Teri Hatcher American actress

December 9th

Ambitious hero

There is nothing wrong with aspiring to hero status, but the trick here is to remember to be the hero of your own story as much as anyone else's. Being ambitious isn't a negative, either, and this can take numerous forms without being selfish. Being ambitious for other people's happiness lies close to the heart of many born on this date, and this can play out not only through your choice of profession but also through the simple gestures you make at home, where you probably have a commitment to domestic harmony, too. Making concessions for other people's perceived weakness comes very easily, but resist the instinct to rescue others when it means denying them the opportunity to learn valuable lessons for themselves. Your instinct for rescue may take you literally into a career in the fire service or animal welfare, or perhaps in less literal ways into social work of some kind. That big heart will always find a connection with others, but you must be careful not to spread yourself too thin. What will support you is an intimate relationship where the balance between you is equal, and this may take some time to achieve, but once the commitment is finally made, it's very often for life.

Numerology

No. 9: An old soul that looks to spiritual awareness to solve life's problems and likes to help others to do so in the same way.

Tarot

Five of Pentacles: The resources needed here are not being used and this suggests you're not always aware that these need to be extended to yourself as much as to others. When you are feeling burdened by the difficulties of those around you, it's important to remember that sometimes others need to find their own solutions.

Famous birthdays

Judi Dench British actress
John Malkovich American actor and director
Beau Bridges American actor

December 10th

Social butterfly

This is how you come across and, indeed, you value your ability to grace a social occasion and also to network, both of which are skills common to many born on this date. You probably wouldn't enjoy a static office job, so something where a bulging contacts book is a bonus and some form of journalism, PR or marketing in a creative industry like fashion or cinema is likely to appeal. Some people who love the spotlight become the centre of every social gathering, but you probably relish being behind the scenes making it happen rather than just turning up for an event. That combination of enthusiasm and graft will help you excel in your role while enjoying yourself at the same time. Your personal social circle is likely to be diverse, but you're probably loyal to those that go way back, even to kindergarten, because you value that longevity of friendship, too. The same applies to your most intimate relationships, in which you're prepared to invest and commit, and these are more enduring than others might realise if they only take you at face value.

Numerology

No. 1: A powerful entity and results-oriented force, all about initiating action and getting things done.

Tarot

The Sun: This card radiates youthful vitality and happiness. It suggests that an ability to retain the optimism of your inner child is part of the secret of your social success, because there's a lack of cynicism about life that helps energise you and to which others happily gravitate.

Famous birthdays

Emily Dickinson American poet
Kenneth Branagh Irish actor and director
Ada Lovelace British mathematician

December 11th

Canny risk-taker

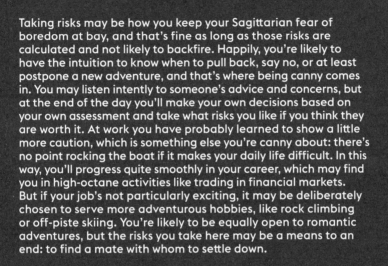

Taking risks may be how you keep your Sagittarian fear of boredom at bay, and that's fine as long as those risks are calculated and not likely to backfire. Happily, you're likely to have the intuition to know when to pull back, say no, or at least postpone a new adventure, and that's where being canny comes in. You may listen intently to someone's advice and concerns, but at the end of the day you'll make your own decisions based on your own assessment and take what risks you like if you think they are worth it. At work you have probably learned to show a little more caution, which is something else you're canny about: there's no point rocking the boat if it makes your daily life difficult. In this way, you'll progress quite smoothly in your career, which may find you in high-octane activities like trading in financial markets. But if your job's not particularly exciting, it may be deliberately chosen to serve more adventurous hobbies, like rock climbing or off-piste skiing. You're likely to be equally open to romantic adventures, but the risks you take here may be a means to an end: to find a mate with whom to settle down.

Numerology

No. 2: Shows resilience and power in gentleness, often provides the role of mediator and linked to psychic abilities.

Tarot

Temperance: This card is designed to prompt us to reflect on the balance in our lives from time to time, and it reminds us that we need to pause occasionally and consider if we are getting this right for ourselves. It's also a card about the necessity of creating downtime to refresh and refuel our bodies and minds, so avoiding burnout.

Famous birthdays

Jermaine Jackson American singer
Donna Mills American actress
Marco Pierre White British chef and restaurateur

December 12th

Charismatic influencer

You probably welcome and respond easily to attention, whether that's to a compliment from a friend, the limelight at a party or even an online Twitter spat because, in your world, these interactions are a positive thing and an opportunity to shine. You didn't necessarily set out to be in the spotlight, but you probably understood from an early age how this game works and were keen to learn how to play it to your advantage. Plus, you enjoy working out the best medium to use to promote the interests and causes closest to your heart, while also having fun. Your authenticity is also part of your charm and one of the reasons why people are interested in what you have to say. You recognise the opportunities that exist, whether for a science boffin presenting a TV show, a jewellery maker with a unique brand to sell, or a social media influencer using a video platform to highlight the latest make-up trends. A happy home life is also a priority, although it may take longer to achieve because, for you, more is at stake and it may come after you've established a professional role in some capacity as an influencer.

Numerology

No. 3: Creative with the gift of imagination and an ability to communicate in writing, art or speech.

Tarot

The World: This card suggests that there are opportunities available to you in your own world and beyond, should you wish to explore them. It also nudges you towards the confidence you may need to take the next step (and the next), and if you do so, reassures you that you have the personal resources necessary to make a success of your efforts.

Famous birthdays

Frank Sinatra American singer and actor
Bill Nighy British actor
Edvard Munch Norwegian artist

December 13th

Resilient philosopher

You may take life a little more seriously than many of your fellow Sagittarians but you're not necessarily a serious soul. You are good company one to one, and probably a great conversationalist, but you don't shy away from thinking about some of life's more difficult challenges. Life isn't so much about what happens with you, but how you respond to it, and if you've been knocked back or disappointed in some way, you've learned how to manage it. This resilience is probably what helps you focus on the good in things and also explains your philosophical approach to what really matters in life. This air of positivity is an attractive feature which many will warm to, and for those that you care about, you're a completely reliable friend. You have all the qualities, including an ability to detach emotionally when necessary, that would assist you in a legal career of some sort, and a good head for figures, which could take you into the worlds of finance and business. You enjoy romance, and your ability to see clearly will also assist you in making positive choices about a partner.

Numerology

No. 4: Invested in the physical world, centred earth energy that is practical in application.

Tarot

Queen of Pentacles: Stable and trustworthy are characteristics embodied in the Queen of Pentacles. She's on your side and offers you the resources you may need for success, although you will have to do the work yourself to be truly effective. If you have doubts about how to proceed, look for the support you need and trust your instincts when it is offered.

Famous birthdays

Christopher Plummer Canadian actor
Jamie Foxx American actor and singer-songwriter
Steve Buscemi American actor and director

December 14th

Resourceful cheerleader

Encouraging others comes naturally to those born on this date, and you're probably already aware of how much you enjoy mentoring others. Whether you make this a professional role or use it when volunteering for a local community project, it's likely that you actively seek out a way to cheer others on without even being aware of it. Sociable and good-natured, you're also surprisingly self-reliant and don't feel you need much back from others. This generous and independent nature will make you popular, but make sure people appreciate the time and effort |you devote to them and don't let them take you for granted. You will thrive in any people-orientated career but especially one where you can make other people's dreams come true, so maybe an event planner or something in retail or sports. You have the ability to take the long view and will be a creative co-worker with the ability to lead by example, should you find yourself in that position. Love, to you, is also an adventure and you'll be happy and committed as long as your partner keeps your interest.

Numerology

No. 5: Impulsive and restless by nature, spontaneous and likes to discover the world through the senses.

Tarot

The Chariot: This card speaks of the merits of moving forward steadily, to overcome all obstacles and achieve our aim by staying focused and avoiding distractions. A chariot needs steering, but success is achieved through hard work, dedication, self-belief and a commitment to a personal vision or goal.

Famous birthdays

Jane Birkin British actress and singer-songwriter
Miranda Hart British actress and comedian
George VI Former King of the United Kingdom

December 15th

Motivational leader

Not everyone who assumes a leadership position has the ability to motivate others, but you're probably already aware that you do. With something of a no-nonsense approach to getting on with the task in hand, your instinct to lead by example is highly motivating to others, and in the workplace you're likely to slip naturally into this role. You've probably got a natural affinity with any form of education and actively enjoy sharing your learning, so you may work in teaching or in roles in which you'll become the trainer for the company where you work. You also enjoy social interaction and know how to party, so there's a nice balance to be struck. You have a gift for negotiation, so may find yourself called upon, either at work or at home, to smooth troubled waters and find a solution that everyone can live with. In your intimate relationships you can be charming and affectionate, seeing no reason to complicate what's really a quite straightforward proposition between two people. You probably think in terms of 'we', not 'me', and so may need to couple up to feel complete.

Numerology

No. 6: Empathic and nurturing, can problem-solve in an emotional and physical way, responsible and cares deeply about family and friends.

Tarot

Seven of Cups: There are multiple choices depicted by this card, which may be a useful reminder to you that sometimes it's important to consider all options when looking for new solutions to old problems. Calmly focusing on these without distraction can help reveal the best way forward.

Famous birthdays

Don Johnson American actor and director
Gustave Eiffel French civil engineer
Chihiro Iwasaki Chinese water-colour illustrator

December 16th

Thoughtful eccentric

You're likely to have a serious demeanour, but this hides something of an unconventional outlook on the world. Keeping your own counsel until you're sure of what you want to say or do is a useful way to avoid criticism or dismissal, so your ideas tend to appear fully formed. This is advantageous because it avoids being side-tracked from your own vision, which, even if others feel it a little eccentric, is usually well thought through. Others may well come to rely on this unique take on problem-solving, looking to you for solutions. It could take some trial and error to find a way to make best use of this professionally, but creative application in engineering research and design may make you entrepreneurial, which is how the wind-up radio came about. You probably have a diverse collection of friends, reflecting your different interests, and enjoy socialising. It may take you some time to find the one you want to share your life with, and it may require you to focus your time and attention to do so, but they are likely to be someone you've got to know well as a friend first.

Numerology

No. 7: Very analytical and detail-oriented, likes to observe and investigate things and has a keen, inventive eye.

Tarot

The Hanged Man: This is not a card about death but about someone who has a different viewpoint and consequently a different perspective on life. Once you realise the potential of this, you can let go of what you thought might limit you and trust in your own vision and potential. Once you trust yourself, others will trust you.

Famous birthdays

Arthur C. Clarke British science-fiction writer
Jane Austen British writer
Wassily Kandinsky Russian artist and art theorist

December 17th

Prosperous enthusiast

What comes first, enthusiasm or prosperity? In your case, born on this date, they go hand in hand. Enthusiasm is a form of energy and once you realise that this can be harnessed to help you accomplish what you want to do, then you're more likely to be successful and prosper. This energy will also help you to focus on what you might need to learn in order to deliver those results, whether through physical or mental application. You may be drawn to building your own business and prosper in this way, and you are likely to be shrewd enough to make good choices about who you team up with to accomplish this. Others enjoy working with you because once you've decided on your course of action, you apply yourself with enthusiasm to achieve success, and that's extremely motivating to others. Travel is likely to be something you enjoy, exploring new places and meeting new people, all of which fires you up. You're probably quite clear that when it comes to a romantic partner you want someone intellectually equal to create a home with, from which you can come and go, but who is also as enthusiastic as you about what you regard as life's adventures.

Numerology

No. 8: Sees the big picture and aims for it, linked to abundance and material wealth and uses financial success to give back to others.

Tarot

Ten of Cups: This is one of the most joyous cards in the entire Tarot deck. Happiness that is the result of companionship and the ability to see the silver lining in every cloud lies at the heart of this card. This positive attitude will help you weather life's challenges and enable you to overcome those obstacles that may arise.

Famous birthdays

Bill Pullman American actor
Milla Jovovich Ukrainian-American actress and musician
Anne Brontë British writer

December 18th

Chivalrous ally

You're unlikely to say it aloud but there's probably nothing you love more than swooping into a bad situation and rescuing someone stuck in its grip. This comes primarily from your general sense of justice, which is probably what ignites your chivalrous side, an old-fashioned idea in many ways but with plenty of scope for it today. Plus, you don't believe in ignoring a situation when you could do something about it, automatically making you an ally and the one more likely to challenge someone's disrespectful colleague or unscrupulous landlord. You're also likely to be naturally curious, which is how you find out about things that need your time and attention. Find a profession that can make formal use of this inclination, perhaps in the legal or charity sector, because making a difference in life is probably always going to matter to you and you'll feel frustrated if you can't. In your more intimate relationships, resist the temptation to seek out lame ducks. You deserve to partner with someone who values and supports the work you do, rather than drains you further.

Numerology

No. 9: An old soul that looks to spiritual awareness to solve life's problems and likes to help others to do so in the same way.

Tarot

Knight of Wands: Power, vitality and creativity are all associated with Wands and the Knight of Wands also suggests something chivalrous and crusading. This is a card that reminds us that rolling up our sleeves to confront or tackle social injustice is much more effective than just talking about it.

Famous birthdays

Brad Pitt American actor
Betty Grable American actress
Steven Spielberg American director and screenwriter

December 19th

Impulsive pioneer

There's a courage associated with pioneers because being the first isn't always easy but, for those born on this date, it's associated with an impulsive streak, which means you've probably done something new before you've fully realised it. How does this play out for you? It may show up in quite simple ways – overcoming a hesitation when offered a new job, for example, or accepting an invitation that might take you out of your comfort zone – because sometimes there's a little reticence to be overcome. As you mature, you'll gain the confidence to fully explore your pioneering approach, so be reassured that what might look impulsive to an outsider is often a useful strategy. At work this may serve you in a sales or marketing role, especially in an area of particular interest to you such as travel, education or fashion. You're probably shrewd about people, too, and able to delegate to others when necessary. Those close to you find you warm, but you can be a little cool with strangers and on initial dates, which may hamper your romantic life, so ease up on this to allow potential partners to get close.

Numerology

No. 1: A powerful entity and results-oriented force, all about initiating action and getting things done.

Tarot

Strength: This strength probably comes from holding your nerve and trusting your intuition, which is often the result of learned experience. Being open to the ideas of others is good, but having the confidence to make our own decisions, and to take responsibility for these, comes from a place of strength, and it's often useful to reflect on this.

Famous birthdays

Edith Piaf French singer-songwriter
Mileva Marić Serbian physicist and wife of Albert Einstein
Richard Hammond British TV presenter and journalist

December 20th

Intuitive problem-solver

It's not that those born on this date rely solely on their intuition, but they somehow trust that this is a facet of problem-solving. Knowing the facts alone isn't enough for you when it comes to finding the right solution; there has to be a sense of what will work best for that particular situation or person. Your ability to problem-solve in this fact-based but intuitive way is likely to be a huge asset in a people-oriented profession like education, conflict resolution, human resources or recruitment. You are also likely to have a good sense of humour, which also helps to balance your more analytical skills, and you may be called upon to mediate in business or family disputes. This is probably because others recognise your ability to balance intellect with emotion when it comes to adjudicating fairly. And while you may dream the Sagittarian dream of being a free-spirited adventurer, your deep need for a stable home life will probably over-rule any desire to remain completely free of an intimate relationship – just take the time to find someone who also shares your travel bug.

Numerology
No. 2: Shows resilience and power in gentleness, often provides the role of mediator and linked to psychic abilities.

Tarot
Four of Wands: This card reveals the importance of a happy union with another, which is something that you value and wish for. The Wands represent communication skills and with this card reminds us of the importance of staying open-hearted and sharing our true feelings with those we love, especially our life partner.

Famous birthdays
Jenny Agutter British actress
Uri Geller Israeli illusionist and magician
Ashley Cole British footballer

December 21st

Scholarly communicator

Depending on your time of birth the year you were born, you may have edged from Sagittarius into Capricorn, which might explain the more grounded approach to the way you communicate, harnessing your facts before holding forth. Often those born on this date are concerned with life's big questions and you will want to share what you believe, giving you a rather professorial air. You're also likely to be very open-minded, so are happy to communicate widely on diverse subjects, while being smart enough to acknowledge that not everyone wants to know what you think. It may be that you choose a research-based occupation as a career but, given your creative talents, you may choose to express yourself in a more artistic way, either in a professional or amateur capacity, but always with a firm grip on reality. You commit to friendships with care but may delay settling into an intimate relationship, believing that you need to have concluded your scholarly exploration before you do. But don't forget that this can also be a shared journey very much enhanced by a like-minded companion.

Numerology

No. 3: Creative with the gift of imagination and an ability to communicate in writing, art or speech.

Tarot

The Sun: This is an auspicious card that expands and illuminates those life choices that will be presented to you, suggesting happiness, joy and harmony will follow from those you make. Trust that the Sun's light will help you see clearly and guide you when it comes to choosing which path in life to follow.

Famous birthdays

Jane Fonda American actress and activist
Kiefer Sutherland British-Canadian actor and director
Samuel L. Jackson American actor

December 22nd

Sure-footed achiever

Given a problem to solve you're probably in your element and seldom overwhelmed by even the biggest of conundrums because, like many Capricorns, you approach these in a sure-footed way. Being blessed with a practical nature, you're capable of breaking things down into manageable steps and achieving your goals in this way. You're also something of an inspiration to others because you dream big and then just do what it takes to push through. Material security is important to you and you're willing to put in the hard work that paves the way for financial success. You're likely to be mistrustful of anything that looks too good to be true and it only took one failure to have you checking the small print every time, so you're unlikely to lose money investing unwisely or taking big risks. If you haven't set up your own business, there's a good chance you will because the responsibility of running your own show will probably suit you, as will the autonomy. If there is a flaw in the way you go about things, it is your tendency to forget that nurturing relationships is important to our well-being and that this is what makes your successes so much more worthwhile.

Numerology

No. 4: Invested in the physical world, centred earth energy that is practical in application.

Tarot

Three of Cups: This card is about celebrating relationships, whether intimate, collegiate, work or community, as our association and friendships with others are what enriches our lives. It's good to remember this when forging a path in life, because nothing is more important, and this card is a timely reminder for you that work isn't everything.

Famous birthdays

Ralph Fiennes British actor and producer
Robin Gibb British singer-songwriter and record producer
Vanessa Paradis French singer

December 23rd

Community visionary

Community, whether that's the immediate group of people you live, socialise or work with, or a wider community to which you feel connected, is something you probably value highly. For you, this commitment to more than just yourself will probably play out in your choice of work. There may be a spiritual element, or it may just stem from a sense that more can be accomplished together than alone, so teamwork and team-building is likely to come naturally to you. This will make you a much-valued work colleague, especially if you move into a large corporation and begin to manage at a senior level. You can do this in any field, whether in business, the creative arts or social work of some sort, but your vision of how best to operate comes from being so comfortable working with other people. You bring this same enthusiasm to your personal life and are likely to have not only a wide range of acquaintances but also a handful of close trusted friends. You're canny about people but can sometimes be a little restless, so it may take you some time to find the love of your life.

Numerology

No. 5: Impulsive and restless by nature, spontaneous and likes to discover the world through the senses.

Tarot

Three of Pentacles: The Pentacles are about our material resources and this card suggests that there may be public recognition for the work you do at some point in your life. It may be related to the service you provide, but it could also arise from a more creative association with something built, like the architecture of a public space or community centre.

Famous birthdays

Carla Bruni Italian model
Chet Baker American jazz musician
Eddie Vedder American musician and singer-songwriter

December 24th

Instinctive peacemaker

You really don't like disagreement or conflict but, unlike some, your instinct is probably to instigate a resolution rather than a revolution. As a child you probably weren't possessive about your toys, trusting that your turn would come or finding something else of equal interest. You're likely to develop considerable charm and emotional intelligence to help resolve disputes when they occur, both at home and at work. This diplomatic approach probably stems from a desire for a quiet life, but you also have a knack for really getting to the nub of an issue between two sides without getting emotionally involved. When it comes to career choices, you're probably very comfortable with a public-facing role and would feel at home in a range of professions, from retail to teaching. There's also a warmth about you that people respond to, all of which stems from a general feeling you have that people are usually well-meaning. You will probably take a similar approach towards an intimate partner, expecting the best of them unless proved otherwise, and this trust is usually rewarded.

Numerology

No. 6: Empathic and nurturing, can problem-solve in an emotional and physical way, responsible and cares deeply about family and friends.

Tarot

Two of Wands: The card of great success, we see a well-to-do merchant gazing out across the sea, perhaps thinking about his next business trip. In his right hand he holds a globe which tells us that he is no stranger to being on the world stage; and his position is elevated – he is standing on a high balcony overlooking the sea – so we know he has reached the top in his own life. He is where you are heading and want to be. He could, in fact, be you.

Famous birthdays

Ava Gardner American actress
Ricky Martin Puerto Rican singer-songwriter
Kate Spade American fashion designer and entrepreneur

December 25th

Good-humoured pragmatist

Depending on your spiritual beliefs or faith, being born on Christmas Day could be a mixed blessing. You may feel somewhat cheated that in some cultures everyone gets presents on your special day, or you may be glad to share the festivities. Luckily, there's a pragmatic component to being a Capricorn, so the chances are, you'll just get on with your day with good humour. And good humour marks out those born on this date, as they genuinely tend to be glass half full types. Often quite individualistic, you are likely to enjoy your own company and even, at times, to prefer it. Others may find you a little detached, and at work you are less likely than some to want to socialise at the end of the day. For you, the home hearth burns brightest and it's where you're prepared to invest considerable time and energy to make it something of a haven for you and your family. Your practical side may enjoy actual house building, home decorating or furniture making, activities that could be extended into your professional life, or vice versa. And when it comes to settling down, you'll be more than happy to share your space with someone you love.

Numerology

No. 7: Very analytical and detail-oriented, likes to observe and investigate things and has a keen, inventive eye.

Tarot

The World: It may not be immediately apparent that you have a spiritually attuned streak, and it may show itself in a love for the natural environment rather than organised religion, but it's there. When it comes to valuing your accomplishments, material success needs to be balanced by the personal happiness you are also keen to achieve.

Famous birthdays

Sissy Spacek American actress and singer
Annie Lennox Scottish singer-songwriter
Humphrey Bogart American actor

December 26th

Devoted intellectual

Developing your intellect is probably important to you and you're also likely to have a very clear idea about why it matters to you, possibly as a means to an end. It may take you into further education or the sort of professional role where your ability to think rationally is imperative. It may also remain just one feature of your life rather than its whole focus, as many born on this day have such a zest for fun that they happily lay their work down at the end of the day and show similar devotion to interacting with family and friends. There's no problem with finding an intellectual focus early in life, as it can be to your advantage, but it's important to recognise that this is only part of the picture in a balanced life, so check that devotion isn't turning into a defence. So, enjoy its rewards but ensure this isn't to the exclusion of the warmth and joy that human connection can bring and take stock if you feel you're missing out in other areas of your life. Close friends are likely to understand your commitment, but it may take equal devotion to find someone with whom to share a life. Bear this in mind and make sure you take time away from your studies to enjoy a social life.

Numerology

No. 8: Sees the big picture and aims for it, linked to abundance and material wealth and uses financial success to give back to others.

Tarot

Two of Cups: This card reflects a possible reluctance to turn your attention from the objective to the subjective, from matters of the head to matters of the heart. The two people are facing each other, but while one appears steady, the other appears less so. Learn to trust your feelings as much as rational thought to ensure a happy union.

Famous birthdays

Henry Miller American writer and artist
Phil Spector American musician and record producer
Kit Harington British actor and producer

December 27th

Emphatic romantic

Romance in life is very important, but if you become over-emphatic it can occasionally blind you to the obvious. Being emphatic can sometimes be confused with certainty, and for those born on this date, as for many other Capricorns, certainty is important. Unfortunately, uncertainty is a feature of life and we have to learn to manage it, and it may be that you are attempting to do this by looking through rose-coloured spectacles for the answers you seek. Pause and reconsider if you feel you're over-romanticising some of life's possibilities to avoid constant disappointment. Alternatively, take that emphasis and prosper from it by writing romantic fiction, because you probably also have the ability to work these ideas hard and make them pay off. There may be other professional roles in which you can exploit this romantic view of things, as a wedding or event planner, for example. Or you may choose to keep it completely separate from your working life. Your personal life may be another matter and here your romantic impulses may ensure you're never short of a date or, in the end, a very romantic partner.

Numerology

No. 9: An old soul that looks to spiritual awareness to solve life's problems and likes to help others to do so in the same way.

Tarot

Ace of Cups: The Cups represent emotions and the most potent card in this is the Ace of Cups. It reveals that you're a deeply emotional person and also explains your generous and giving nature. This may spill over into romantic gestures but, in your case, it also reveals a deep commitment to the staying power of love.

Famous birthdays

Marlene Dietrich German actress and singer
Gérard Depardieu French actor
Louis Pasteur French biologist and inventor of pasteurisation

December 28th

Reliable entrepreneur

Confident and capable, you probably have the drive, ambition and focus to launch your own business projects and make them successful, so if you're not an entrepreneur, you will probably look for work that gives you the same kind of autonomy. There's a simple reason you need to be the one in the charge and that's because you're often the one most qualified to run the show. This is because you tend to work hard, listen to others and lead by example, but you have the self-confidence to trust in your own instincts and to take responsibility for your actions. You also know which battles to fight and which to walk away from, and people are likely to admire this in you. You are also generous with your time, which could occasionally lead to you being taken for granted, so be careful not to neglect your own needs. You probably have more than a passing interest in spiritual matters and whether or not you have a conventional faith, you may look to this when it comes to making the important choices in your life. As a partner, you are kind and reliable, which is often under-rated but a huge plus in a relationship.

Numerology

No. I: A powerful entity and results-oriented force, all about initiating action and getting things done.

Tarot

The High Priestess: Also referred to as the Eternal Student, this card reflects your capacity to learn new things and to do so diligently when in pursuit of new ventures. Being open to this is a great strength and the key to success, and the focus of any studies you pursue are likely to be wide-ranging, from the esoteric to the practical.

Famous birthdays

Denzel Washington American actor
Maggie Smith British actress
Sienna Miller British-American actress

December 29th

Charismatic organiser

Whenever you're in company, whether just a few family members or a large work crowd, you're likely to be the one making sure everyone is having a good time. Introducing people to each other, dishing up food or refilling glasses. This instinct may stem from being shy as a child and learning how to engage with others by organising nice times to share or just because you want to make any gathering more enjoyable for those participating. Either way, this isn't really about looking to be the centre of attention, but because you enjoy seeing people socialising and having a good time. There may also be something of the showman in you, a natural raconteur of some charisma, and this may be something that comes naturally or which you develop over your lifetime. With a reputation for generosity and thoughtfulness, you may find that others come to expect you to do all the organising for celebratory events and this may become a career option, too. What you will also appreciate is the security of your home where you can be peaceful and recharge your batteries. While a partner may be attracted to your charismatic side, they will come to appreciate this facet of you, too.

Numerology

No. 2: Shows resilience and power in gentleness, often provides the role of mediator and linked to psychic abilities.

Tarot

Strength: A young female with a tamed lion, which suggests that her power comes from gentleness and not brute force, depicts strength in this card. This can be a lesson that takes time to be learned, but an openness to learning is also a strength and those who recognise this tend to make better progress than those who don't.

Famous birthdays

Jude Law British actor
Marianne Faithfull British singer-songwriter and actress
Jessica Andrews American singer

December 30th

Grounded enthusiast

As warrants an earth sign, there's a grounded quality to your approach to life that often goes unobserved because by nature you're an enthusiast. But what those close to you will come to learn is that often what you're most enthusiastic about are those things that are tangible and can make a collective difference. It's very seldom all about you, as your ideas and plans are so often extended to others that you probably can't book a holiday without inviting friends or extended family along. Your generous spirit is also likely to be evident at work where you can hardly accept praise for a job well done without also mentioning your team-mates. In time you may find this makes you a natural leader, heading up projects or a business that needs to be securely based in reality, while imparting an enthusiastic confidence that the most ambitious of plans can be realised with a steady hand. This also extends to what you probably offer a life partner: a really secure basis for a relationship, about which you'll be equally enthusiastic once you've found the right one.

Numerology

No. 3: Creative with the gift of imagination and an ability to communicate in writing, art or speech.

Tarot

Knight of Wands: There's an energy about this knight on his horse, armed with a wand (a symbol of vitality), that's demonstrably enthusiastic about whatever quest he's on. This reflects your own ability to find genuine meaning in what you do and communicate it to others in such an enthusiastic way that they'll follow your lead.

Famous birthdays

Patti Smith American singer-songwriter
Rudyard Kipling British writer
Tiger Woods American golf champion

December 31st

Independent reformer

It seems symbolic that for those born on the last day of the Gregorian calendar year the word 'reformer' comes up, however this plays out. It may be in simple ways, where you regularly take stock of your domestic surroundings, for example, or on a larger canvas in social welfare, but for you, reform is something of an instinct. There's a confidence in this that others will appreciate because you're more than likely to have done the groundwork that informs your ideas and decision-making. There's something about this end-of-year date that makes everyone consider what's past and what's to come, and how what we've learned might be useful to us in the future. You're likely to have a commitment to collective reform as much as personal, and this may see you working in a role in local government or education, where your clear views may set you apart from the crowd. However, on your birthday and the eve of your personal new year, you are likely to be celebrating with those you love because, however much you value your independence, you probably value close companionship more.

Numerology

No. 4: Invested in the physical world, centred earth energy that is practical in application.

Tarot

The Tower: A card of great promise, this primarily represents the possibility of change through the knocking down of obsolete structures. Transformation – and reform – is made possible by the letting go of old ideas. It's also symbolic of how we can rebuild ourselves, adapting to change and trusting in this process.

Famous birthdays

Val Kilmer American actor
Anthony Hopkins Welsh actor
Donna Summer American singer

About the Author

Stella Andromeda has been studying astrology for over 30 years, believing that a knowledge of the constellations of the skies and their potential for psychological interpretation can be a useful tool. This extension of her study into book form makes modern insights about the ancient wisdom of the stars easily accessible, sharing her passion that reflection and self-knowledge only empowers us in life. With her sun in Taurus, Aquarius ascendant and Moon in Cancer, she utilises earth, air and water to inspire her own astrological journey.

Acknowledgements

As ever, my appreciation to the best team at Hardie Grant for all their hard work in making the Seeing Stars books a reality. In particular, thanks are due to Kate Pollard who commissioned the original series and to Kate Burkett for picking up the reins on *AstroBirthdays* with such enthusiasm and efficiency, while an equally big thanks must go to the illustration and design talents of Evi O Studio, who has made all the books look so beautiful.